DARK ALBION

A Requiem for the English

David Abbott

SPARROW BOOKS
www.sparrowbooks.webeden.co.uk
sparrowbookpublishers@gmail.com

Dark Albion
A Requiem for the English

David Abbott

Published in 2013 by Sparrow Books

PO Box 475, Ramsgate CT11 1BN
www.sparrowbooks.webeden.co.uk
sparrowbookpublishers@gmail.com

Copyright © Sparrow Books 2013

ISBN: 978-0-9572289-0-0

Contents

'So the world gets on step by step towards brave clearness and honesty!'
- George Eliot upon publication of *On the Origin of Species*, 1859

'We will remodel this country in an Islamic image'
- Omar Bin Bakri, London, 1989

WAITING FOR A BUS
A whiff of Frank incensed

OUR inheritance has been turned over to strangers, our homes to aliens.

At dusk on a freezing December weekday afternoon, I have to take a bus down Westcombe Hill to the North Greenwich Underground Station on the Greenwich Peninsula, which defines a loop of the Thames. At the bus stop I meet an old man named Frank who was a friend of my late father. Frank, wearing a check cloth cap, has a grey moustache. The last time I saw him, which was at my father's funeral, his moustache was auburn. His eyebrows are still coppery. I too now have a grey moustache that was once auburn, with coppery eyebrows.

'Wotcher,' Frank says, his lips blue from cold. 'How are you? Still a journalist?'

'No,' I say. 'Retired. I write books now.'

'You write books?' he says. Had I confided that I was a ballet dancer he could not have looked more ill at ease. To make him feel better I add, 'Just a hobby, really; something to do, like making matchstick models.'

Although the pavement is packed with people waiting for a bus, we are the only ones speaking English. Where in the past there would have been an orderly queue of Cockneys is now a haphazard crowd of settlers. Some stand by the gutter, some to the left of the covered stop, some to the right, some in the middle of the snow-covered pavement and some at the back by the glass-fronted estate agents or the chemist's shop. On this freezing day, with snowflakes hovering in the air and dusting shoulders, several are dressed in tropical clothes. No one has any concern for who was there before them. This is the new way of waiting for a bus. The likes of Frank and me, heirs to a different custom, find it disturbing. On the other side of the road is the Green, a cross between a small park and a big roundabout, where I played football as a child, using the trees as goalposts. It is white with frost, the trees shrouded in ice. As I kicked the ball around, I could not have foreseen that fifty years later I would stand across the road waiting for a bus among a crowd of brown-skinned foreigners.

Suddenly there is a commotion by the Green. Several groups of children going home from school have seen their bus coming and have merged to break into a stampede across the busy Royal Standard junction, ignoring vehicles and causing drivers to brake sharply. The children all come from a local Church of England secondary school, which was founded in 1700. Its website says it 'values diversity and is sensitive to the range of traditions and cultures represented in the community it serves'. In reality the diversity of the local community is not represented. All of the school's pupils are black. They consist of adolescents of both sexes but mostly boys, all in a perpetual state of high excitement. For about forty minutes every afternoon in school term Old Dover Road and nearby streets are taken over by them. Most of my neighbours avoid going out at this time and look forward to school holidays and weekends, when they can reclaim the streets. The children block the pavements, walking in groups of half-a-dozen and constantly yelling to each other between the groups, so unruly and aggressive that police are routinely deployed. Recently while going home from school one of the children stabbed another with a knife. Four policemen are standing now by the bus stop in yellow fluorescent jackets, where they will wait until the children have dispersed. On the last day of term and every Friday more trouble than usual is expected and two mounted police are deployed as well. In the past, four policemen at a scene signified a serious crime, while mounted bobbies were only seen at big football matches. Now they signal obnoxious children going home from school. The stampede is as incongruous as a herd of wildebeest streaming across an English road.

Unfortunately, the bus the children saw coming was a 108 - my bus. They noisily join the throng in front of me. Always heedless and overexcited, they are now further excited by their stampede and the snow and are jabbering and whooping uncontrollably. Some of their jabber is a sort of self-conscious patois, which they adopt whenever they realise they have been talking normal English for a while.

The red single-decker bus pulls up, its windscreen wipers slowly brushing off the snowflakes. My father used to take a 108 early every weekday morning to work, greeting workmates with a sleepy 'Wotcher'. He was a hammerman at the gasworks on the peninsula - 'slinging a sledge-'ammer', as he used to say. In those days it was a double-decker Routemaster.

On this 108, all the seats are taken, a brown face framed in every window. I will have to stand, or maybe wait for the next one. The boarding flow stops because someone's Oyster card does not have enough money on it for the fare and the harassed Sikh driver cannot explain because the swarthy holder is pretending he does not understand English, not even the basic 'Not enough money'. The Sikh lets him on without paying a fare.

By the step, a bespectacled long-limbed young black man says over his shoulder to an Indian pressing and banging a heavy wheeled shopping basket against his calves, 'You're breaking my legs, man.' The Indian responds with slight sideway motions of the head. A Nigerian is so engrossed in a mobile-phone discussion, negotiating a deal in Yoruba peppered with the word 'percentage', that he rudely pushes some other type of male ethnic; a policeman has to sort out the ensuing inter-ethnic unpleasantness, hindered by them understanding neither English nor each other's language. With everyone getting colder by the minute and the bus becoming so packed that there is a real danger the Sikh will shut the doors and exclude them, impatience and frustration now grip the multi-cultural throng.

Though Frank and I have lived in this area all our lives, we feel out of place. Our existence does not register with the pushy newcomers who surround us. We have a strange, unpleasant feeling of irrelevance. We are invisible.

Frank becomes angry. He mutters, 'What are they all *doing* 'ere.'

I put a finger to my lips. Such talk could get him jailed.

He nods. 'I'll walk dahn the 'ill,' he says.

'Be careful of the ice,' I say.

As he turns away he asks in a whisper, 'Can you describe this in one of yer books?'

'I can,' I say, and he smiles fleetingly.

THE COMING OF THE ENGLISH
and their going

THROUGHOUT the second half of the fifth century Teutonic tribes made frequent incursions into southern Britain. From the north of modern Germany came the Saxons, named, some antiquarians believe, after their distinctive bone-handled, single-edged curved knife, called a sæx, carried everywhere for household tasks and used in fighting. To this day the flag of the county of Essex ('East Saxons') consists of three of these knives. From a district north-east of Schleswig on the German-Danish border that is still called Angeln came the Angles; and from the Rhineland (not Jutland, as is often, reasonably but erroneously, believed) came the Jutes.

Although there is little documentary evidence outside the writings of the great Northumbrian historian-monk Bede three hundred years later and the *Anglo-Saxon Chronicle* even later still, archaeological discoveries on Britain's eastern seaboard, mainly objects from graves in pagan cemeteries, confirm their account of the waves of incomers. The remnants of a timber village at the mouth of the River Weser in Old Saxony indicate that the place was abandoned in about 450, apparently in consequence of rising sea levels.

With the natural fertility of southern Britain and the evidence that its inhabitants' leaders invited foreign mercenaries, this flooding of coastal settlements across the Channel and the North Sea helps to provide an explanation for the migrations. Another reason may have been that those realms, which had been outside the Roman Empire, once the Roman defences of the Rhine collapsed in 407 suffered a northward migration into their territory, providing further encouragement for the Saxons and others to move westward across the sea to the fertile lowlands of Britain.

Meanwhile, following the Romans' withdrawal from Britain in 410, regional leadership had reverted to tribal chieftains. The most powerful overlords in fifth-century Britain were Vortigern, Cunedda, Ceretic and Cunedda's father-in-law, the wise ruler of the northern kingdom of Rheged, Coel the Old, remembered in nursery rhyme as Old King Cole.

In the middle of the fifth century, at the request of Vortigern, Cunedda and his sons led their armies into North Wales to expel unwanted Irish settlers. The Picts of Caledonia in the far north took advantage of Cunedda's absence to launch a series of border raids across Hadrian's Wall. Vortigern invited a band of Jute mercenaries, led by two brothers, Hengist and Horsa, to help repel the invaders. The mercenaries' three ships arrived at Thanet in Kent, at Pegwell Bay, now a nature reserve. A replica longship with the typical tall twisted prow and row of round shields along the hull commemorates the spot. Chroniclers' dating of this event, 'the coming of the English', to 449 is backed by no evidence (though this did not prevent an anniversary enactment in 1949, when a longship sailed from Denmark and landed at Thanet). Ambiguity of the early sources of information makes it impossible to assign a precise year to the beginning of the English settlement in Britain. But the coming of these three ships on the beach at Pegwell Bay at the foot of the eroded chalk cliffs with their flint-encrusted strata is an historical event as important as the landing of the *Mayflower* and of the *Empire Windrush*.

Let us try to imagine this legendary landing. As a winter crossing was unthinkable, let us say it was summer - a cloudless, sunny day, the parchment sky reflected in the sea, but windy.

The newly-built oak-timbered ships look beautiful - long-keeled, wide-beamed and beak-prowed - but they leak, as new ships will, especially when cobbled together as quickly as these had been, the shipwrights knowing they were expendable and the warriors who commissioned them not caring about quality. Approaching the wide eastern end of the Channel, there just a narrowing of the North Sea, those of the men who have never been to sea before are delighted by the ocean's fecundity. The luminescent water teems with life. Behind them, half a mile away to starboard, a family of humpbacks spouts in turn, revealing their backs and dorsal flippers. Porpoises race alongside the boats, leaping into the air. Those men making their first sea voyage have never seen or heard of these strange fish before, fish as big as a deerhound, with a triangular fin, their backs glistening in the sun as they arch out of the water. The few men who know about them say they are reputed to give sailors luck, which heartens the superstitious warriors. The porpoises swim off to chase a shoal of mackerel they have seen just beneath the sea's surface, visible also to the men.

They had been warned that the sea off Thanet was a treacherous place of mudbanks (now called Goodwin Sands, and still dangerous, a yacht running aground there as recently as April 2013) and feel relieved when these have been safely navigated.

As the ships approach the shore the waves surge and the swell mounts higher. The men ship their oars (a dozen each side), the square single sails rattle down and the helmsmen on the steering platform work hard at the big steering oar to hold a true course, for if their ship, with its shallow draught, goes even slightly across the surf it will certainly capsize. The ships are now going faster than a galloping horse; the surf thunders in the men's ears, the waves break around them in walls of foam and suddenly the ships crash up the beach scattering shingle as yet another breaker smashes over the stern and rushes past the men.

Here the tumbling of the tide upon the pebbly shore resembles the familiar cry of a pack of hounds in hollow echoing woods, a pleasing murmur reassuring to the warriors in this unaccustomed marine adventure, and, the discomfort and danger of the sea voyage ended, they are now shouting like children, roaring with laughter at the joy of it all.

They jump over, soaking their woollen leggings and leather-thong cross-gartering and tossing the salt water from their flowing, light-brown hair, in order to help the last push of the waves to get the ship a few yards further up the rock-strewn beach to where the receding spent water resembles filigreed lace. Maybe one trips, banging his face and making his nose bleed. Maybe one of the ships has capsized, and snapped its mast, for which Hengist now rages at the helmsman.

Presumably, some locals are waiting on the clifftop to welcome them, having been alerted by Vortigen's men that they come as allies, one with a glinting chain about his neck, suggesting he is of high rank. Possibly some have misgivings. Even unarmed (axes, swords, round shields and leather helmets still stowed away in the bilge in large, heavy hessian sacks) and laughing and shouting like excited children, the newcomers look ferocious. Their tatty elongated ships are obviously expendable warboats, and they are clearly warriors. They are lean and tough, quick and wiry and light on their feet. Several have a scarred face or a mutilation. Maybe a long scar runs across the cheek of one, drawing the corner of his mouth up in a sinister curl, and perhaps another has lost the top of an ear. Although the welcoming party has encountered Jutes, Angles and Saxons before, the others had been straggling groups cultivating difficult marginalised land with their superior heavy ploughs. The injuries of these newcomers had not been inflicted while they were drawing a plough. And warriors always too much relish acquiring things by force. These men with the blond flowing locks and blue eyes will be more enamoured with the thought of fighting than of sailing away to their own country in their long ships.

The misgivings proved justified. After helping to repel the Picts, Hengist and Horsa were joined by more Jute warriors, with whom they sought to acquire territory for themselves. Provoking a dispute over provisions, they took up arms against Vortigern. Horsa was killed in a battle at Aylesford in Kent but Vortigern bought off Hengist by offering him the kingdom of Kent, which Hengist ruled from his base on the Isle of Thanet (which ceased to be an island in the sixteenth century when the channel separating it from the mainland silted up). His son was king of Kent for twenty-four years, from 488 to 512.

The Jutes' success in founding a kingdom encouraged Saxon and Angle warriors to invade from north Germany, landing on the stretch of Kent coast known as 'the Saxon Shore'.

Many years of inconclusive warfare followed. The Britons had lost much of their military strength when the Romans departed. After having learnt to fight in a trained manner like the legions, they now once again fought ineffectively as separate tribes, as they had done before the Romans came. But a major British victory, about the year 500, at an unidentified place called Badon Hill, halted and even reversed the Anglo-Saxon advance for more than a generation. (According to a monk named

Nennius in his *History of the Britons*, a British chieftain named Arthur fought in this battle, personally killing nine hundred and sixty men.) Shortly after the middle of the sixth century the historian Procopius wrote that the Angles had been crossing in great numbers from Britain to the Continent. A reverse migration of English peoples to the Continent at this time implied that the invaders had outgrown their first settlements and abandoned the attempt to find new ones. After the defeat at Badon Hill they were restricted to their original Kentish coastal territory with no chance of providing for a growing population by the establishment of new inland colonies.

But the Anglo-Saxons eventually returned and when they regained the initiative new kingdoms emerged. Reinforced by a continual stream of immigrants, the invaders pressed further and further west, until eventually they held almost the whole of what is now England, the east of Scotland at least as far north as the Forth, and the Solway Plain. The sixth century British monk Gildas lamented that Britain's rulers 'sealed its doom by inviting in among them (like wolves in to the sheepfold) the fierce and impious Saxons, a race hurtful both to God and men. Nothing was ever so pernicious to our country, nothing was ever so unlucky. What palpable darkness must have enveloped their minds! Those very people whom, when absent, they dreaded more than death itself, were invited to reside, as one may say, under the selfsame roof'.

Bede too noted the fatal stupidity of inviting hordes of foreigners: 'Swarms of the aforesaid nations came over into the island, and the foreigners began to increase so much, that they became a source of terror to the natives themselves who had invited them. They over-ran the whole face of the doomed island.'

Britons fled in such numbers to the nearest safe land, the Armorica peninsula, that it became known as Brittany.

The invaders meanwhile divided up England among themselves. Saxons took the south of Britain, developing the kingdoms of Wessex, Essex, Middlesex and Sussex, while the Angles occupied the rest of the land (excluding Wales) from the Severn estuary up to Hadrian's Wall, comprising Northumbria ('north of the Humber'), Mercia and East Anglia. By the end of the sixth century the invaders were in permanent control of half of Britain, though kings rose and fell quickly, gaining great power briefly. The longest reign was that of Penda, who ruled Mercia from 632 until his death in battle in 654. One of the first kings in England to mint a coinage of his own, his name survives in the word 'penny'. The Anglian, Saxon and Jutish peoples who lived between the Humber and the Channel are often referred to in early charters as the *Sutangli*, or southern English.

Thanet was again the site of an important landing when, in 597, Augustine reluctantly arrived there with forty other reluctant monks to begin his Papal mission to convert the English race to Christianity. King Æthelbert of Kent, afraid of the strangers' magic if he crossed a building's threshold (they could have buried some magical object underneath it, with dire consequences for anyone who stepped over it), insisted on meeting them outdoors. The interview, which took place in Thanet, convinced him of their honesty, and although he refused to give up immediately what he and the whole English race had hitherto always believed, he gave them a dwelling-place in Canterbury, supplied them with food, and allowed them to preach their religion. They on their part lived a simple communal life in Canterbury. The first stage in their mission ended successfully, despite Augustine's tendency to panic under pressure, when Æthelbert himself accepted Christianity, undoubtedly influenced by his wife Bertha, who was already a Christian. From Æthelbert they received the beginnings of an endowment in land, and, though the Kentish church itself almost expired after the death of its royal protector, the tradition of Augustine always prevented Canterbury from becoming a mere local diocese. Æthelbert's grandson Eorcenbert was the first English king to order the destruction of idols throughout his kingdom.

In other kingdoms too Christianity had been established at court and preached around the country, and by 664 was the dominant religion throughout England, though it took a long time to percolate down from court to the populace. The reformation was too radical to happen quickly. Christianity was at first an aristocratic indulgence. But over a century the new religion spread down through society and out, north and west, across all the pagan island.

In practice, the old festivals did not altogether disappear, remaining as Christian festivals. The word Easter comes from Eostre, the old Germanic goddess of spring. Rituals related to Eostre focused on new beginnings, symbolised by the Easter egg, and fertility, which was symbolised by the hare, who became the Easter bunny. And, following the advice of Pope Gregory, pagan sacred places were taken over and turned to Christian use.

By 695 the Kent king Wihtred, while issuing laws granting complete freedom from taxation to the church, also felt the necessity to include provisions against offerings to devils. (His law-code also excluded from the country foreigners who would not conform!)

The seventh century was an age of continual wars. Even in the early eighth century the bishops and abbots attending a king's court seem incongruous members of an assembly that was still essentially a warband. Kings were glorified warlords, and their nobles leading warriors.

Linguistic evidence shows that the immigrants whose settlements formed these original English kingdoms all belonged to a single group of closely related Germanic peoples. This evidence establishing a basic connection between them is the first sure fact in English history. There was no difference of race or culture. They were of the same stock. And they knew it. They remained highly aware of their Germanic origin. Bede's older contemporary, St Aldhelm, used 'our stock' and 'the German race' as parallel expressions, noting that the English so identified with the continental Saxons that they were wont to say, 'We are of one blood and one bone.' They were conscious of an essential unity that distinguished them from the subjects of the Roman empire to the south and the barbarians to the east. It rested on a fundamental similarity of political structure and social convention. Beowulf came from the middle of what is now Sweden; the poem about him was known in every Germanic country. It is preserved in West Saxon English of the tenth century but contains many ancient forms of words showing that an Anglian original lies behind the existing texts, composed for an audience sufficiently familiar with northern tradition to grasp the meaning of the most casual reference to other stories. The small amount of English epic poetry that has survived plainly represents a mere fragment of a body of tradition once common to the whole Germanic world, with its mutually intelligible dialects. All the Germanic languages shared enough basic vocabulary for their peoples to adequately communicate.

The family feuding that ruined dynasties became a major problem when the Viking raids began in 835. During the next three decades attacks from Scandinavia came almost yearly, culminating in the arrival of a full-scale invading army, which the disorganised kingdoms were ill-prepared to repel. It was hard for any ninth-century king to improvise an effective programme of resistance to invaders who could disembark 5,000 seasoned fighting-men at any one of a score of undefended ports. The once-great kingdoms of Northumbria and East Anglia ceased to exist. Wessex was better organised, and when its king, Æthelred, died in the middle of the crisis of an impending invasion, his brother succeeded to the throne with no disunity. This brother's name was Alfred, later to be called the Great because of his success, against seemingly hopeless odds, in repelling the Vikings.

A sickly youth, he collapsed at his wedding in 868 and throughout his life endured bouts of pain, possibly from Crohn's disease. He also suffered badly from piles. His greatness did not only consist in defeating enemies in battle. He was the first English town planner; carried out a programme of education to revive literacy and learning, including writing and translating books himself, for which he studied Latin; and, caring about justice, codified laws.

The English tribes who came over from the Continent already had an elaborate and developed legal system, whose basic principles were shared by other Germanic nations. Evidence exists that long before William the Conqueror's invasion England already had a tradition of belief in the rule of law. Alfred's codification of laws in 871 recognised that without the ability to rely on people when they gave undertakings, society could not function ('Every man should strictly hold to his oath and pledge'). Anglo-Saxons had always set great store by the keeping of oaths. The habit of law was deeply ingrained in the English.

And Englishness goes back a long way. Alfred, in the preface to the translation of Pope Gregory's *Cura Pastoralis*, alludes to 'Angelcynn', the English kin, and 'Englise'. In one treaty he is associated with 'the councillors of all the English race', and in the last years of his life always referred to himself as 'King of the English'. By that he meant all the land in Britain where the Saxon languages were spoken.

Although this described an ambition rather than a reality, his ambition was realised by his successors - his son Edward, his daughter Æthelflæd and Edward's son, Æthelstan.

Alfred used the term 'Anglo-race' and consistently called his native language English, not Saxon, even though he himself was a Saxon. Bede, in his *Ecclesiastical History of the English People*, takes it for granted that the English people are a specific and identifiable race sprung out of Saxon and Old English roots. King Harold's army that fought at Hastings consisted of Angles, Jutes, Danes, Frisians, Saxons and even, from the forests of Kent and the western shires, Celts, all of whom called themselves English. Fewer Angles than either Saxons or Danes were in it, but no Dane would call himself Saxon, nor vice-versa, so they were all happy to be called Angles or English.

The concept of Englishness had wide circulation in the Anglo-Saxon world. The peoples of England were not so very different to one another and were wonderfully pliant and malleable in their admixture with those they settled among. All belonged to the same broad culture.

The later Norsemen - first the Vikings and then the Vikings' descendants the Normans - were also of the same stock. The rulers of Normandy were Vikings who had settled on that peninsula. Some Normans still had Scandinavian names at the time of the Conquest.

Numerically, the Normans who remained to settle in England after the Battle of Hastings were insignificant. Mercenary units hired out to William by enterprising nobles made up a substantial portion of his invading army, and these soldiers returned home immediately after the battle. The Norman aristocracy simply became the ruling class of a country whose army they had destroyed. Even the initial antagonism described in Sir Walter Scott's classic novel *Ivanhoe* was really between classes, not races.

The Normans were racially the same as the English, adhered to the same set of beliefs and relatively few settled here. Alfred's vision of a unified state called England was not threatened.

That was all very different to what is occurring now.

Nations have their eras, which may last longer than a millennium or shorter than a century. Eventually, sooner or later, everything grows rigid, everything ossifies, everything withers and decays. The most ancient people of whom we have any knowledge, the Sumerians of Mesopotamia, were conquerors from the north and east who arrived in the fourth millennium BC, who thrived for a thousand years, irrigating the country and filling it with their towns before being conquered themselves, by Semitic tribes. So we can accept that our civilisation too has to end some time.

But not like this. Not cravenly, in denial, shamefully led by traitors.

In the past, a doomed people, knowing their fate, usually anyway resisted angrily. Occasionally their rage was so powerful it stemmed the course of history. Before modern times, rage was mentioned and described in literature far more often than love. Indeed, 'rage' is the first word in the West's first great work of literature. The rage of Achilles - its cause, its course, its disastrous consequences - is the theme of Homer's Bronze Age epic poem *The Iliad*, the mainspring of the plot. Achilles, the leading warrior in the Greek army besieging Troy, is enraged when the king who commands the army, Agamemnon, takes for himself a captured girl Achilles has claimed as booty. Achilles withdraws his warriors, thereby nearly causing the Greeks to lose the war.

Nowadays, 'rage' is most often used in newspapers to describe the feelings of football managers upset at a referee's decision, being a shorter word than 'irritation' to fit in headlines. Some genuine, justified, righteous rage is now required by the likes of me if our civilisation is to last at least until the end of the century, which is probably the most that can be hoped for it. We need a rage that is cold, lucid, rational; a rage that eliminates any detachment, any indulgence. We have no choice but to try to preserve a semblance of our identity. England's wealth is also its danger. Carelessness with wealth always evokes audacity. With bold settlers swarming over our land, our culture is already dead. But the dead must be buried, and with due rites. A requiem must be sung.

We can record the ethnic autism of the settlers among us, a condition in which ethnic groups become so absorbed in themselves they cannot see the misery of others and cannot imagine themselves having caused it, so that they are incapable of seeing that the likes of me have a valid point of view, dismissing the idea that we could have excellent reasons for not wanting them here among us in their millions. We can express our anger at the treachery, naïvety and stupidity of our leaders. We can document the origins of their betrayal and, surmounting our fate by scorn, reveal the nature of those who are displacing us. We can note the impact of mass immigration on our daily lives.

Nothing is sadder than an obsolete race. The English people who once walked tall and proud, now hang their head in sorrow. But they have a birthright to England and must be prepared to angrily defend that birthright, defying their treacherous leaders who strive to deprive them of it. Their turbulent history should not be cited as an excuse to deny their existence as a people. If God chose a race of people, the Hebrews, and created them as twelve distinct, separate and independent tribes who collectively became known as Israelites, then so too can the English nation be historically made up of Angles, Saxons, Jutes, Danes, Normans… The blood stock is still the same.

Traitors desperately deny there is such a thing as the English people. This is important to them. If the English are deemed not to exist the hordes of settlers cannot be accused of subverting English customs and traditions, of usurping the country.

The word indigenous when applied to the English is often written with contemptuous inverted commas (but not when applied to the native people of New Zealand, Australia or America, or red squirrels) implying that no such people exist.

But surely a race that has lived in a land for fifteen hundred years, with that land being named after them, has the right to be called indigenous. Those who deny this are falsifiers. And denying one's ancestors is the first step to the exit of history.

THE LANDSCAPE OF OUR LIVES
Changing it 'ern 'alf bad

MOST indigenous people believe the cost of having so many settlers as guests is too high - especially when they start to rearrange the furniture.

First, they have no responsibilities, a lack normally regarded for adults as unsatisfactory. Our problems are not their problems. They can, if they wish, regard their emigration as a flight from the boredom and banality of the everyday.

Another problem is that settlers are, by their nature, hard to satisfy. They are, after all, people who did not like their own country enough to stay there. And so they complain more than they should, which angers the locals. I personally know a settler, IN BRITAIN ILLEGALLY, who complains about the NHS! Complaining settlers pose a logical contradiction. They complain about the country in which they find themselves, yet they are here by choice. Why do they not go home?

Settlers answer this question by thinking of themselves as exiles - if not in a judicial sense then in a spiritual sense. Something within them had drawn them away from their homeland. They even actually envy the dramatic situation of the real exile. Life abroad is an adventure. I have lived abroad. The novelty of everything all around is stimulating. You become more alive. Not necessarily happier, but that is a separate issue: by definition an adventure has the possibilities of hardship, difficulties, misery and failure. And the more different the new country is to your home country, the bigger the adventure.

In order to heighten this adventure, many settlers, who have emigrated voluntarily and could easily return home, dramatise their position to match that of the few genuine exiles. These settlers have an incoherent relationship with this, their country of residence. Its wide aspirations make the culture of their parents and grandparents look puny and marginal. Casting back to the ancestral homeland for great dramas to participate in can offer fulfilment.

These modern settlers are like a child playing a game in which reality is excluded. They could go back home at any time, but it is more fun to pretend otherwise. Persuading themselves that they are dogged by foes, they sublimate any real difficulties into a more pleasurable fear. As part of the game, they dream up persecution, hostility and suffering. They invent enemies - locals, unbelievers, rival gangs... Their world is that of a wounded Red Indian pursued by vindictive cavalry in a suburban back garden. The indigenous people they settle among have to live with the consequences of this childish behaviour, which, combined with other behavioural problems, can be calamitous.

If the settler comes from a lawless part of the world, he fetches his lack of respect for law; if being devious is a way of life where he comes from, he brings his deviousness; if getting all upset at the least little thing is in his culture, he imports histrionic behaviour. Harshly bureaucratic peoples have fetched their delight in causing problems when in a position to do so; religious fanaticism and intolerance have been introduced into our formerly peaceful and rational secular country. The rudeness endemic in backward countries has been imported wholesale. The settlers' offspring inherit their parents' traits, at the same time as tiresomely moaning that they did not ask to be born in a country where they do not feel they belong, implying that this is somehow the fault of the indigenous people and not a consequence of their parents' decision to emigrate. The young males, fuelled by testosterone and their sense of grievance, engage in anti-social activities and crime. The indigenous people are expected to put up with all this. Our rulers, fearing our objections might get out of hand, have passed restrictive legislation, banning any criticism of the newcomers. Journalists acquiesce in deception, obscuring both the extent and the consequences of the mass immigration.

Our culture eroded, modes of behaviour that have existed for many centuries in England have changed. People need a culture. Without one, they degenerate.

A culture is neither education nor law-making: it is a heritage and an atmosphere. What makes a culture specific is the way in which over many centuries the elements have combined, developed and affected one another and eventually formed a system. The strengths of a people lie in continuity. To break with it is perilous.

Histrionic behaviour, now so prevalent, is not natural behaviour in England, where understatement and reserve have been noted national characteristics for a thousand years. Bede wrote about them in the eighth century. At the same time as Bede was writing, and probably also in Northumbria, the most important Old English poem, *Beowulf*, was being written down: and in this too, the voices possess 'eloquence and understatement'. The phrase 'sword-play' to describe the painful confusion of battle comes from *Beowulf*. It is typically Anglo-Saxon. There are many such examples of laconic understatement in the poem. A warrior says, 'Little courtesy was shown me in allowing me to pass beneath the earth-wall' whereas in fact he had to kill a dragon to get inside. The dragon, fifty feet long and breathing fire, is repeatedly called a worm. 'This hoard was not less great' means it was much greater. Beowulf uses the negative twice in one sentence: 'Not easily did I survive the fight, I performed this deed not without a struggle.' This means he almost died in a hand-to-hand struggle with a monster. Ironic meiosis and the use of the negative is still used by Cockneys when they say, 'It 'ern 'alf good', meaning it is excellent. George Orwell, in advising writers to avoid the 'not unworthy' style of phrasing, parodying it with phrases such as 'not ungreen grass' and 'not unbrown fox', missed the point that such understatement was part of the national mindset.

This characteristic, until recently embedded in the English manner and language, mirrors the English terrain.

The influence of terrain on national character has often been noted. Willa Cather writes in her novel *The Song of the Lark* about the pine trees that dominated the land of the Navajos in northern Arizona:

> The great pines stand at a considerable distance from each other. Each tree grows alone, murmurs alone, thinks alone. They do not intrude upon each other. The Navajos are not much in the habit of giving or of asking help. Their language is not a communicative one, and they never attempt an interchange of personality in speech. Over their forests there is the same inexorable reserve.

John Milton too noted in several of his works that climate and topography nourish consciousness as well as fruit. More recent studies have confirmed the associations between locality and behaviour, suggesting that the power of the ground on which generations have lived is greater than deities in the heavens in determining human destiny. Geography makes people who they are. It shapes human behaviour. Landscape is usually responsible for the form a civilisation takes.

The lands bordering the southern part of the North Sea have a quality that the terrains of most other countries lack, however more flashily dramatic. It is a deeply satisfying, enchanting quality, the charm of small things. No geographical feature in it has any claim to a world record.

In my travels further abroad I have dutifully expressed rapture at some grandeur or other, to the gratification of the natives, but believe this undulating countryside has its own grandeur.

Some may think that calling undulating scenery 'great' boastful but I believe this adjective can fairly be used to describe the English terrain, even though William Blake's famous phrase 'green and pleasant land' is now often quoted ironically by recent settlers and their descendants, in derision.

And its beauty lies precisely in its sense of restraint, its calmness, its very lack of spectacle or flashy drama.

Surely it cannot be a coincidence that the people who lived among this scenery for generations have been known for exactly the same quality? It cannot be the merest chance that the main characteristic of the English landscape is also the main characteristic of the English people.

Remnants of English traditional calmness and understated manner of expressing themselves still exist but the quality is vanishing. And the new loudness and excitability should not be dismissed as an unimportant change, for it is not natural to these shores; it is an alien way of behaving, and it accompanies other challenges to the traditional English manner.

Thirty-five years ago, the philosopher Isaiah Berlin wrote a tribute to his Austrian friend Raimund von Hofmannsthal, who had settled in London after the war. 'England seemed to him,' Berlin wrote, 'the embodiment of a quiet, honourable, humane existence, above all of a civilisation singularly free from violence, hysteria, meanness and vulgarity.'

Since then, the civic virtues, good manners, ingrained personal habits of self-control and moderation, and the national mistrust of excess, have all been jettisoned or destroyed. In the last few decades there has been a catastrophic collapse of English manners and habits. England now is a moral swamp in which the hug-and-confess culture is extirpating hardiness and self-reliance from the national character in favour of a banal, self-pitying, witless and shallow emotional incontinence.

Traditional English virtues have been largely destroyed, widely regarded now as emotional disorders or obsolete. In 1954 Geoffrey Gorer wrote, 'The English are a truly unified people, more unified, I would hazard, than at any previous period in their history.' The country had just been through a terrible war, which had required discipline and sacrifice shared by a population that was still homogenous. Over the following decades a rot set in as the country spurned the moral consensus that underpinned the era of the television series about a bobby on the beat, *Dixon of Dock Green.*

A number of things combined to inflict the damage on traditional self-control and self-respect. They include the institution of the welfare state in the 1940s; the destruction of community spirit begun by misconceived urban rebuilding programmes in the 1960s and completed by Margaret Thatcher's monetarist government in the 1980s; the degrading spectacle of shrieking pseudo-emotion of American films and television; and the incessant melodrama and confrontational behaviour in popular programmes such as *EastEnders*.

What cannot be denied is the impact of American popular culture. But I believe the most important factor in this degradation of a people is the massive influx of settlers. No culture can withstand such an influx, which amounts to an invasion. The reassuring bonds of community have broken down in towns and suburbs where dozens of different languages are spoken and where the main one is not English but some patois or an oriental language. The very word 'community' has become so debased as to be meaningless. When a pervert was murdered some years ago, the police appealed for information from 'the sado-masochistic community', and on March 2nd 2011 the London *Evening Standard* ran a news story about 'thieves from the travelling community' as though the criminals were commuters and not gypsies. This politically correct lumping together conveys a spurious dignity to groups of people no more a community than packs of hyenas scattered throughout the veldt. A strong culture, pride in one's background, could also have resisted Americanisation.

Every society needs some philosophical base to bind its members into a coherent whole. Our country has lost ours over the last fifty years, which have been years of immigration on a scale and at a speed unparalleled in world peacetime history. I have observed over those five decades multiculturalism creating enclaves within the society and the peoples of these enclaves demanding special prerogatives using the excuse of prejudice.

My generation has been the subject of a societal experiment amounting to a covert revolution, a social upheaval unacknowledged and denied. We have seen the very landscape of our lives stealthily transformed. The country we grew up in has changed so much it is another country. Like Soviet citizens in the 1990s, we have become strangers without going anywhere.

Some say it is a brave thing to be a settler, to cast off from your old reference points and certitudes and set out in quest of a better life, but many of the likes of me are in a similar position. Cut off by cultural changes from the world we thought we would inherit, we live in interior exile. In one respect we are in a worse position than settlers - we did not choose this disruption. For many of us, expulsion from our parents' culture is the story of our lives. That being the case, it seems fair to demand that settlers who want to stay in England give up the ways of their own parents.

I was three years old and presumably asleep in bed at home in Greenwich overlooking the Thames when, in the early morning of June 22nd 1948 the rusty old steamer *Empire Windrush* berthed at Tilbury Docks downstream on the other side of the river at the end of a month-long crossing from the Caribbean. On board were five hundred West Indians seeking a new life in 'the mother country', including several stowaways. The revolution had begun. The mother country would soon be another country.

NAZI SHIP GREETED IN THAMES
Black to the future

AS the *Empire Windrush* passed through the English Channel those émigrés who went up on deck would have seen gleaming in the moonlight the famous white cliffs of Dover. Before transatlantic crossings that terminated at west-coast ports such as Cardiff and Liverpool, and air travel, these cliffs were usually the first part of England visitors saw. Because of this, some believe the ancient poetic name of England - Albion - came from these cliffs. Albion is mentioned in the Greek of Ptolemy and the Latin of Pliny, in which 'white' is *albus*. The name of the Alps definitely comes from the fact that they are permanently covered in snow and so always white. But the etymology of Albion is not so clear and this name could have derived from a proto-Indo-European word for 'hill'.

Rounding the Isle of Thanet, the ship entered the Thames estuary and sailed up the river. One passenger said the water was 'brown and red'. The Thames in those days was indeed brown, from pollution, and as it was 7am maybe the red was the reflection of the low sun. At Tilbury the stowaways jumped overboard and swam ashore, where they vanished, never to be found, to become Britain's first illegal immigrants. Whether they survived the diseases that could be caught from swimming in the filthy waters of the Thames is unknown.

A mist rose from the river for a while but when it cleared the tanned sails of the sailing barges downriver would have been clearly seen, russet clusters of canvas sharply peaked, as the barges drifted up with the tide trailing eddies of effluvia and swooping flocks of frantic gulls. The tidal current of the Thames' lower reaches was flowing in its age-old 'good service to the race that peopled its banks', as Joseph Conrad put it.

But upriver the air would seem condensed into a mournful gloom, brooding motionless over the capital. The first Clean Air Act was not passed until 1956, after the Great Smog of December 1952, when a smoke-filled fog shrouded London for five days, bringing to a standstill the entire transport system.

As the sun rose, lights along the shore, at Erith, Woolwich, Greenwich, Deptford, would have started to disappear, switched off. I would by then have been up and toddling around, making a nuisance of myself as my father prepared to leave for his job as a hammerman down the gasworks (which was a major cause of the river's pollution).

Many of those on board the *Empire Windrush* waiting to disembark had dressed up stylishly for the occasion, the men in a felt fedora and a suit with a tie, and the women wearing white gloves and hats and subdued, formal dresses as if on their way to a celebration such as a wedding or Sunday worship. Officials from the Colonies Ministry came on board with a qualified greeting. Loudspeakers summoned the passengers to a talk in which they were told things would not be easy and they were handed leaflets that said they would have difficulty in England and should not have come.

Several politicians and senior civil servants had expressed misgivings. These unregistered newcomers were not really wanted or needed. There was a housing shortage (large parts of London were bombsites); strict food rationing remained from the war (in fact rationing in Britain was worse after the war than during it); the feeling of a need for control over every citizen, necessary in wartime, had not yet dissolved; and, in spite of the myth of a shortage of labour that was later propagated to justify them coming, no industry was seriously undermanned. Labour Minister George Isaacs had said, 'I can give no assurance that they can be found suitable work. I hope no encouragement will be given to others to follow them.'

And two days after the ship docked, eleven Labour MPs wrote to Prime Minister Clement Attlee, 'An influx of coloured people domiciled here is likely to impair the harmony, strength and cohesion of our public and social life.' These Labour MPs, unlike their successors, were writing with knowledge of, and concern for, the feelings of their constituents. Most people in those post-war years had instinctively retreated to familiar ways, familiar rituals, familiar relationships, all in the context of austerity. They lacked the strength and means to cope with any more disruption. (Attlee replied, 'I think it would be a great mistake to take the emigration of this Jamaican party to the UK too seriously.')

Two years before, the BBC, as part of its celebration of victory in the war, had broadcast on the wireless a doggerel poem in praise of the contribution made to the war effort by 'unimportant people who are not in the parade', declaimed in suitable gung-ho fashion by musical comedy star Cicely Courtneidge. Listeners might have raised an eyebrow at the line 'We've got England, shabby, hungry, but England with a future still'. Post-war Britain was a country of ration books and clothing coupons. The London Olympics held a few weeks after the arrival of the *Empire Windrush* became known as the 'Austerity Games'. Competitors were asked to fetch their own towels and, where possible, food, and many made their own sports clothes. No new venues were built for the Games, the athletes being housed in existing accommodation such as schools and wartime barracks instead of an Olympic village.

It was generally believed the settlers would return home after their first experience of an English winter, especially as the previous winter had been by far the worst in memory and one of the harshest ever recorded. It was the reason food rationing was more extensive now than during the war. Bacon was limited to one ounce per person per week. Even potatoes were now rationed, to 3lb a week for each person, the crop having been badly damaged by the prolonged harsh frosts, the snow and the floods. Londoners were living on not much more than Spam fritters and dried egg powder, one tin of which was claimed by the Ministry of Food to be equivalent to twelve fresh eggs but which left cakes and Yorkshire puddings made of it as flat as when they went in. The unfair feeling that the government had not handled the winter crisis well contributed to it losing the next general election. For five months the cold had continued, on and off, the lulls only making everything worse. Short thaws followed days of blizzards, melting the accumulated snow to cause flooded streets. Gutters overflowed with rushing water that poured over and around the full drains. Then the cold returned, so suddenly that the water froze in mid-flow, creating strange configurations of ripples, whorls and bumps. Pavements became almost impossible to walk on, bodies slipping and flopping helplessly on the hard, smooth surfaces. More snow followed, then another thaw; more floods, more black ice. Supplies of food, already rationed, were disrupted. It was dispiriting when going out shopping for food to have the inconvenience of putting on several layers of warm clothing, be aware with every step taken of the danger of slipping over, and then discover that the grocery shop did not have what you had gone out for. Five months of this sort of life, especially coming so soon after the war, was intensely wearying.

The following winter did not turn out to be as brutal as this one but no one could have known that in advance and the first serious cold spell brought back all the bad memories of the previous year. Panic mounted in the streets, the desperation of the people as they braced themselves for the onslaught. The folk memory of the awful winter and a lingering fear of another one did not evaporate for several years. London was a bleak, chilblained make-do-and-mend town, where bombed-out survivors lived with overcrowded relatives.

Into this tense atmosphere of apprehension, discomfort and shortages came strangers. The newcomers expected to be fed and housed. Locals' unease was first disregarded and then made illegal, kindness enforced by Act of Parliament. Many more ships arrived from the Caribbean carrying settlers after that first docking.

The *Empire Windrush* was built in Nazi Germany as a troop carrier. Initially named the *Monte Rosa*, it was launched in 1930 as a cruise ship, and became the favourite cruise ship of top Nazi officials. When the war began she was first used as a barracks ship, and then as a troop carrier for the invasion of Norway. Stationed in Norway, she became an accommodation ship attached to the *Tirpitz*. At the end of the war, as the Germans fled the Red Army, she was used as an evacuation ship. In May 1945 she was seized by the Allies and handed over to the British Ministry of Transport. Two years later she was renamed *Empire Windrush* and, run by the New Zealand Shipping Company on behalf of the British government, was put to service carrying troops between Southampton, Gibraltar, Suez, Aden, Colombo, Singapore and Hong Kong. Over the years in which she ran this route, extended during the Korean War to Japan, in 1948 she made one other journey - from Australia to Britain, via Kingston, Jamaica, where the emigrants, enticed by a newspaper advertisement offering one-way berths to Britain for £28 10s each, embarked.

Three years after the defeat of Hitler, the ship that heralded an ineradicable change in the complexion of Britain was a Nazi troop carrier.

A convoy of charabancs took the new arrivals over the river to Clapham Common in south London, where they could be accommodated in cavernous wartime air-raid shelters. The Women's Voluntary Service distributed mugs of tea and parcels of precious rationed food, while Communists and churches offered moral support. The immigrants had been informed at Tilbury how to register for unemployment, and the Labour Exchange (job centre) nearest to the Clapham shelters was at the Brixton end of the long Coldharbour Lane, so this was where they went for their registration documents.

Despite politicians and officials continuing to express misgivings about the influx of immigrants, they were powerless to prevent it, for, as an internal Minister of Labour memo stated just days before the *Empire Windrush* arrived, 'There is no logical ground for treating a British subject who comes of his own accord from Jamaica to Great Britain differently from another who comes to London on his own account from Scotland.'

It recognised however that a political problem was being created, and recommended dispersal as the solution: 'If only they could be dispersed in small parties, then even though they did not get immediate employment, they would cease to be recognisable as a problem.'

But most remained to put down roots in Brixton. One became a Brixton Market trader, a barrow boy, earning his living at this until his retirement. Over the years, especially after a USA Act of 1952 limited immigration there, many others followed, so that Brixton eventually became inhabited largely by West Indians. Immigrants' families and descendants also spread north to the district of the Old Kent Road and eastwards, to Peckham, New Cross, Lewisham - and Greenwich.

I still remember the surprise I felt a few years after the *Empire Windrush* anchored at Tilbury when I first heard a negro child speaking with a Cockney accent just like me and my friends and our neighbours. It was strange to hear this accent coming out of the mouth of someone with so much melanin in the skin.

Nowadays, when everyone knows what a negro looks like, it is hard to recall how odd and foreign the first ones appeared to us. Of course they acted differently to the indigenous people. How could it be otherwise? They were informal where we would be respectful (and sometimes the opposite) and careless when we would be scrupulous. Their body language was different, which led to misunderstandings. But nobody felt any alarm about them, and the first wave of interest soon ebbed away. Blacks were, admittedly, a bit weird - but that was, after all, just because they were novelties. People had felt the same about novelties of other days - about kangaroos, giraffes, giant lizards... In time, the public grew out of thinking negroes freakish. They could be amusing but not greatly interesting. Attempting to understand their accent was usually more trouble than it was worth. In the general ignorance naturally some falsehoods thrived. It was widely circulated and casually believed that the settlers ate tinned cat food. The locals were not interested enough to question this rumour or to consider that, even if true, it could only be because the settlers were too poor to buy decent meat. When the pre-war fascist Sir Oswald Mosley returned from exile abroad to fight North Kensington in the 1959 general election on behalf of the 'British Movement' he finished bottom of the poll and lost his deposit. Most Britons remained unexcited by Mosley's appeal to racism.

Because the people were not racist, successive governments, especially Labour ones, for years acted with extraordinary complacency. Settlers increased even under Winston Churchill, who was against immigration. When he regained power the numbers rose anyway, from 3,000 arrivals in 1953 to 42,650 two years later, including, it was rumoured, a former Caribbean Minister of Education. Afterwards the numbers steadied, fell, then increased again to reach 136,400 in 1961. When the Macmillan government the following year set up a voucher system for settlers, the Labour Party called the government racist and when it returned to power scrapped the system. Immigration was already a political problem.

It was noticeable that the settlers encroached. You would one day see a lone individual or a family in an area where none had ever been seen before - then, soon, you would regularly see several individuals or families in that area: then you heard it being said, 'They're taking over the district.' Their wide distribution led to puzzled speculation more than their original sudden appearance. By 1976 a cricket Test match between England and the West Indies at The Oval in south London was regarded by the West Indies as a 'home venue', a feeling enhanced by the Caribbean heat of that summer.

Only then, three decades after the first arrivals came, did there begin to arise serious widespread misgivings among the indigenous people. As the West Indians multiplied, their presence affected more and more English people, and so more noticed how loud and flamboyant they were in an un-English way. They spoke louder, their adolescents' horseplay was louder, they played their music louder and they dressed louder. Their cars hurtled along too fast, with headlights blazing and horns blaring at the mistakes of other motorists or pedestrians crossing the road. They kept finding occasion to shout to a friend on the other side of the street. Worst of all were the noisy all-night parties. Complaining neighbours were informed by way of explanation that, in the Caribbean, dwellings were spaced some distance apart so the noise did not bother neighbours. (We have here one of the early examples of modern settlers refusing to adapt. It did not occur to them that noisy parties are inappropriate in England, where most homes are flats or terraced houses. Unfortunately, this lack of consideration was imitated by some young whites, and is now regarded as normal behaviour.)

And then came the hideous commercial parties, which featured the new pounding sound systems (a sort of amplified juke-box) and which, for reasons of extra profit, never ended before the early hours of the morning. Five hundred invitation cards were printed and given to every black person the organising 'hosts' met. Word went round and groups of black youths would go from party to party throughout the night, speaking of 'raiding' these parties.

The English had always called loud and flamboyant types 'flashy', regarding them as not only alien but even abnormal. Estate agents and journalists began describing areas in which many blacks lived as 'bustling' and 'vibrant' but to the whites who had lived in these areas for generations the newcomers did not seem to 'liven things up'. Instead, they seemed to introduce something rather ugly that had not been there before, a sense of chaos, which then remained in the area like a kind of contamination.

Impartial observers such as visitors from abroad were not certain, either, whether the newcomers and the indigenous people were quite as friendly as they were supposed to be, as full of bonhomie as journalists and politicians made out. These observers noticed that they did not talk to each other unless it was absolutely necessary, and seemed to avoid looking at each other altogether.

Other peoples followed the Caribbeans. The first big group to come from the Indian subcontinent was Punjabi Sikhs. Next came Hindu Gujaratis. Then it was Muslims, first from north-east Pakistan, then from Bengal, then from what is now Bangladesh. The East End of London is now inhabited largely by immigrants and their descendants from a region in the north-east of Bangladesh named Sylhet (a reality not reflected in *EastEnders*, in which most of the characters remain chirpy Cockney sparrers, admitted by the BBC's controller of drama production John Yorke when he said *EastEnders* 'may be significantly white compared with the real East End.'). Within fifty years of the docking of the *Empire Windrush* the racial complexion of England had changed utterly. Most big towns had areas in which white people had become rare. Already, talking about immigrants in those places as 'minorities' sounded perverse. By 1998 it was indigenous children who had become a minority at local-authority secondary schools in inner London and even in the suburbs they made up only 60 per cent of the secondary-school population. More than a third of inner London's children did not even have English as their first language.

Since then the situation has become catastrophic. A report in March 2012 revealed that in London 98,000 schoolchildren do not have English as their mother tongue, as opposed to the 79,000 native English speakers. And many of the latter are not indigenous.

More than 1,600 schools across England are now in the minority when it comes to having English as the first spoken language, and the number is dramatically rising weekly. Almost one million children who now attend schools in England do not have English as their first language at home.

Now settlers include Afghans, Africans, Albanians, Arabs and many others all the way through the alphabet up to and including Zulus.

And now, six decades after the *Empire Windrush* arrived and I first heard a negro speak like me, I am invariably the only indigenous Cockney on a packed double-decker 53 bus in the Old Kent Road, the thoroughfare down which Chaucer's pilgrims began their journey to Canterbury in *The Canterbury Tales* and celebrated in the music hall song 'Knocked 'em in the Old Kent Road', the chorus of which captures the flavour of Cockney speech:

'Wotcher!' all the neighbours cried,
'Who yer gonna meet, Bill,
'Ave yer bought the street, Bill?'
Laugh - I thought I would 'ave died,
Knocked 'em in the Old Kent Road.

Known then for its shops selling jellied eels and pie and mash, now you see only food shops such as the Ryad Halal Emporium, the Chittagong Grocers and Caribbean takeaways advertising jerk chicken. Virtually all the pedestrians on the crowded pavements are ethnics.

So it is on the bus also. And they are noisy. Passengers travelling alone used to be silent. Now they all yell into mobiles. So on the bus I hear Yoruba and Hausa, and Nigerians shouting English with a Yoruba or Hausa accent; rattling Tamil and other Indian languages, and their accents; Arabic; Somali; black youths self-consciously speaking Anglo-Lewisham; and many other languages and accents. The 53 bus is a Babel on wheels.

Multi-culturalism seems to me more and more like cultural murder.

The *Empire Windrush* has acquired an iconic status almost equal to that of the *Mayflower*. With good reason. Both ships heralded a great tragedy for the indigenous people, who helplessly watched vast numbers of aliens settle on their shores to utterly change the nature of their land. And in our case this catastrophic change is lauded by some as being good for us! Would you Adam and Eve it!

DOWN WITH XENOPHILIA!
Human rights all gone wrong

IN the same year that the *Empire Windrush* arrived the Labour government ratified the British Nationality Act, which gave every Commonwealth citizen the legal right to settle in the United Kingdom. It was passed with little debate because MPs believed few of them, living as most did in pleasantly warm countries, would want to come and live in cold, dank Britain.

There were 800 million of them. The number looks more spectacular in figures - 800,000,000. Unfortunately, the MPs were mistaken and many of these millions DID want to come and live in cold, dank Britain - and not only did hundreds of thousands do so, but, surprise, surprise, they were all from the pleasantly warm countries.

Indian leader Mahatma Gandhi, who had been assassinated by a fellow Hindu on January 30th of that year, when asked while on a visit to England in 1931, arriving at Buckingham Palace absurdly wearing only a loincloth and sandals, what he thought of British civilisation, had wittily replied, 'I think it would be a good idea.'

Over the following decades millions of his compatriots have chosen to live in that civilisation rather than their own.

Word had spread around the Commonwealth that the English were extraordinarily tender-hearted - and it would have been an offence to universal common sense not to audaciously lead a people like that around by the nose. Having heard that kindness reigned in England, foreigners came, saw and took outright possession of many of our towns.

Visas were eventually introduced, which, though they did not stop Commonwealth immigration, belatedly set limits, thus ending the illusion that it was perfectly reasonable and quite feasible to let 800,000,000 foreigners have the right to come and go at will. But then, with several English cities already resembling Calcutta, and the capital an unpleasant mix of all sorts, exactly fifty years after the Nationality Act another Labour government passed another act, which once again allowed in all and sundry. Among the new beneficiaries were many asylum seekers, who only needed to be prepared to tell silly lies to be allowed in, with no means of ever getting them out.

By now England was the new land of milk and honey. Like the 'happy valley' in Samuel Johnson's 1759 novel *The History of Rasselas* it gave 'constant gratification for every kind of appetite, the blessings of nature collected and its evils extracted and excluded'. Its inhabitants, luxuriating like heedless children in the vacuity of ease and plenty, their childhood Canaan incompatible with the process of growing up and looking after themselves, were vulnerable to covert invasion by cunning, energetic, virile foreigners attracted by the riches. All it needed was a few influential traitors; and these were duly supplied by Labour governments.

Vast hordes of different peoples have now crammed onto our island. But why are there all the denials and protean and retroactive excuses and justifications? How was it allowed to happen?

Up until 1997 nobody said, 'Let us invite millions of foreigners to settle among us. This will achieve many things: they can willingly do the dirty jobs our layabout working class, spoilt by the welfare state, now refuse to do; they can fill the job vacancies caused by the indigenous people ageing at an alarming rate and not reproducing sufficiently; it will alleviate the suffering of the world's poor, who, by coming here, can better their lot; it will give the vulnerable in conflict areas of the world (which includes much of Africa most of the time) somewhere to escape to; it will benefit the economy; increase our GNP; and we can observe and appreciate at close quarters their funny ways. Let us all live together in comfort and luxury and celebrate diversity.' No one reasoned thus.

But then Labour came to power and, dreaming up such dubious arguments, within a year passed the Human Rights Act, which dismantled the few remaining flimsy barriers, enabling fresh hordes to stampede into Britain despite the backlog of asylum seekers growing by 3,000 a month, four hundred and fifty immigration staff resigning and a new computerised system collapsing.

Most settled in London. Suddenly, within a few years, as well as the millions of ethnics already in the capital, the streets, shops and public transport were full of new arrivals not even speaking English. This has been followed in the last couple of years by another, sinister, phenomenon - a massive influx of Nigerians. In Greenwich, they are suddenly everywhere. Pushy, expansive and confident, loudly speaking Yoruba, Hausa or Igbo, they often seem now to dominate the borough. Something is happening we have not been told about.

London is being ethnically cleansed - of Londoners. It is no longer an English town. Nowadays, whenever you pass someone in a London street, he or she is more likely than not to be speaking a foreign language. Three million out of London's eight million inhabitants do not speak English as a first language. And these are in addition to the offspring of the earlier arrivals. London has become a town of ethnics, where Cockney spoken by an indigenous Londoner is rarely heard. It has been officially announced that most babies being born in the capital are aliens. This sounds like the plot of a science fiction novel such as John Wyndham's *The Midwich Cuckoos* in which, nine months after a visitation by an unknown life form when all the inhabitants of a village fell asleep, all the women of child-bearing age in the village give birth at the same time. The children are all aliens from a civilisation that plans to take over the world.

We had better watch out. Aliens now fill our maternity wards.

Indigenous Cockneys are supposed to call this phenomenon 'diversity' and to 'celebrate' it. Why should we? What have we gained? We had a culture, and the British class system was sufficient diversity for us, thank you very much.

Multi-culturalism is an evil concept, truly invidious. It has caused much suffering, and in the coming years will cause a lot more. People of two cultures do indeed in a way belong to both - but in other ways do not fully belong to either. A nation has a history, a culture, an identity. England is not France, Spain is not Germany, and none of them are Bangladesh or Nigeria. Nor do their citizens want them to become so. People do not want to be over-run by foreigners of a strange religion, a different race or exotic (and sometimes repulsive) customs, even if it does mean a temporary one per cent rise in economic growth. No amount of lecturing or legislation will change these attitudes.

The lectures and the laws usually contain the phrase 'human rights'. Coined in 1942, it was at first simply a war slogan. The spread of its wider meaning later was caused by the tendency of socialists to go beyond their remit and speak and act on behalf of all suffering humanity. One of the earliest uses of the term 'human rights' with its extended meaning came in 1959, when the Labour MP for Brixton, Marcus Lipton, in his contribution to the local *West Indian Gazette*'s 'Election Guide', wrote, 'The Labour Party has always fought for social justice and human rights because our socialist creed is based on the equal value of every human being.'

In the 1960s socialists increasingly declared that religion and race did not matter, that immigrants and natives alike were members of the working class or the brotherhood of man whose common interests were more important than their superficial differences.

It was a wildly romantic, unrealistic view.

The British Communist Party had a perfectly good daily newspaper called the *Daily Worker*. This was known by everyone in the country and respected even by political opponents. But then, in 1966, it was changed to the *Morning Star* because, it was argued, 'We Communists speak not only for the working class but for everyone who is in any way oppressed throughout the world.' Many years after the name change few had heard of the *Morning Star*, especially when the tabloid *Daily Star* appeared, a title that the *Morning Star* challenged in the courts as being too similar to their own, to be rebuffed by a judge who ruled that, 'Only a moron in a hurry could not tell the difference between the two papers.'

In the same way, Labour politicians, who, for the most part, unlike their Tory counterparts, traditionally represented something more than their own personal interests, also became universal goody-goodies. Instead of striving to keep traditional British values alive and relevant they strove to be everything to everyone throughout the whole world. Concern for the indigenous working class, which the Labour Party was founded to represent, expanded and metamorphosed into concern for suffering humanity.

It seemed ever more obvious to the likes of me that as suffering humanity poured into Britain in ever-increasing numbers, this concern became at the expense of the indigenous working class. We saw projects for jobless negroes, not all the jobless; for disadvantaged Indians or Muslims, not all the disadvantaged. When we saw newspaper headlines such as 'Studio gives teenagers role in the movies' we knew without reading the article that the adolescents being given a chance in the film industry were ethnic adolescents only. In July 2010 we read of Channel 4 being upbraided by MPs on the Culture, Media and Sport Committee for being so obsessed with diversity that whites were under-represented in its workforce. Tory MP Philip Davies told the broadcaster's heads that recent schemes such as a bursary for African, Caribbean, Bangladeshi and Pakistani students were effectively depriving white people of the same equal opportunities. We heard mild and respectable indigenous Cockneys say matter-of-factly of council houses in a prime location, 'I couldn't get a house there, I'm the wrong colour.' Labour politicians, in their concern for humanity, ignored their own constituents, who know, like all normal people everywhere in the world know, that strangers' tears are only water. People only feel comfortable in sharing with those they regard as 'one of us'. It is not healthy when nations live within a nation.

This has long been known by sensible rulers. Aristotle wrote about leaders who drove out settlers, fearing they would in time increase so greatly they would supplant them and bring down the state.

Ancient wisdom all over the world on the rules of hospitality made a clear distinction between those strangers to whom one should be generously hospitable and those who over-stayed their welcome. Captain Cook was fêted when he first arrived at Hawaii and killed when he unexpectedly returned (to repair a mast damaged in continuing bad weather).

Anyway hospitality as a virtue is over-rated, tainted with the sense of possession. It is a type of showing off.

Aesop noted 7,000 years ago that people often give enemies the means for their own destruction. History and classical myth are full of examples of settlers being welcomed and the hosts' descendants suffering the baleful consequences. In Virgil's epic poem *The Aeneid* the king of Latium agrees to help the Trojan prince Aeneas and his vagabond followers settle in Italy. Their settlement became Rome. After five centuries of incessant warfare only the Roman kingdom remained; every other kingdom in Italy had ceased to exist - including Latium. Its language became the basis of Latin but the race was wiped out.

Ominously for Albion, its principal city, destroyed by Rome in the seventh century BC, was named Alba.

Likewise, the Algonquin tribe, who fed the starving English settlers on the mysterious east coast of North America in 1584, taught them how to survive the terrors of the 'wilderness' and guided them on their forays inland, unaware of the ethnic disaster awaiting them as a result.

And, on the eve of the Pequot war fifty years later, further up the coast, as Captain John Underhill recalled in his 1638 *News from America*, 'The [Pequot] Indians spying of us came running in multitudes along the water side, crying, "What cheer, Englishmen, what cheer, what do you come for?".' Unhappily for them the English had come for their land, and the Pequots would soon become, as Herman Melville put it, 'As extinct as the ancient Medes'.

The band of Wampanoag led by chief Masssasoit who celebrated the first Thanksgiving with the *Mayflower* settlers in 1622, fetching five freshly-killed deer to the feast, were soon to regret befriending and helping the newcomers. In later years Massasoit, gazing out at the ocean from where the *Mayflower* had come, must have often thought, 'What have we done? What if we had taken a different course of action in dealing with these people?'

Similarly, in Australia the local members of the Eora people, the Cadigal clan, who danced hand in hand with the Redcoats who had arrived with the eleven ships of the First Fleet in 1788, also soon had cause to regret their friendly welcome. The oldest civilisation on Earth was henceforth doomed.

In all these cases, and in many more throughout history all over the world, those among the indigenous people who advocated repulsing the settlers were the wise ones.

Welcoming and aiding settlers is a perilous enterprise best avoided. It has never been a good idea.

Among politicians in England now there is a widespread uncritical, unnatural acceptance of anything foreign in our country, the exact opposite of xenophobia - xenophilia.

Xenophilia in politics produces a variety of evils.

Sympathy for settlers creates the illusion of an imaginary common interest in cases where no real common interest exists. It leads to the hosts' leaders ignorantly accepting all that the settlers say, even when detrimental to their own country, and to grant concessions to settlers denied to indigenous people, which injures those being forced against their will to collectively make those concessions. These reluctant philanthropists, from whom not only are equal privileges withheld but who are also unnecessarily forced to part with what should have been retained, are provoked to envy, ill-will and, eventually, a disposition to retaliate. And it gives to those ambitious, corrupt or deluded politicians who devote themselves to the settlers the opportunity to betray or sacrifice the interests of their own country without odium, gilding their ambition, corruption or delusion with the glitter of altruism.

Xenophilia is the true morbid and irrational condition, not the stigmatised xenophobia. The demand that in the course of just one generation we accept millions of foreigners to live among us goes against reason and human nature. A caveman who looked out of his cave and saw a stranger reached for his club. This was the reaction of human beings for hundreds of thousands of years. This is how we evolved.

William Golding suggests in his novel *The Inheritors* that the Neanderthals were wiped out because of a naïve trust in malevolent Cro-Magnons, early modern humans, believing the arrows fired at them to be sticks thrown as presents. Too late do they understand that harm is meant by the sticks of the new people. The extinction of the Neanderthals was in fact genocide. Some paleontologists have endorsed this theory.

'Phobia' is inappropriately over-used. A phobia is an irrational dislike or fear. But dislike or fear of strangers is not irrational at all. It is a perfectly reasonable instinct evolved over many millennia of experience. It is always the likes of me, the reluctant hosts, who are deemed xenophobic. There exists a European Monitoring Centre on Racism and Xeno-phobia, indignantly keeping tabs on these crimes against ethnics, with no Asian or African equivalent.

It has never occurred to any of our leaders to flick the ethnics into a startled awareness that there is another background, another history, another outlook, another breed, than the ethnics' own. For decades there has been nothing but self-abnegation, grovelling apologies for existing. An individual behaving like this would clearly be needing psychotherapy.

Down with xenophilia!

The word 'altruism' appeared in Britain in 1852, in a *Westminster Review* article on the coiner of the word, French philosopher Auguste Comte. One English admirer of Comte wrote, 'Our duty is to annihilate ourselves if need be for the service of Humanity.'

It is all very well and goody-goody for such an individual to annihilate himself in such a cause; it is quite a different matter for a country's lead-ers to annihilate their country; fair enough if they wish to groom the aliens (each to his own) but why should the rest of us acquiesce in sharing our island? We were not consulted. Mass immigration could only happen if it was encouraged by the elites with no reference to the people. A referen-dum has been held on the country's voting system and there has been loads of talk about holding a referendum on membership of the European Union. This is playing games, pretending that the wishes of the public shall be followed, that we live in an exemplary democracy. Not a dicky-bird has ever been said about holding a referendum on the issue that smacks us in the face each time we look out of our window or enter a shop or catch a bus or train.

Not only has it never even been suggested that there be a referendum on such a colossal change in the complexion of our country in the space of one generation - do-gooders have deliberately hidden the facts.

In the same year that the Human Rights Act was passed they kept quiet about an enormous rise in successful refugee applications for fear of a backlash against asylum seekers. One of them, an official of Amnesty International, said, 'We are not making much of it because we want the government to continue paying regard to human rights.'

The public, it seems, were not competent to decide who should come and live among them.

Do-gooders do a lot of harm. When they pause for breath from their tireless do-gooding, it is just to draw on an everlasting stream of pure virtue. Of course, they will argue that multi-culturalism is a worthy end in itself - although you will not often hear that said in places such as

Reading, where more than a hundred languages are spoken in schools, or in Peterborough, the shoplifting capital of Britain, where I recently got lost and could not find a single person who spoke English and where migrants refusing to return to their home countries had set up camp on fifteen busy roundabouts.

Ten years ago I, as a Cockney visitor, was regarded jovially in somnolent market towns as a 'foreigner'. Now real foreigners have engulfed these towns, as well as many of our major cities, with our rulers either denying it is happening or claiming it does not matter and even that it is beneficial. Older citizens such as I are baffled that such a huge thing could have erupted into our peaceful lives without anyone warning or asking us.

Because Nigeria is classified 'an unsafe country' everyone from there is allowed to come and live in Britain if they so desire, can get here and can concoct some lie, no matter how implausible. One hulking Nigerian said he had managed to escape from prison by walking out wearing a nurse's skirt.

Clearly those sleek, loud, expansive Nigerians now so common in London are not piteous victims of persecution. I have not seen a body of strangers bear themselves more proudly. It is not exile but adventure, I am thinking, boldness of spirit, which brings them to England. They are predators who have settled in with forged documents.

Sophisticated certificate factories now operate in many English towns producing high-grade forgeries of birth certificates, marriage certificates and other papers that are hard to tell from the real thing. This is why many Nigerians are called by such names as Smith. (A lot of people in London are reporting they have received a scam telephone call from a man speaking with a thick Yoruba accent who says his name is Peacock.)

It requires a criminal mind and criminal contacts to approach these gangs. And we are expected to believe that such types as Mr Peacock have needed Oxfam or Amnesty International.

Genuinely vulnerable asylum seekers are so rare they barely count. The phrase 'asylum seekers' conjures up pictures of columns of refugees winding their way out of burning towns, of people being tortured in unspeakable third-world prisons, but very few are anything of the sort. Most are able-bodied young men sent by families who can afford to pay a gang £6,000. They are the bold, the aggressive, the cunning - all attributes typically possessed by criminals.

Timid Vietnamese stay at home tending their paddy fields; the go-ahead ones come to Britain and open cannabis factories. Instead of rice they cultivate hash. We get the world's dregs, the enterprising fiends. To equate them with the humble, frightened Jews who fled to Britain clutching their little cardboard suitcases to escape the Nazis is laughable.

If you pander to a child too much, give in to its every whim, you end up with a spoilt brat. This is what has happened with Britain's ethnics. Like spoilt children, they keep pushing for more and more until their demands go beyond all reason; they sense there is no limit to what they can get away with. The steady drip of political correctness backed up by the occasional tantrum will secure them anything.

They despise our largesse even as they accept it. People naturally despise those who court them, but respect those who do not give way to them. Attraction is not the same as admiration. You can be attracted to a pretty woman alone late at night in a pub without admiring her. Settlers' whining buzzes around us incessantly. Too many of them are avidly and relentlessly determined to be mortally offended as often as is humanly possible. Lacking the maturity to shrug off things they find offensive, they have become preternaturally sensitive to almost everything, exploiting the tendency of high-toned altruists to over-estimate the sufferings of those they sympathise with.

Enforcement of the few laws that technically were on the books to limit immigration has been so lax that custom has rewritten them. Aliens have grown up with the understanding that to head to England is simply what people do - since that is what their cousins did, and their uncles, and their neighbours. Whatever people have always got away with ceases to seem like getting away with anything and becomes the least you can expect, one's birthright, one's due. This attitude is adopted by the likes of Amnesty International, and emigration to the UK becomes a 'human right'. That is why the latest wave of settlers to engulf us, all those Nigerians and Somalians, are so full of themselves. They know their rights.

Because settling here has become a 'human right' for foreigners, the slightest hint that they might be deprived of this 'right' provokes indignation among them and among our treacherous leaders, who, attempting to justify immigration, often cite the precedent of the French Protestant Huguenot refugees around 1670, as though 50,000 Christians from a neighbouring country can be compared to three million settlers from all over the world including peddlers of religious charlatanry incessantly seeking fresh opportunities to get their hooks into the state.

And still the settlers have poured in. According to a government report of October 2009 the number of immigrants in Britain nearly doubled under Labour, an estimated three million arriving since 1997, more than seven hundred a day. In 2008 alone, no fewer than 735,000 National Insurance numbers were handed out to newly-arrived foreigners.

Labour leaders, in, at best, allowing this to happen, or, at worst, positively encouraging it, erected a vast edifice of deceit. Everything they said about the issue was as fraudulent as the claims of bogus asylum seekers. Immigration ministers have actually claimed that most settlers work for a while, 'contribute to the economy' and then return home, seemingly expecting us to believe this as though we were a nation of Noddies. You have to belong to the intelligentsia to make such claims: no ordinary person could be such a fool. The general public, being less affected by political correctness, and thus able to think more logically, are on many issues far wiser than their leaders.

In reality, Britain is becoming an indiscriminate mongrel mixture. Within a couple of years 96,000 new primary school places will be needed for migrant children.

Albion has been so overwhelmed that the politicians do not know what to do next. Their first concern is to deny it has happened, 'overwhelmed' being yet another of the many taboo words in any discussion on immigration. Like cowards vowing not to give in to provocation, like timid men calling their celibacy morality, they call their paralysis policy. Weaklings who think themselves good because they lack claws, they have passed and repealed so many useless and contradictory laws on immigration they obviously have no idea whether they are coming or going. Only the settlers have a clear head - they are definitely coming and certainly staying. It is easy to outwit the witless.

Even professional practitioners find it hard to give guidance, as one of them, Habib Rahman, chief executive of the Joint Council for the Welfare of Immigrants, has admitted.

In the face of this paralysis, judges and lawyers now have the final say on who can stay and who must go. Interpretation of immigration law in the courts, written in dense legalese incomprehensible to normal people, with many a courteous reference to the decisions of other learned friends, is what decides the fate of millions, usually in their favour.

Recently it was felt necessary to remind these suave legal folk that documents produced in court by a supplicating ethnic might just possibly be, heaven forfend, not genuine.

The government asserted that only 15,000 migrants would come when eight East European countries joined the EU, the Labour ministers having voluntarily forfeited the right to defer unrestrained entry from these countries. More than 600,000 arrived. (One happy consequence of this was that for the first time you could raise the subject of mass immigration without being accused of racism.)

Ministers later admitted as well that their estimate that there were 800,000 foreign workers in Britain was also wrong. The figure should have been twice that. Home Office ministers were unable to say how many convicted murderers, drug dealers and other criminals had been granted British citizenship; how many deported foreign offenders turned round and flew straight back again; how many times the police and ambulance services had been called to riots at immigration centres, one of which was deliberately burnt down by ethnics to destroy the vital records on them kept there. In the run-up to the 2010 general election the question was often asked: 'Can anyone control immigration?' That this question could be asked so often, with no affirmative answer ever given, means that Britain cannot defend its borders. A civilisation as weak as this does not deserve to survive.

The indigenous people resent above all the newcomers' claims to rights that they themselves do not have. This resentment is not an aggressive dislike but a sheepish aversion that whispers around dim corners. The rulers, fearing more than anything else that this passive dislike will boil up into active hatred, use all sorts of tricks to prevent this happening. The London mayor, announcing that he is 'immensely proud' of his city, sends out a questionnaire asking citizens to indicate from a list their main concerns in order that they can be addressed, with the main concern of the vast majority of indigenous Londoners, the swamping of the city by settlers, left off the list. It is as though a deranged Basil Fawlty, instead of famously repeating, 'Don't mention the war!' in order not to offend a group of Germans staying at his Fawlty Towers hotel, keeps saying, 'Don't mention immigration!' so as not to offend black, Indian or Muslim guests.

O no
Xanadu-on-Thames

THE packed, snow-plastered 108 bus continues on its route down Westcombe Hill, with me the only indigenous English passenger. Yesterday I unknowingly dropped my mobile phone on the pavement outside North

Greenwich Underground Station, and a bus driver had just called my landline number, which was in the mobile, to tell me he has picked it up and if I catch him there either this time or next time round he will return it to me.

He tells me his bus number, 161, which, he says, is a double-decker going to Chislehurst, and his name, which is Pedro. He has a West Indian accent. On the way I will do some shopping at the giant Sainsbury's down there.

The snug ethnics occupying all the seats look out at the icy surroundings, the pavements covered in snow. The bus is muggy with twice-breathed air and the smell of wool. Several of the swarthy women have dark shawls over their heads and around their shoulders. Some hold shopping bags on their laps. The only passengers speaking any sort of English are the loudly jabbering black schoolchildren lapsing every and now then into their patois, and a standing black youth in baggy trousers managing to clutch three mobile phones, making and receiving calls on all three in loud Anglo-Lewisham pidgin as he hangs on. He has incredible lips like tyres. One of the conversations is about a forthcoming court case in which he is the defendant, from which we are to gather he is a petty criminal. From the manner and volume of the conversation I get the feeling that he wants us to know this, that he is proud of it.

Prominent among the foreign languages are those of the Nigerian diaspora. This is a new phenomenon. One of the Nigerians speaking in one of these tongues into a mobile is a gross woman dressed in gaudy African finery partly covered by an overcoat, who has an enormous arse. Although many passengers are having to stand, she is unashamedly taking up two seats. The seats of London buses are not made for Nigerian arses. To emphasise her point (if she is making a point rather than being simply grotesquely selfish), she has placed her shopping bag on the sliver of aisle seat not covered by her arse. In the bag she has a loaf of bread, from which, with fingers adorned with rings, she scoops up lumps straight into her mouth. Crumbs are everywhere. She is also spitting them into her mobile as she speaks loudly in Yoruba (or Igbo, Hausa or Swahili, or whatever). It is so unbelievably grotesque that the passengers remain silent, unable to interfere and stop this outrage against public decency - in fear, perhaps, of being regarded as racist, disrespectful to some peculiar way of life, even though they are all themselves ethnics. Is she deliberately testing the famous tolerance of the English public, unable to recognise, with her typical ethnic autism, utterly absorbed in herself, that no one on the bus apart from me is in fact English?

The five seats ranged along the back of the bus are taken by a pair of young male blacks, two middle-aged Indians not with each other and some other dark-skinned ethnic who could have come from any southern town or village in the world.

I hang on for the swaying, lurching ride, downhill. Standing next to me a black girl opens a fine embossed hardback edition of *Nicholas Nickleby* at the beginning and keeps chuckling at the humorous description of the founding of the United Metropolitan Improved Hot Muffin and Crumpet Baking and Punctual Delivery Company. A Chinese girl appears to be talking to herself in Mandarin but presumably has a mobile microphone tucked away somewhere. A pretty little Arab girl muffled up to the shoulders in a merciless *hijab* offers me her seat but I ungraciously decline. I do not want to take her seat, I want her pretty little bum to be on a camel in Saudi Arabia where it belongs, not incongruously on a 108 bus going down Westcombe Hill.

I feel angry. I never aspired to live in a hodge-podge of world cultures, to see and hear only foreigners in the area where I grew up. They clearly do not belong to the genus 'Londoners', about which journalists are so fond of writing. It must not be forgotten that I knew a time when Londoners all spoke the same language with the only difference in accent being that of class.

I am aware that my reaction is not politically correct but it is clear that noble qualities such as an abstract love of humanity must atrophy in a standing-room-only environment. It is unreasonable to expect a people with their own traditions and customs to absorb so many foreigners. Few English faces have been seen on 108 buses for a long time and now, for some reason, you rarely hear English spoken either. Something is happening here I do not understand. Recently I was on a 108 and at one point there was a black man in front of me, a black man behind me and a black man next to me all speaking on a mobile in some African language. It seems to me perfectly acceptable in these circumstances to wonder what is occurring. Nothing in the bus suggests we are in England. The only clue is that it is going down the hill on the left. Britain is neither the sole country with significant minorities of citizens who are not identifying with the indigenous people, nor the only state with links to diasporas, but this district I grew up in seems to have lost its identity utterly.

Throughout London now are new settlers of strange nationality with whom relations are uncomfortable and ambivalent. My senses are constantly bombarded by incongruous sounds and sights. Politicians who pretend that immigration is solely an economic issue without political, social and cultural ramifications, call such a bombardment 'diversity'. Presumably some, if not most, of the dark-skinned passengers wearing tropical clothes babbling in an incomprehensible language have British passports. I am expected to regard them as compatriots. This is clearly absurd. They no more want to have anything to do with the likes of me than we do with the likes of them.

At the bottom of the hill the pretty Arab girl gets off but a family of twelve of her ilk gets on. One of the women is draped in a head-to-toe *jilbab*, a garment that, like the *burka*, implies utter rejection of the wearer's host country and its values. She frantically castigates the older children for not helping with the buggies or for getting in the way or for being too slow. No one else on the bus knows the precise nature of the Arabic rebukes. All the other passengers belong to different hordes. Several are speaking Urdu (a word that is closely related etymologically to horde). For all I know, some of those speaking in their foreign tongue are cursing the Arabs in a manner that, if expressed by the likes of me in English, would cause a hoo-ha and a possible court conviction for inciting race hatred under one of the seven laws set up for such eventualities.

What with the toddlers and the buggies the boarding takes a long time and then the buggies clog up the aisle, so that when an elderly Pakistani wants to get off at the next stop he encounters problems. A male Arab says something in Arabic, presumably an apology, and the Pakistani mutters something in Urdu.

While the difficulties are being sorted out at the exit in the middle of the bus, at the entrance by the driver a white man is getting on. He presses an Oyster card against the Oyster pad and remains there, unable to go further in. A white man! Dr Livingstone, I presume. Alas, he speaks on his mobile and turns out to be a Pole. More like Dr Livinsky.

Three swarthy, thinly moustachioed youths, possibly Afghan, take up three seats, two next to each other and their companion in the aisle seat in front of them. This one has fallen asleep. His head lollops dangerously close to the shoulder of the discomfited passenger next to him, a middle-aged South Asian. The Afghan's outer leg is stretched out so that it is blocking the aisle. All disembarking passengers, some with heavy shopping bags, are obliged to step over it. When he wakes up he puts his arm on the back of the South Asian's seat in order to turn round to speak to his companions, further irritating the South Asian. I have been to Afghanistan, and recognise this nonchalant disregard for others' personal space. Maybe this explains the rise of the Taliban.

Two other swarthy youths are conversing in their language. A dusky girl seated near me next to a window is upset by something her companion has just said in *their* language and is frowning at the light snowflakes swirling about outside. It feels strange that in the district where I grew up I now rarely understand what anyone is saying. Because of the bad weather many of the passengers are coughing, and I worry about catching tuberculosis, which is now being spread at an alarming record rate in London by immigrants, or some contagious tropical disease. An Indian is irritatingly cracking his knuckles, the way Indians do, for some reason.

The girl reading *Nicholas Nickleby* has got so engrossed in the story, giggling and chuckling, she misses her stop. Glancing up to see where we are, she hurriedly gets off at the next one, which is the stop for Sainsbury's, where I also alight, pushing past the group of hyper-active schoolchildren, back out into the frost. The Chinese girl also gets off, still jabbering into her hidden microphone, and heads for the giant Chinese supermarket across the main road, called See Woo Foods, where the customers are exclusively Chinese.

On the wide pavement opposite the store, by the vast car park, is the resident swarthy Roma *Big Issue* seller for this patch. A young male with a very dark complexion wearing a Father Christmas hat, he is extraordinarily full of himself. Strutting around the wide pavement as if he owned it, he approaches passers-by, calling them 'friend', even loudly hailing people on the other side of the road. He is an able-bodied young man, cocky, bursting with energy and confidence - why does he not have a proper job? Also, this brash, expansive youth obviously does not live in a hostel for the homeless. He feigns homelessness the better to extort charity from compassionate passers-by, gullible people easily persuaded to give alms. Those insufficiently compassionate he threatens, saying menacingly, 'You vill buy on vay back!' Like so much else in this country, the *Big Issue* is being exploited by settlers for whom it was not meant. Few indigenous sellers remain. Those genuine down-and-outs, usually abject alcoholics, seem now part of a bygone era. The usurpers are quite a different kettle of fish - sharks, not sozzled sprats. The only reason I can think of that they are being allowed to practise their deception is that the *Big Issue* has been infiltrated at high level by Romas, an assumption reinforced by the case of Lavinia Olmazu, who, as well as campaigning for gypsies' rights, once even addressing the UN, also helped compatriots make hundreds of illegal claims for state benefits - and who, it was reported at her trial, had a top post at the *Big Issue*. Presumably the brash Roma at Sainsbury's has decided to come to work in such cold as it will elicit more sympathy and therefore more money; but he probably envies his compatriots working the Underground pickpocket shift.

The patch he has commandeered is beneath the two poles of the wind generators that power the store. This Sainsbury's was the first purpose-built low-energy store in the country. By the shop entrance are long rows of interlocking trolleys. A pound coin has to be inserted in the end trolley to release it. An employee, a South Asian youth also wearing a Father Christmas hat, is pushing in a new batch. I bang the snow off my shoes. Inside, by the stacks of blue plastic shopping baskets are shelves of potted red-leaved poinsettias. Two burly black security guards are staring at the screens of closed-circuit television cameras. Sainsbury's resembles a sanitised oriental bazaar. Most of the shoppers and all of the staff are dusky. Many customers are not even speaking English. Africans predominate. A Pakistani couple have piled up two trolleys with half-price fizzy drinks, to sell in their grocery shop at the full price. Christmas songs are being played over the Tannoy; at the moment a female American is singing *Jingle Bells*.

I quickly collect the few items I require and join a queue at a checkout. A middle-aged East European woman stands in front of me. A female African with an ugly snub nose approaches her to continue an altercation they had just had when the African had rudely bumped into her and was not going to apologise. The East European afterwards tells me what had happened. The African had only reluctantly said 'Sorry' when given a dirty look. The East European woman had then said, 'I should think so too,' and the African tart had now chased her to the check-out queue in order to say, in some thick Nigerian accent, 'I no need you to say me when to apologise.' She then struts off, her Nigerian arse protruding like a camel's hump. It is obviously important to her not to let Whitey have the last word.

The East European pays and departs and then it is my turn, I am next. I am served by a charming Indian girl who seems a bit shy. The name tab on her uniform says, 'Aloka'. In the oriental ambience, I almost feel inclined to haggle - 'I'll give you 60p for that packet of Weetabix' - but desist. I carry my shopping in its orange carrier bag to the bus stop across the road to continue my journey to collect my mobile, my breath turning to fog round my face, the air is so cold. The Roma hails me: 'Hello, my good friend!'

My bus comes, over-full with settlers, but enough alight to enable me this time to get a seat. I board it gladly. I have only waited a few minutes but in that time got seriously cold. My face feels icy.

Approaching the station we pass on the right the disused David

Beckham Football Academy, which resembles two adjoining aircraft hangars each big enough for a full-sized pitch, and which was closed down a few months ago. You can see behind that Antony Gormley's giant artwork Quantum Cloud. It is his tallest sculpture, taller than his Angel of the North. Made of sections of tetrahedral steel units that from the bus resemble twigs, the sculpture looks like a steel tree in winter. If you look carefully, you can see the outline of a human figure in the middle, the trunk of the tree.

The Greenwich Peninsula used to be called Greenwich Level, as it is flat, a place of 'wet land and dry water'. The area that the marsh covers is a finger of land projecting from the southern shore east of Greenwich so that the river forms a long main boundary to north, east and west. A southern boundary is neatly defined by the main road between Greenwich and Woolwich. In 1390 Chaucer, a courtier in a top position in what we would now call the Civil Service, was put in charge of the repair of walls, ditches, sewers and bridges along this stretch.

Before 1800 nothing was built on the marsh except a few sheds and barns. No one lived here other than a watchman stationed to keep out the relatives of pirates gibbeted in a deep part of the river here trying to reclaim the bodies before the stipulated time. The pirates were hung at Execution Dock and their corpses chained in a cage here until three tides had passed over them. Only then could their relations take away the body for burial.

There is a photograph of a haystack that dates from as late as the 1920s, and until the 1880s the only commercial activity that had nothing to do with a rural economy was the storage and distribution of gunpowder. The marsh's remoteness from human habitation was a factor in the establishment of this one early industry, and it was the gunpowder industry here that led to the founding of the famous Woolwich Arsenal along the road. But then many industries were started up, including a sugar refinery, which continues to this day, and two that had a profound effect on the world - the cable for the first transatlantic telegraph was made here and the first shot fired in the American Civil War came from a gun manufactured on the peninsula.

Then, in 1880, was built here Europe's biggest gasworks. This made coal gas in a process that produced toxic waste, including arsenic, asbestos and cyanide, and when the area was chosen as the site of the Millennium Dome and its supporting infrastructure the ground was sealed with crushed concrete, plastic and clay and each building had to have a gas-tight membrane underneath. The blackened, sterile topsoil was buried in landfill sites in Bedfordshire. Decontamination cost British Gas millions of pounds. Towering against the sky alongside the Blackwall Tunnel approach road to the west is the sole remaining gas holder, with its latticed girders, erected when the gasworks was first built.

The *Daily Telegraph* described the atmospheric effect of the gasworks, scenes I remember from my childhood: 'By day the red hot coke was withdrawn from the retorts, great clouds of steam vapour would rise into the sky as water was applied. By night the sky was lit up by the reflected glow of the red hot coke.' As I sit at the station's bus terminal waiting for Pedro's bus, the Dome looming a few yards away to my right, I ponder that most of my father's working life was spent on this very spot. The ground here, black with crushed coke and coal, had smouldered and smoked beneath his feet. Where there is now a bustling hub of transport served by a catering kiosk called the London Diner selling burgers my father used to eat his meat-and-two-veg dinners in the staff canteen. Where hundreds of thousands of commuters now come and go he used to 'sling a sledge-'ammer' in a blacksmiths' forge. Not a single passenger alighting from the endless stream of buses nor any of those waiting for a bus resembles him.

He and all his workmates were made redundant by North Sea natural gas. The gas produced from coal was no longer required. The buildings were demolished (I got a temporary job at this as a fitter's mate, despite not knowing which way to turn a spanner) and the site lay derelict for many years, the soil saturated with a century's filth and pollutants.

Then the Dome was built, amid much scandal and misgivings, initially as the venue for the country's glitzy national millennium exhibition, devoted, ironically, considering my reflections, to the theme of Time. The prime meridian line runs through the site, which was chosen for the millennial celebrations after a challenge from Birmingham, whose claim was that it was the centre of England. The Dome is the biggest building of its kind in the world, as tall in the middle as Nelson's Column and taking up space equivalent to two Wembley Stadiums.

Waiting for Pedro, I regard it, in awe of such profligacy. Millions of pounds were squandered on it, to a stupid, senseless and disgraceful purpose, its background story a tale of the stupidity, cynicism and avarice of fools and rogues.

A politicians' whim, it was conceived simply because it resembles a fingernail at the end of the finger of land that is the peninsula. The preceding Conservative government had dreamed it up, vaguely liking the idea of a vast tent in the London borough that, being on longitude zero, is 'the centre of world time', to celebrate the new millennium, and Labour Prime Minister Tony Blair decided to continue with the project, and even expand it, despite the opposition of the cabinet, including the Secretary of State for Culture, Media and Sport who had inherited the responsibility for it.

Between them, cabinet members predicted every aspect of the approaching fiasco, identifying the absence of an animating idea, accurately estimating the eventual losses and voicing the resentment of the provinces. In a free vote the idea would have been rejected but its sole supporter happened to be also the most powerful, and, after telling his colleagues he wanted it to go ahead, Blair swept out of the room like some autocratic monarch, forestalling any discussion.

If the *polloi* had been asked they too would have opted for something useful and lasting, such as hospitals. At the other end of the old Blackwall Tunnel approach road, Tunnel Avenue, Greenwich District Hospital, founded in 1904 as St Alfege's Hospital in buildings dating back to 1840, was so dilapidated that only a few years after the Dome was erected it had to be demolished. Greenwich was short of hospitals.

As the locals feared and expected, the exhibition flopped. Only half the predicted number of visitors turned up, which was a third of the number who went to see the 1951 Festival of Britain. The reason was simple and obvious. The 1951 exhibition succeeded because it was exactly what it said it was - a festival of Britain. The organisers knew what to celebrate. At the start of the opening ceremony - a service in St Paul's - the king praised the nation's courage in the world wars; the official handbook declared categorically that 'Britain is a Christian Community'; brightly coloured pavilions on the South Bank paid tribute to picturesque countryside, seaside holidays and an unparalleled tradition of Parliamentary government. Commemorating the centenary of the Great Exhibition at a time of economic shortages and much gloom in overseas affairs, it had seemed to some jaundiced critics hardly the right time for a festival of national rejoicing but it proved a triumphant occasion, testimony to a people still vital and vigorous in its culture, still at peace with itself and secure in its heritage. Appointed roles and rituals were strongly marked. Institutions and traditions were firmly in place, sustained by great confidence. A people can overcome every obstacle if they have the will to succeed - which means acting collectively.

The Dome guide book, on the other hand, put the word British in inverted commas, indicating the writers' unease with the idea. The word was used hesitatingly. This was apt, in a way, for it set the trend for the new millennium. The Dome's exhibition celebrated a negation.

The Dome itself was a celebration of hypocrisy, built with funds from the Lottery, which only the foolish enter, and from a foreign billionaire businessman, who, though he had businesses in Britain, dodged paying British taxes that, if paid, would have been enough to build the Dome without his sponsorship. Before he was persuaded to sponsor the Dome, Rupert Murdoch's *Sun* attacked it for wasting public money that might have been better spent on the NHS, when his British media companies paid negligible corporation tax. Between 1987 and 1999 his papers made £1.3 billion. *The Economist* calculated that if full corporation tax had been paid at prevailing rates the Inland Revenue would have collected enough for seven new hospitals. One could have been a new Greenwich District Hospital.

Then Murdoch was talked into becoming a Dome sponsor. He promised £12m; upon which the *Sun*, literally overnight (they had to take out articles and replace them with stories saying the opposite), ceased its attacks; only to renew them later when a scandal involving other foreign sponsors could not be ignored.

The exhibition was divided into zones, including a Learning Zone, a Mind Zone and a Body Zone. Someone, probably a bishop, said there should be a God Zone. Hardly anybody outside the cabinet wanted a celebration of religion. The exhibition was, after all, not only welcoming the 21st century but welcoming it in the most atheist country in the world. But, unluckily, leading British politicians in 2000 were the most religious for many decades, Tony Blair and Jack Straw being particularly pious. Most twentieth-century British politicians were irreligious, regarding going to church occasionally on a Sunday as an insincere duty like kissing smelly babies at voting time. By the start of the twenty-first century most of the electorate too were atheist. A third did not know what Easter was supposed to commemorate. But this cabinet chose this time to advertise religion. (Unfortunate too that men with a respect for religion should be in power when Islam launched its assault.)

The religious zone was called first 'Soul', then 'Spirit Level', then 'The Faith Zone', then 'Faith Zone'. The definite article was dropped because the 'the' suggested there was only one faith, established Anglicanism, which was more important than the other varieties of Christianity, let alone Hinduism, Sikhism, Judaism, Zoroastrianism, Buddhism and, heaven forfend, Islam. Faith Zone paraded the ecumenical lie that all established religions were basically the same, with just a few unimportant minor differences. Try telling that to honest Muslims.

In the past, Labour politicians tended to profess some degree of allegiance to socialism and the working class. They knew that religion traditionally was used by cynical ruling classes to keep the plebs subjugated. Why all these highly educated people with a background in socialism should now be adopting Bronze Age beliefs, and that at a time when the plebs were rejecting these beliefs, is a mystery. It is possible that only Blair had a genuine, deep-down belief in supernatural beings and that the others cynically reasoned they would stand a better chance of advancement if they too professed to be believers.

But because of this, a space devoted to religion was agreed. Then it had to be decided what should fill the space. Clerics representing all the religions met to earnestly discuss this, disregarding the incompatibility of their beliefs and the many massacres committed over the previous two millennia in the name of their religions as their adherents slaughtered each other.

While they debated, the cabinet minister responsible for the exhibition, Peter Mandelson, was facing another big problem - who was going to pay for Faith Zone? No one in business could see anything to be gained by being seen consorting with religion in an atheist country. Finally he found people who had something to gain - a family of Indians. They gained British passports.

The Hinduja brothers, in ingratiating themselves with the British establishment, resembled the deceitful financier Augustus Melmotte in Anthony Trollope's classic novel set in the 1870s, *The Way We Live Now*. Melmotte plotted to use his wealth to gain admission into the top levels of British society, one tactic in both cases being to invite aristocrats and political leaders to lavish balls and dinner parties. In September 1999 the Hindujas held a reception for Keith Vaz to celebrate his appointment as the first Asian minister in recent times. Like so many of this sordid crew, Vaz also would be heavily involved in various scandals (see essay, 'Keith Vaz'). Mrs Blair turned up at one of the Hinduja parties wearing an Indian costume and a jewel on her forehead. The brothers met the queen. One of them said he agreed with Prince Charles and believed in the 'shared values of each faith'. He wanted the Dome to recognise that the human race must sow the seeds for peace, development and co-operation. They announced that they believed in 'multi-cultural and inter-faith understanding, tolerance and respect between the different people and their faith'.

These promoters of understanding, tolerance and respect were also arms dealers. And while Labour was trying to raise funds for the Dome, the Indian authorities were accusing the brothers of corruption in a deal to supply India with Bofors 155mm field howitzers that went all the way up to Indian leader Rajiv Gandhi, who was accused along with several others of receiving kickbacks from Bofors.

Mandelson resigned from the government in 2001 after it was revealed he lobbied on behalf of the brothers in their bid for British citizenship, his second scandal. Having once said Labour was 'intensely relaxed about the filthy rich' he seemed throughout his career to be infatuated with them, holidaying with Tory tax exiles and Russian oligarchs who any Labour politician should have regarded with disdain and even hostility. Just as Frank Sinatra got a thrill from socialising with Mafiosi, so Mandelson came over all unnecessary from being with dodgy filthy rich businessmen. It is surprising what despicable dolts people are when they desire to be deceived. Mandelson seemed not to realise that those who snuggle up to filth get dirty.

In 1998 he had authorised Wessex Water to be bought by Enron, America's seventh biggest corporation that was no more than a criminal conspiracy. Enron sponsored that year's Labour conference.

For fifteen years, Labour ministers, the heirs to honourable champions of the working class, embraced dubious business organisations from all over the world. Unprecedentedly, a Labour government will be known to history for its corruption and its treachery.

Labour used to take pride in its past and the legends surrounding the Labour movement. Generations treasured their sites of memory, what the French call *lieux de mémoire*. It was an often sentimental tradition, with its own heroes, providing a robust alternative chronicle. Nothing more signally diminished the Labour government of 1997-2010 than its lack of interest in the party's history. Blair and his crew thereby emphasised their own lack of roots. It was a disastrous rupture. Those who do not know where they come from cannot find the way ahead. Puny ambition replaced a grand vision, and personal greed and unwise decisions filled the moral void. There seemed no reason for Labour to be in government.

Brown unwittingly revealed this as prime minister in his most memorable speech of the 2010 election campaign when he did not speak of Wat Tyler or John Ball, or Jack Cade, Tom Paine, Jimmy Reid or Mary Wollstonecraft, but of three black foreigners - Martin Luther King, Nelson Mandela and Barack Obama. It was as if the struggles of people thousands of miles away were more relevant than those of the country he wished to continue to lead. The Brown government boasted in its final days that it had created 1.7m new jobs since Labour came to power in

1997. More than 1.64m of those jobs went to foreigners.

Mandelson had told the head of the New Millennium Experience Company in a memo, 'I agree that the Hinduja brothers are an above-average risk, but without firm evidence of wrongdoing how could we bar them from involvement in sponsorship?' He was playing games, as was his wont. If you see billionaires facing accusations of taking part in a major arms scandal, you are under no obligation to get involved with them. Recently, I was about to hire someone who called himself an electrician when a neighbour told me he had done a job for her that was botched, and she suspected he was unqualified - someone known in such circumstances as a cowboy. With this opposite of a recommendation, I chose someone else. Why could not Mandelson, in a similar situation, have done the same? Why associate with dodgy people, even if you have no absolute proof of their dodginess?

Blair said in 1998, 'This will be the most famous new building in the world. I am determined to do all I can to ensure that the Dome stands as an enduring legacy for the future.'

Unfortunately, it will only stand as an enduring legacy for twenty-five years, ten of which have already passed. The original plan was for it to be made of indestructible PVC but after a contract had been signed with a German company to supply this material, it was realised PVC contains a lethal dioxin, so it was replaced with a sort of Teflon, the same stuff that coats non-stick frying pans, giving the tent its short lifespan. The German company had to be paid off with £8m.

The Dome is actually more of a tent than a dome, for it is not self-supporting but is held up by twelve giant yellow masts with cables ranged along its rim. From the air it must resemble a poached egg stuck with matchsticks. The Blackwall Tunnel runs under it before going beneath the Thames, necessitating a big hole in its roof for the chimney of the ventilation shaft that disperses the exhaust fumes. This inconvenient, unsightly hole was airbrushed out of all the official photos. Another publicity ploy was ensuring the Dome received a positive mention on all television soap series, and on revising the credits of *EastEnders* to prominently include it, just as the credits of *The Sopranos* were changed to omit the destroyed twin towers of the World Trade Centre.

Erecting this preposterous Teflon tent was a mistake, a major and uncomfortably visible blunder, a fraudulent and boastful folly that soaked up funds - £760m - that could otherwise have been spent on building hospitals, including a new Greenwich District Hospital. It was appropriate that the creepy Mandelson was appointed the minister responsible for it.

Justifying it, he felt obliged to point out in a cabinet office document that 'millenniums only come once in a thousand years'. Eloquent in defence of the original material of choice, he later enthused equally about its replacement. Dreadful is the scourge of such cabinet ministers.

The Dome's design was based on that of the Dome of Discovery at the 1951 festival. A visitor to that exhibition noted in his diary, 'The only noticeable foreigners I saw were 2 Asiatics, 2 American servicemen, 1 black, and 1 woman talking French.' Happy days.

Two other differences between then and now are that the 1951 festival was a huge success and the site was afterwards dismantled, while the millennium exhibition attracted fewer visitors than expected, leading to recurring financial problems, and its Dome remained. The politicians had claimed that after the exhibition closed on December 31st 2000 the Dome would not become a white elephant but, of course, it did. Unused, it cost a fortune in routine maintenance just to stop it falling down. Early on it was almost sold to a property company that wanted to turn it into a business and residential zone. Then the BBC wanted to build a theme park; as did the Tussauds group. At one point it looked like it would stay in public hands, and at another that it would be demolished. A football club run by a leading gangster named Dogan Arif had applied to use the site for a new stadium as part of their ambitious plans for expansion but all such plans had to be abandoned after its funding by drugs money ceased when he was imprisoned .

After stunning losses, the Dome was sold on extremely generous terms to the world's biggest leisure operator, Anschutz Entertainment Group (AEG), which is headed by Philip Anschutz, an American billionaire.

And guess what? Philip Anschutz is a dodgy character! The story of the Dome teems with dodgy characters. According to the National Audit Office, the paperwork for dozens of contracts had disappeared, and the police were investigating sixty contracts that had been awarded without being put out to tender, as required by law. And now along comes Anschutz.

At the time of the sale he, like the Hinduja brothers when they became involved with the Dome, was facing serious charges. The New York district attorney was investigating wheeling and dealing common in the years preceding the collapse of the world economy. The British government rejected as ridiculous calls from its opponents to stop the sale of its symbol to such a dodgy executive, pointing out that accountants of his telecom company Qwest, the subject of the investigations, had done nothing to raise the alarm about the state of the corporation's books. The auditors were from Arthur Andersen, a firm that also approved the books of Enron, which in 2001 would break all fraud records. In that same year, Enron chairman Kenneth Lay told the *San Diego Union-Tribune*, 'I believe in God and I believe in the free market.'

Blair too would increasingly worship both God and Mammon, since 2007 accumulating a fortune believed by some to be as much as £60m, mainly from consultancy. The government of Kazakhstan alone shells out £8m a year to Tony Blair Associates. He travels the world advising Arab despots and African dictators and thieves. The exact figure for his wealth is unknown because he has set up a complex web of companies through which he channels his earnings without having to publicly declare them.

One of his companies, provocatively named Windrush Ventures - turnover £12m - managed to spend £11m on administration in 2011, leaving it with a taxable income of barely £1m. Of those administration costs, £8m were not explained in the accounts.

As the publicity for Faith Zone verily said, the Dome explored 'the values that underpin our society'.

Philip Anschutz planned to build a 'super casino' as one of the attractions, as this would create a huge investment for his company and would allow for business opportunities and further developments of the area. The association of Deputy Prime Minister John Prescott with Philip Anschutz gave rise to serious political controversy, with allegations that Prescott used undue influence to support Anschutz's casino licence bid. Prescott had met Anschutz several times and even stayed at his ranch.

Despite Prescott's best efforts as a guest cowboy the 'super casino' plan fell through, the bid going to Manchester, and, following all these political and financial shenanigans, the Dome now houses a big entertainment complex. AEG have constantly stated they wish to abolish its name as 'the Dome' due to its bad reputation as a failed project.

Eventually, the naming rights to the district were bought by mobile-phone and broadband provider O2 plc, now Telefónica Europe plc, from AEG. The O2 is visually typeset in branding as The O_2, the logo of the company.

The Dome is now just a commercial theatre, an Americanised pleasure dome, a Xanadu-on-Thames, for which a standard concrete rectangular structure would have been perfectly adequate at a fraction of the cost of putting it up. A third of its space is still waiting to be filled. And all locals still call it 'the Dome', not 'the O2' as desired. While waiting for Pedro's bus I glance at the posters advertising forthcoming attractions. They are all music events targeted at adolescents. I have been down here late at night when such an event had just finished, and the departing audience consisted almost entirely of young blacks.

Most of those waiting alongside me at the bus stop are also blacks - Africans, to be precise. I wonder why, and then realise the number 472 also stops here, which goes to Thamesmead, the south-east London suburb known as Europe's credit-card fraud capital, most of the fraudsters being Nigerians.

Pedro's bus arrives, and he hands me my mobile. As expected, he is a West Indian. I proffer a fiver in gratitude but he declines any reward.

Even though the pavements are icy and I am carrying shopping I decide to walk home rather than take another bus packed with ethnics speaking gibberish.

I pass Edmund Halley Way, which is supposed to be named after the world-famous astronomer who was the first to predict the return of a comet, who died in Greenwich in 1742. Except that it isn't. The name on all the street signs (and on all maps of London) is spelt wrong.

Further evidence of the lack of concern for the past is all around. The peninsula has become unrecognisable. It has been developed because of the overcrowding in London. More homes and transport facilities were needed. But London is overcrowded because there are too many settlers. Many more continue to arrive, the pressure of newcomers incessantly mounts, their numbers increase all the time, and it is settlers and their offspring who have mostly relocated here and travel here.

The enormous cost, the vast expenditure of energy, the interest of a top gangster, the involvement of dodgy arms dealers with an ulterior motive, of admired 'filthy rich' businessmen, of greedy politicians abandoning everything a Labour government was supposed to believe in, the new roads, the silly big artwork, the extravagant entertainment complex, the eco-friendly giant grocery shop staffed solely by ethnics, the supermarket that sells only Chinese food to only Chinese customers, the transport hub - all because of settlers, and for settlers.

The short, narrow cobble-stoned little streets that once ran through the district, crowded with local people, including children playing, have now been replaced by wide concrete avenues along which heavy lorries and ethnic-packed buses come and go all day. In the past, games of football would be interrupted every half-an-hour or so with a casual warning of 'car coming', upon which the participants would go to the side of the road until the vehicle had passed.

The only thing that has remained unchanged is a row of eight terraced cottages, front doors opening straight on to the pavement, with the adjoining Pilot pub at the end. My father 'used' the Pilot (in the phrase of that time), which was established in 1801 and which most people assume refers to the Thames' river pilots but it more likely derives from a song about former prime minister William Pitt in which he is called 'the pilot that weathered the storm'. The pub sign depicts neither Pitt nor pilot but a sailing barge.

The cottages remind me of when this area was crammed with similar houses. My father grew up in one, in adjacent Deptford. Fog from the river merged with the smoke spiralling in ribbons from the dockyards, factories, gasworks and, in winter, innumerable chimney-pots, to form choking smog, sometimes so thick that people carried torches when they went outside and even then could hardly see anything. Coughing children clutched their mother's hand for fear of losing touch and getting lost, unable to recognise any landmarks in the 'pea-souper'.

Partly to escape the worst of the smog, when my mother was pregnant with me my parents moved up the hill, to a rented terraced house at the top of sloping Northcombe Road, from where you could see at the bottom a patch of the Thames. This was the house I grew up in. It was a big, fine, Victorian two-storey brick house with bay windows, half-a-dozen steps down to the pavement and a porch decorated with embossed shiny tiles depicting flowers. My childhood friends and I, usually dressed in Fair Isle patterned woollies, played marbles and swapped cigarette cards of footballers on this porch. The house was semi-detached, a narrow alley separating it from the next house. This alley led only to our back garden and that of our next-door neighbours.

Many in Deptford lacked the means to move away from the poor air, and also quite a few preferred to remain in the old familiar neighbourhood despite it. Over the years tenants installed inside toilets, often leaving the outdoor privy in place, so that inhabitants of this humble district actually had the luxury of two toilets. On Sundays there was always a roast for dinner, which the wife cooked while listening to the wireless, a popular programme being *Two Way Family Favourites*, in which troops stationed in occupied Germany exchanged messages with relatives at home and asked for a favourite piece of music to be played. It was the husbands' chore to clean the windows every Sunday, and there was often a tiff over it if he did not feel like doing it, possibly because he'd had too much to drink at the pub while the missus cooked dinner. Cockles and winkles made up Sunday tea.

The first task every winter morning was to light the coal fire. When an electric fire replaced coal the coal cupboard in the scullery was used to store other things but the smell of coal in the cupboard never went away. A man clothed in black like an undertaker regularly came to collect the rent of every household. A rag-and-bone man, a 'totter', often went slowly through the streets on a horse-drawn cart calling out 'Ol' lumber', the saucepans and cookers rattling, the horse's hooves clapping on the road. The totters used the railway arches as stables.

The milkman's van was also drawn by a horse. I used to help the milkman, Bert, on his round, joining him at the start of the round outside my house at the top of Northcombe Road and accompanying him to where it ended down here on the peninsula, passing on the way many bombsite clearings cluttered by thrown-out stained mattresses and other dumped rubbish, the destroyed houses delineated by knee-high brickwork like an archaeological digging and the devastated sites covered in 'bombweed' - rosebay willowherb, which had sprung up in this new environment, producing sheets of magenta blossom and subsequent blizzards of downy seed-fluff.

One day's payment from the round was enough for my ticket for Saturday morning pictures at the Roxy in Old Dover Road. At the end of the round Bert would hand me a tanner - sixpence, in the ridiculous complicated old currency. Customers paid their milk bill on Fridays, when I had to stand on doorsteps calculating payment and change in farthings, halfpennies ('appenies'), pennies, dodecagonal threepenny bits, 'tanners', shillings, florins, half crowns and pound notes. There were four farthings to a penny, twelve pennies to a shilling and twenty shillings to a pound. And some older people, including my father, could never adjust to decimal currency! This just shows you the power of what you are used to. That should be a lesson to those imposing hordes of aliens on us. Unfortunately, it is not, as is shown by merely looking around the peninsula.

All around on it now is a meaningless jumble of incongruous buildings for incongruous settlers, brutally blocking out the long and complex history of thriving industry and vibrant streets. Coloured low blocks of flats and tall, shiny glass-fronted office buildings tower over fenced-off expanses of wasteland.

The peninsula is a strange, eerie district, a partially tarted-up ghost town, the cosmetics overdone in some places and not applied at all in others. Structures on it are monumental but lacking substance. To me everything feels artificial. Local conditions and traditions have been ignored in the attempt to propagate community architecturally, in the paternalistic and naïve belief that well-designed urban squares can create citizens - in the absurd assumption that slapping down a few windswept plazas will magically engender a kind of idealised version of southern European street life. I feel the planners would have dyed the Thames a Mediterranean blue if the river had not been so tidal. No doubt the authorities have their schemes but the district has been like this for many years and the schemes keep changing. Most of the properties seem vacant and few pedestrians are on the pavements.

I gaze at the painted desolation, remembering the people who once frequented this area, feeling nostalgic. There is a lack of continuity. The old and the new do not gel. The peninsula resembles an explosion in a jig-saw factory, the disparate pieces falling to the ground to lie mixed up together higgledy-piggledy, impossible to interlock.

No one living in the area has any long-term connections with it. The people on the peninsula now, a hybrid populace with a split sense of belonging, inhabiting two cultural worlds, astride value systems often incompatible, are not my people. They are alien, foreign, out of place, an intrusion. They do not belong here. They have nothing to do with the likes of me. I desperately wish they were not here. I long to be back among manners, gestures and speech that I know. I yearn for people speaking Cockney, for orderly bus queues; for familiarity. Multi-cultural London is one vast provocation. Oh, to shake the dust of it from my feet!

LONDON BOROUGH OF BROWNWICH
A borough discoloured

HAVING been brought up in Greenwich and lived there all my life apart from four years working abroad, I like to spend time walking along the riverfront and in London's loveliest park.

Greenwich Park's architectural masterpieces, the Queen's House designed by Inigo Jones, and the Royal Naval College of Christopher Wren, both at the bottom of the park on the river, were vital to Britain when it was a nautical power. Wren built the college in two symmetrical halves so that the view of the river from the Queen's House behind it was undisturbed - the distance between the two sections is exactly the width of the Queen's House. Hence from the Queen's Steps on the river foot-path you can see through the gap in the college the National Maritime Museum and the park beyond and then up the hill the observatory (now also a museum, with a fine planetarium).

Nelson's bloodstained uniform, showing clearly the hole of the bullet that killed him, is now displayed in a glass case in the maritime museum. His body arrived back from Trafalgar at the Queen's Steps pickled in a barrel of brandy. Transferred to a coffin, he was taken from the ship to lie in state in the naval college's Painted Hall before being rowed upriver for a state funeral.

At these steps the explorer Martin Frobisher stopped off for an audience with Queen Elizabeth I on his way to seek the Northwest Passage. Sir Walter Raleigh was a regular visitor. The famous episode in which he gallantly covered a puddle with his cloak so that Elizabeth could walk across it is probably apocryphal, first recorded decades after the supposed event, but was said to have taken place in Greenwich Park.

At the end of the footpath is the Trafalgar Tavern, a big old draughty Georgian building of fading grandeur where Charles Dickens regularly dined and whither House of Commons politicians would decamp every year for a whitebait dinner to mark the end of parliamentary sessions.

The naval college was built as a refuge for disabled sailors left on the streets at the conclusion of the naval wars of the seventeenth and eighteenth centuries. When full it housed 3,000 sailors. It was taken over by the Royal Navy and converted to academia in the nineteenth century.

In 1997 the college was moved to the RAF College at Cranwell, and Greenwich's last working link with the sea was gone, its decline mirroring that of Britain as a maritime nation. The Queen's House has not housed a monarch for more than two centuries and now forms part of the maritime museum.

Two buildings on the riverfront have connections with my father. After being made redundant by the gasworks he worked for a while as a porter at the tiny, whitewashed seventeenth-century Seamen's Hospital, and then, having moved from his house up the hill in Northcombe Road after my mother died, unwilling to remain there alone with the memories, he eventually secured himself a flat in the nearby Trinity Hospital almshouse.

The almshouse, dwarfed by the massive brick walls of the adjacent power station, was founded by Henry Howard, Earl of Northampton, in 1614 for twenty-one retired, respectable Greenwich workmen: 'No common beggar, drunkard, whore-hunter, haunter of taverns nor ale houses, nor unclean person infected with any foul disease, nor any that is blind, or so impotent as he is not able, at the time of his admission, to come to prayers daily.'

The picturesque building resembles a child's toy fort. A passage underneath a clock tower leads into a small, cloistered courtyard with a fountain and a large, well-worn bench, on which my father liked to sit in mild weather.

In the park, by the observatory, the home of Greenwich Mean Time, a brass strip runs through the tarmac representing zero degrees longitude. Tourists straddle the line to be photographed with one foot in the western hemisphere and the other in the east. Here, at the top of the slope that rises from the river, in front of General Wolfe's statue, is seen London's most dramatic and detailed panorama. The Canary Wharf complex of skyscrapers is straight ahead, the City, St Paul's Cathedral and the Tower of London far off to the left and the O_2 dome to the right. On the stretch of river immediately below was where, during the reign of Æthelred the Unready, the Viking fleet anchored, to remain for three years, the army encamping on the hills above as a base to make raids on London and Kent, including Canterbury, where they captured the archbishop, Ælfheah, having been admitted into the town by treachery.

Ælfheah was held to ransom by them here in Greenwich for the vast sum of £3,000, which he refused to let his people attempt to raise and pay, and was brutally murdered one night when the Vikings guarding him got drunk and pelted and hit him with the bones of slaughtered cattle and the hafts of their axes. The Viking leader, Thorkell the Tall, who had tried to intervene, offering all that he had except his ship in return for the archbishop's life, was so distressed (and insecure now as the leader of a band of pirates who had got out of hand and successfully disobeyed him) that he changed sides and joined Æthelred, taking with him forty-five ships, which Æthelred used to form the basis of the first English standing fleet. A riverside parish church called St Alfege marks the site of the martyrdom. Vestiges of those times may be traced in the names of Northcombe and Westcombe, 'combe' being an Old English word for a deep hollow, especially one on the flank of a hill. And the place was already named Greenwich, spelt Grenewic in records of 964.

The park is peaceful, even with the tourists milling around. I often walk through it on the tarmac paths that conveniently criss-cross it. Flotillas of ducks quack and stretch their wings on the pond, and deer graze in an enclosure by a beautiful extensive flower garden, in which the branches of ancient trees hang so low they nearly reach the grass. The park contains many old trees - oaks, and chestnut trees that drop conkers every autumn for children to collect, for their shiny beauty and to have contests with, threaded with string and smashed against each other to see who has the champion conker.

The conkers that break open from their spiky shells when they fall are collected also by the thousands of grey squirrels that live in the park, so tame they take nuts from outstretched human hands. They run down the trunks of the trees or along the grass, grab the proffered prize and scamper away, their long bushy tails resembling monstrous furry caterpillars, their black eyes looking sharply around, incessantly alert. They either dash into the undergrowth to bury the nut or nibble it several yards away.

The grey squirrel is not native to Britain. It came from America and, being more aggressive than the native red squirrel, expanded its range, eating all the nuts and occupying all the holes in the trees, making the future of the reds increasingly uncertain. There are estimated to be only 140,000 red squirrels left in Britain, with more than 2.5m greys. The Forestry Commission is working with partners in projects across Britain to develop a long-term conservation strategy that deters the invaders and encourages the native population. It occurs to me that while this policy is sensibly being applied to squirrels, the opposite situation prevails with regard to humans.

Tourists and grey squirrels are not the only habitual aliens in Greenwich Park. Indians are also usually there in great numbers, especially in the summer, when their extended families picnic in the flower gardens - the food and drink on a cloth spread on the grass, toddlers toddling, older children playing ball games, parents, grandparents, aunts and uncles chatting peacefully, no one dropping litter or quaffing alcohol. I used to think, 'How nice, how civilised' until I realised that Indians were often the only people in the flower gardens. It was as though, like the grey squirrels, they had superseded the native of the species.

This has happened in my lifetime. The cultures in South Asia are still thriving, in Pakistan, in the Punjab, in Gujarat, Bengal, Bangladesh, Tamil Nadu... but by coming here in their millions these people have helped to destroy my parents' culture.

I often wonder how this was allowed to happen. Clues can be found on the website of Greenwich Council, which runs, and pays for, many services 'for people from black and ethnic minorities'. Here are some, with their services:

❑**Greenwich Council for Racial Equality** 'We provide advice on black business development... and on immigration, homelessness, housing benefits and welfare benefits. There is no charge for this service.' In 2012 treasurer Hardev Singh Dhillon and director Makhan Bajwa were convicted of fraud, siphoning off £47,000 of the £248,000 this organisation receives a year in funding from Greenwich Council. Astonishingly, they were let off. A staff member said Bajwa was a nepotist as well as a thief.

❏**Asian Resource Centre** 'We provide help with completing forms, dealing with benefits, bills, etc. We offer courses such as literacy and numeracy [they teach the three Rs] and basic computer skills as a pathway to courses. We support people to develop their confidence. We have Punjabi, Urdu, Hindu [*sic*], Gujarati and Bengal speaking members of staff. There is no charge for this service.'

❏**Asian Health Project** 'Has been set up to work with people from the Asian Community [*sic*] in Greenwich. Children can come to the centre to participate in activities [play] such as football and cricket. There is no charge for this service.'

❏**Indian Cultural Society** 'We are the oldest Asian organisation in Greenwich Borough. We provide advice and information. We are involved in arranging cultural festivals and celebrations. We advertise in the local media and in places of worship. There is no charge for this service.'

❏**Greenwich Network Trust** 'We provide a service for African people, African/Caribbean people and people of African descent. We also provide a service for black, non-English speaking refugees... There is legal services department covering issues such as immigration, benefits, etc. There is no charge for this service.'

❏**Greenwich Vietnam Community** 'We provide advice and information on welfare, housing, education, health and training. Support for Chinese and Vietnamese women. There is no charge for this service.'

❏**Woolwich Simba Project** 'This service is a multi-community resource centre providing a range of services that meet the needs of African and Caribbean people across the borough. Simba is currently providing welfare and benefit advice to the general public.' It is unclear if this 'general public', in view of the sentence preceding it, includes Whitey. However, hurrah, there is a charge for some classes and play schemes! Not everything is down to the taxpayer!

Apart from the cultural implications, how much is all this costing? Is the cost ever questioned?

The interpreters and translators alone must be costing us a fortune.

As well as providing such services, Greenwich Council makes available leaflets in Chinese, Gujarati, Punjabi, Somali, Turkish, Urdu and Vietnamese. The leaflets in these languages usually concern such things as welfare benefits. A leaflet on 'Promoting responsible dog ownership in Greenwich' was one of the few published only in English. And the council's website is translated into FIFTY-THREE languages!

The council, like all local government throughout Britain, is always keen to provide multi-lingual services; but discouraging people from speaking English by pandering to their ignorance of it is profligate. In 2004 London's 999 emergency services employed linguists to translate emergency calls into one hundred and fifty languages, from Arabic to Zulu. Speaking to the London *Evening Standard*, Professor Tim Connell, the Director of Language Studies at City University, welcomed the move: 'It is really key that public services embrace these languages because everyone has a right to basic services.' But translators cost money. If everyone spoke English this money could be invested in the emergency services and save more lives. Saving lives should take precedence over promoting cultural diversity.

Many people raised in Greenwich are fed up with all the ethnics. In September 2009 a mosque was set on fire for the third time. Greenwich Islamic Centre caretaker Mohammed Kohelee heard a noise late one night, and discovered the building ablaze. The arsonist hit him with a hammer. 'Mohammed tried to put the fire out by throwing buckets of water,' said mosque director Tariq Abbasi. 'They want to damage this place for some reason or other. They're not happy that we've got a mosque among them. But they don't realise, we're only doing like churches or synagogues - we are only praying to, we hope, the same god.'

This statement is typical of Muslims. Everyone knows that they chant all the time, 'There is no god but Allah... ', that they deny all other gods, that, indeed, it is the intolerance of Islam that makes it so dangerous and abhorrent, but when it suits them, such as in this case to garner sympathy as pious victims, they chant a different mantra. Predictably, Abbasi has been awarded an MBE 'for his work to promote community cohesion', upon which he came out with more sleek hypocrisy.

In 2011 the mosque was revamped to extend its prayer halls and to create the facilities for an Islamic primary school, 'to meet the needs of the growing Muslim community', which was now 'more than 10,000 families'. Given the size of Muslim families, this means at the very least 80,000 people and probably much more, and this does not even include the many Greenwich Muslims in Britain illegally.

We are certainly not happy at having a mosque among us. Why should we be? Having a vast horde of Muslims among us in the borough we played in as children feels like being invaded by troglodytes. Of course we did not desire it. The idea is preposterous. On the contrary, we do not understand how it was allowed to happen.

Thousands of culturally different people have been imported into Greenwich, including in the last couple of years the sinister massive influx of Nigerians, who seem to have arrived all together and all at once, like flies on the first hot day of summer. Roaming the streets, engrossed in loud mobile-phone conversations in Hausa or whatever (rarely English), they seem unaware that the land they are making their own could possibly have belonged to others already. Nigeria, the most populous country of Africa, is incapable of feeding its inhabitants even while it spends more than half its oil revenue to buy food. The oil will soon be gone. Of course all Nigerians want to flee.

So they come to Greenwich. Documents published by the council's planning department in 2011 showed that 13 per cent of Greenwich residents are African. Thirty-five per cent are ethnics. The population of Greenwich grew from 213,000 in 2001 to 235,000 in 2010 and is expected to reach 288,000 by 2027 - an increase of more than 35 per cent. (None of these figures include the many illegals.)

How do you expect the likes of me to feel on seeing our ancestral borough being turned into a third-world slum? Naturally we want to lead a Western way of life, with our own kind of people. Pubs that have stood for longer than a hundred years, with the area named after them, are closing down all over the borough because the Muslims that now predominate in the vicinity do not enjoy a convivial drink. So we now have a Sun in the Sands roundabout with no Sun in the Sands pub. Some of the pubs have been turned into grocery shops, run, to add insult to injury, by Muslims. And a couple have been turned into mosques.

Luckily for you I have a poor memory. I cannot bore you with too much about my childhood because I remember so little of it. But still I recall things and feel nostalgia. And even I remember quite a lot about my childhood house in Northcombe Road.

When the original landlord died and his son inherited it, as we were 'sitting tenants', according to the law he could not evict us. Because he did not want the responsibility of owning it he offered to sell it to my father at well below its market value. It was such a bargain my father had no choice but to take out a mortgage and buy it - but deep down he too did not want this responsibility, and the worry of keeping up the mortgage payments tormented him so much he succumbed to a severe nervous breakdown from which he never fully recovered.

After Mum died, by which time I had left home, he entrusted its sale to estate agents and took no further interest. When informed they had a buyer he simply signed the documents and moved out. I had no reason to go there after that and did not visit the street until several years later, when I had occasion to walk down it; and coming out of our house, pausing on the porch decorated with shiny tiles depicting flowers where my childhood friends and I, wearing our Fair Isle patterned woollies, had played marbles and swapped cigarette cards, was a bearded, turbaned Sikh.

The sight upset me. It is unpleasant to picture aliens living in one's childhood home. The image of them in the familiar rooms that you will never see again affects all your memories of scenes in those rooms, contaminates all recollections.

The council house on its right had been occupied by an Indian family even before my father left the area, and when I checked I discovered the house on its left was now also the home of Indians.

I think of the street where I grew up, named from Old English of a thousand years ago, and am heart-tied and cannot speak.

BLACK MYSTERY MONTH
Annual celebration of nothing much

RACIAL discrimination was declared illegal in 1965. I was surprised therefore to read an article in the London *Evening Standard* in 2009 about a blatantly discriminatory event. 'A London theatre is to host its first "white only" season,' it announced. 'Three leading white writers have written commissioned pieces examining the state of white Britain.'

I jest, of course. I have replaced the word 'black' with 'white'. The three playwrights, Bola Agbaje, Kwame Kwei-Armah and Roy Williams, were all black. Agbaje wrote about immigration, Kwei-Armah about the possibility of a negro ever becoming London's mayor and Williams about the prison system. One feels that the 'white' version would not get past the law. I wrote to the theatre asking if they were certain that what they were doing was legal but received no reply.

The Tricycle Theatre in Kilburn, which hosted the event throughout that autumn, prides itself on its 'inclusivity' and receives vast amounts of public money in funding - nearly a million pounds a year. Tricycle Theatre's grants from statutory bodies in 2008 totalled £995,841; in 2007, £976,495. In the year ended March 31st 2009 it received £752,000 from the Arts Council alone. This particular black-fest was sponsored additionally by giant American financial software, news and data firm Bloomberg.

This would not matter if there really was ever a comparable season for white playwrights and if the theatre in its website did not go on so much about its 'inclusivity'. (Top of the list of those 'targeted' in its 'social inclusion programme' are 'young refugees and asylum seekers'.) The likes of me were not included in this event, and you will never see such a season for indigenous playwrights.

The theatre's Artistic Director, Nicolas Kent, justified the season by pointing out that in London now, 'Black and Asian children outnumber white British children by about six to four'. Oh, so that's all right then. In the course of one generation, my lifetime, indigenous Londoners have become outnumbered by aliens, and instead of us wondering what was occurring and feeling grossly hard-done-by, we are invited to 'celebrate' the new diversity and to go and watch plays by and about the newcomers.

A play by Williams is in a book published in March 2011 called *Plays by Black British Writers*. In an introduction, Lynette Goddard both laments 'institutional racism in the British theatre sector' and claims that 'black British playwriting is thriving'.

This is not necessarily a contradiction, of course. Black British playwrights could be so talented, such powerful writers, that they thrive in spite of being victims of institutional racism. But I doubt it. I have never seen any of these plays but one supporter of 'black theatre' admits most are awful, staged purely out of political correctness. Lindsay Johns, in an article in the *Standard*, wrote, 'Contrary to the all-pervasive mood of multicultural bonhomie and self-congratulation, there is actually something rotten in the state of black British theatre.' This is of course exactly the opposite of what Ms Goddard wrote. As she is also the author of articles such as 'Staging Black Feminisms' and 'In-yer-face Black Womanist Playwriting' and as calling a book *Plays by Black British Writers* is itself a segregationist gesture, I think we can safely assume that she is a typical confused champion of victimhood and that Johns is right.

He wrote that black British theatre is 'languishing in an intellectually vapid, almost pre-literate cacophony of expletives, incoherent street babble and plots which revolve around the clichéd staples of hoodies, guns and drugs. At best, these plays succeed by masquerading as the voice of the marginalised black underclass, which by dint of acute white guilt and a commitment to diversity get an immediate audience at the capital's most prestigious venues.

'Constrained by political correctness, critics dare not challenge these works for their lack of artistic merit, for fear of being deemed racist.'

I used to be interested in agitprop theatre, and know that most of such theatre is embarrassingly bad - artistically naïve, intellectually clumsy and lacking in psychological veracity. I walked out of many plays at the interval. I am sure black theatre must be the same, and survives only through politically-correct funding, just as Soviet propaganda plays were funded by the state while better plays were ignored.

Do you imagine that the Tricycle Theatre, for all its 'inclusivity', would consider staging a play about the effect of multi-culturalism, the alien invasion, on the likes of me? Of course not. You know it sounds silly. For a start, it would not get any Arts Council money. But do Cockney pensioners not have feelings? When we are struck, do we not bruise or bleed? When affected by colossal injustice, do we not get the raving 'ump?

It would also not matter if its black only season was unusual, a passing whim. But such events now saturate Britain.

The biggest is the annual Black History Month.

Like so much else in British blacks' culture, Black History Month comes from America, where the idea first appeared in 1926 as Negro History Week, becoming a Month fifty years later after a proclamation by President Ford. Some American blacks resent the fact that it occurs in February, the shortest month of the year. In Britain it happens each October.

Here it consists of a wide range of cultural events, including exhibitions, lectures and workshops. The problem with black British history, even though there is an Oxford Companion tome devoted to it, is that it is boring.

American blacks' history is full of tragedy and drama. It consists of picking cotton in sub-tropical heat and lines of men walking six hundred miles to their new owner connected together with a rhythmically clinking chain; daring escapes, desperate uprisings, the Civil War, emancipation, segregation, the civil rights movement, Martin Luther King, Angela Davis, the Black Panthers, great speeches, assassinations, crosses burning in the night, hooded vigilantes, men lynched on a tree, unending dread; and when they died, blacks could only be legally buried in specially designated cemeteries by a licensed black undertaker.

This history has inspired epic films such as *Glory*, the true story of the valiant failed frontal assault by an all-black regiment on Fort Wagner in the Civil War; *The Journey of August King*, in which a young widower in the Appalachian mountains of North Carolina in 1815 reluctantly helps a runaway slave rather than let her be caught by her cruel owner, and in doing so loses everything; and *The Autobiography of Miss Jane Pittman*, the life of a fictional slave from the Civil War to the civil rights movement, which ends with her, aged 110, defiantly drinking from a water fountain marked 'Whites Only'.

How can you make an epic film about being taunted by Teddy Boys?

American blacks, the descendants of slaves, were angered by having to use separate facilities; settlers in Britain, who came voluntarily, felt mild irritation with *The Black and White Minstrel Show*.

Albion is not Alabama; the Pennines are not the Appalachians; the *Empire Windrush* is not the slave ship *Amistad*; the Mersey lacks the grandeur of the wide Mississippi, which many runaway slaves had to somehow cross to reach freedom. A song entitled Ol' Man River when the eponymous river was the Mersey or the Medway would be risible.

The British Black History Month has no truly great figures or stupendous events to celebrate. And this absence is revealed by the dominance in it of all things American. Greenwich Council's newspaper *Greenwich Time* published an article on how one primary school in the borough staged a play as part of a Black History Month. It was called Black Heroes. All the heroes were American. The teacher who wrote and directed it appeared in it as American singer Ella Fitzgerald, and, 'Figureheads portrayed in the show varied from well-known political and sports icons like Martin Luther King and Michael Jordan to lesser known inventors like Howard Latimer [born in 1848 in Chelsea - er, Chelsea, Massachusetts, that is] and Garrett Morgan [born in 1877 in Paris - Paris, Kentucky).

The teacher said, 'We live in a multi-cultural society and it's important that children are interested in cultural diversity to appreciate other cultures. The play included musical interludes from Louis Armstrong; rap battles [?] and even a spot of basketball.'

The deputy head said, 'Our community is 51 per cent ethnic minorities, and it is important that kids understand all aspects of history.'

The paper added, 'Youngsters who took part in the performance spoke about some of their heroes of the play's title. Bola Oyetade, nine, said: "Rosa Parks is a role model. She wouldn't give up her seat on a bus and got arrested for it." [The bus was in Alabama, not Albion.] Ten-year-old Kelecha Chukwuadinulo added: "Martin Luther King changed the world from all the racism to how it is today".'

So we have African children celebrating American history at the expense of English taxpayers. And what do the few remaining indigenous pupils do while these celebrations of victimhood are being held? Is little Jane Smith supposed to sit through them and then go up to Bola Oyetade and Kelecha Chukwuadinulo and apologise for her ancestors enslaving theirs?

Great emphasis is placed nowadays in the teaching of history in schools on the Atlantic slave trade. The slaves can reasonably be shown as nothing but the victims of oppression, and therefore the world can be neatly divided into good and evil. Black pupils naturally revel in this interpretation. It is hugely damaging, inculcating in them a feeling of eternal victimhood and in white pupils a sense of perpetual guilt. The textbooks ignore the 17,000 seamen and marines of the Royal Navy's Preventive Squadron, who, in six decades of dramatic and daring action on the high seas in the nineteenth century, died in battles that liberated 160,000 Africans enslaved by Arabs and fellow Africans.

In England now there are many events and organisations that exclude the likes of me, countless groups, associations and publications that would be unacceptable if they were working for whites. The Society of Asian Lawyers actively promotes the career opportunities of lawyers solely on the basis of their Asian ethnicity; the London borough of Tower Hamlets in 2005 opened an 'Asian only' housing development; an event was held in London in October 2009 'designed to inspire, empower and inform Black, Asian and Minority Ethnic women about the business of social enterprise'; there exists a glossy forty-eight-page monthly listings magazine called *Lime*, stocked at public libraries, 'Your Essential Guide to Cultural London', which is devoid of any mention of a white person; and there is Sporting Bengal United Football Club, formed in 1996 'to encourage Asian football in London'; and Imkaan, a 'national charity for Black and Asian victims of domestic violence'.

The Lewisham Park Housing Association provides sheltered accommodation for elderly ethnics only. My father, who needed sheltered accommodation in his old age, would have been excluded from the Lewisham Park Housing Association. And in Lambeth there is Aashna House, a residential care home exclusively for the South Asian elderly.

The first racial discrimination legislation was aimed mainly at landladies putting 'No Coloureds' in their windows. Are not the many organisations that now exist such as the Lewisham Park Housing Association and Aashna House applying exactly this same sort of discrimination?

Also in Lewisham, at the other end of the age scale is the Black Pupils' Achievement Programme, 'aimed at helping improve the academic performance of black students of Caribbean heritage'.

Black-only jamborees are too numerous to list. They include:
❑**Miss Black Britain.**
❑**The Black Youth Achievement awards.**
❑**The Black Tie Comedy awards** (for black comedians - what a joke!).
❑**The Black List awards**, an annual ceremony held by the blacks' newspaper the *Voice* for black footballers ('the black football fraternity') that

is 'designed to highlight the growing contribution of black people in football at all levels'.(In fact blacks now dominate the game.)

❑**The Birmingham Black International Film Festival**.

❑**Black Fathers in the 21st Century** (I am not making this up), deemed necessary I suppose because in today's Britain 59 per cent of Caribbean and 44 per cent of African children grow up fatherless.

❑**London Schools and the Black Child awards**, for 'young black students [pupils] who are contradicting negative stereotypes by achieving very high academic grades', which implies that black pupils typically fail because white teachers have low expectations of them, not because they neither do homework nor pay attention in class.

❑**Reach**, a desperate and patronising initiative that took twenty 'great black role models' around the country to inspire black boys to success, as though they could not be inspired by anyone around them who is positive, including white teachers.

❑**The Black Entertainment, Film, Fashion, Television and Arts awards**.

❑**The Music of Black Origin awards**.

Launched in 1996, the MOBOs every year receive enormous media coverage despite being blatantly racist. It highlights the double standards of all these discriminatory events. Imagine the uproar if someone organised a Music of White Origin awards, presumably called the MOWOs. You would have every race discrimination law in the book thrown at whoever was behind it.

And the same applies to many other events, such as Tricycle Theatre's black season of 2009, where, if the word 'black' was replaced with 'white', collars would be felt by Politically Correct Plod.

British blacks revel in a sense of victimhood. It became popular in the 1960s, when they realised that if they succeeded in gaining this status in perpetuity they could do no wrong. Every black hooligan and criminal has learnt to blame slavery and colonialism for his behaviour. Black pupils, poor things, have been traumatised by four centuries of racism, slavery and oppression.

Their chip on the shoulder seems almost as generic as their colour. Many have no measure to understand their lives other than that of the victim. They have all the language and discourse of the race relations industry but nothing much to complain about. What is known as black culture is actually an exploitation of negritude for commercial reasons.

The obsession with American blacks supports a commercial empire that mass-produces books, films, cartoons, television dramas, comics, clothes and, of course, music. British blacks have acted as a fifth column for the Americanisation of Britain. They talk like American blacks, do the lupine American black walk and dress like American blacks, including wearing beltless jeans, hanging halfway down their bums, in unknowing imitation of black prisoners, who are deprived of belts in the American penal system, lest they hang themselves. This Americanisation would doubtless have happened anyway but British blacks hastened the process, for which we have no reason to be grateful.

A doctor who has worked in Birmingham and as a prison doctor, who writes under the pseudonym of 'Theodore Dalrymple', has written that the worst of his patients are the offspring of the first generation of Jamaican immigrants. 'How has such a charming and humorous community been turned into the sullen, resentful people that so many of their children (or grandchildren) seem to be today - particularly the males, possessed as they are of an arrogant sense of radical entitlement that renders them almost extra-territorial both to the laws of the land and the laws of good manners?' he asked.

He blames not racism but 'radical anti-racism (a kind of employment opportunity for bureaucrats of limited ability)' that has persuaded many young men of Jamaican descent that when someone asks them at three in the morning to turn their music down, or upbraids them in any other way or circumstances, he is motivated by racism. 'This is convenient for the young men themselves,' Dalrymple continued, 'who are enabled thereby to behave badly while convinced of their own moral superiority, based upon permanent, insuperable and existential victimhood; and it is also convenient for the anti-racist bureaucracy, who thereby assure themselves of "work", that is to say, a salary, for the foreseeable future.'

He concluded, 'The Jamaicans are a goldmine - for the record companies and welfare bureaucrats alike.'

Many people have suffered far more than British blacks - including millions of British children in the nineteenth century, who were forced to continue working sixteen-hour days in the textile factories for long after African slaves were emancipated. Pauper apprentices were just as much slaves as Africans in the plantations but the campaign to free them began many years after the abolition of recognised slavery.

It is the mark of a civilised and mature people that they accept that what was done in the past was done in the context of the age in which it took place. The idea of a collective sin relayed down the generations permanently staining a people is insidious. Contrition is not a policy. A hereditary transmission of the status of tormentor does not exist, any more than a transmission of the status of victim exists. Righting wrongs retrospectively has no virtue other than its poetic alliteration. Those who claim to be victims of a crime committed more than two centuries ago are saying, 'Don't judge us!'

These perpetual victims are making themselves comfy in an impregnable place, that of the damned of the Earth, seeking to gain esteem cheaply and effortlessly by inhabiting an accursed legend. They resemble those Japanese soldiers on remote Pacific islands in the 1980s who did not know the war had ended long ago. It is a vocation to be a victim once the suffering has ended. Because of what happened more than two hundred years ago, Britain owes Africans and their descendants housing, healthcare, education, decent wages, weak punishment for their crimes, tolerance of their loudness, immediate consideration and respect for their identity. Before they have even arrived they have legal and moral claims based on the principle 'your ancestors enslaved mine.' Once here, based on these claims, they are extraordinarily aggressive. The great ordeal of the oppressed must develop in the wake of the slave ship: in reality most African slaves were never transported but remained in Africa, enslaved by fellow Africans.

In fact slavery seems to have been more prevalent throughout Africa than anywhere else in the world, thriving extensively for a thousand years before the Europeans' arrival. Sir Samuel White Baker, who helped to discover the sources of the Nile, said of his travels in the Sudan region between 1862 and 1865, 'The institution of slavery is indigenous to the soil of Africa, and has not been taught to the Africans by the white man'. Between 1300 and 1900 in Senegambia alone almost a third of the population were slaves; in the nineteenth century among the Duala of the Cameroon, the Igbo and other peoples of the lower Niger, the Congo and the Kasanje kingdom and Chokwe of Angola, more than half the population were slaves; a third of the population among the Yoruba were slaves. Tribes enslaved each other constantly. Dahomey chief Gezo said in 1840, 'The slave trade has been the ruling principle of my people. It is the source of their glory and wealth.' Also guilty were the rulers of Benin, the kings of Ashanti and Congo and the Vili chiefs of Loango, all of whom sold great numbers of slaves over many generations. Throughout the continent, it was a custom that had begun centuries before the transatlantic slave trade and persisted long after Parliament abolished it throughout the British Empire. When other countries and illegal slavers continued to abduct people from the coasts of West Africa, the British sent warships at great cost to their own people to destroy this trade. Most of the 160,000 slaves freed by the Preventive Squadron chose to settle in Sierra Leone, run by the British, as they would not have to fear being re-enslaved, a danger in any other part of Africa.

Only recently have many African states outlawed the practice; in northern Nigeria in 1936, in Ethiopia in 1942 (under pressure from Western war allies), in Niger as late as 2003. In the region of Say on the right bank of the River Niger, it is estimated that in 1905 three-quarters of the population were composed of slaves, and that more than 870,000 in Niger still live in conditions of forced labour despite the new law.

Muslim religious leaders in Africa have always opposed emancipation, teaching their black slaves that they, the slaves, would not go to Paradise if they did not obey their masters. One *imam* said in 1997 that abolition was 'contrary to the fundamental text of Islamic law, the *Koran*... [and] amounts to the expropriation from Muslims of their goods; goods that were acquired legally. The state, if it is Islamic, does not have the right to seize my house, my wife or my slave.' In the Islamic state of Mauritania, on Africa's West coast, hereditary slavery continues, with Arab Muslims owning an estimated 90,000 blacks. Mauritania banned the slave trade only in 1980 and only buying and selling slaves, not owning them. The Arabic word *abid* has meant both black and slave for more than a thousand years.

Islam sanctions enslavement of infidels. Indians co-operated with the British Empire because it brought them unprecedented order and civility following eight hundred years of the plunder and depravity of the Mughals - Muslim rulers who came from as far west as Turkey. Delhi was razed eight times in that period, great pyramids being built with the skulls of its inhabitants. Indians were sold across the Islamic world in such numbers that the international price of slaves collapsed. The Hindu Kush, the mountain range of Afghanistan, means 'Hindu Slaughter', and is named after the huge numbers who died there while being marched to the bazaars of Central Asia and Arabia. The British, as well as combating other barbaric customs, also outlawed slavery at a time when 10m Indians were slaves - up to 15 per cent of the population in some areas.

Blacks in Britain fail to acknowledge that Britain not only did not invent slavery but was the first country in the history of the world to outlaw it.

One might have thought this would be a cause for self-congratulation rather than self-abasement.

Britain's record on slavery compares favourably with that of other countries. There is no evidence that other countries in Britain's position of prominence would have behaved any better, and considerable evidence that they might have behaved very much worse. Slavery is as old as humanity, and has been carried out by most peoples whenever they had the chance. It was sanctioned by classical authorities in all civilisations and by major religions, and was carried out by enthusiastic black and Arab intermediaries, who merely sold them on to Europeans.

Over the centuries, one million Christian slaves were carried off from Europe by pirates from the north African coast, who raided occasionally as far north as Cornwall and Cork.

The West developed the idea of abolition before it was disseminated in black Africa and in east Asia. Blacks are not angered by fellow blacks whose ancestors enslaved their ancestors in vast numbers for centuries, nor by Arabs who still maintain that enslaving other peoples is sanctioned by the *Koran*; they are angered only by the likes of me.

And the do-gooders who presume to speak for the likes of me, all those liberal, passive, gullible masochists, agree that we have only one duty, to endlessly atone, to accept constant flagellation.

Guilt has gone too far. It has become a pathology, the slaver's lash superseded by the tingling thrill of dusky Madame Dominatrix's whip. Albion should be renamed Algolagnia, which means pleasure from pain. It is almost compulsory nowadays to surrender to masochism and guilt where the British past is concerned.

It was not until early modern times that there began to appear, first in north-west Europe, a handful of countries where slavery was not woven into the social fabric. It was practised in ancient Mesopotamia, India and China, among the Aztecs, Incans and the Mayans, in Greece and Rome. It is estimated that the Roman Empire needed to find up to 400,000 new slaves a year just to keep the slave population steady. (Freed slaves, if they prospered, as they often did, themselves then took slaves.)

Slavery was a feature of most societies of which we have record - including Anglo-Saxon England. The earliest commodity to be mentioned as an export from England is slaves. In England during that period the usual price of a slave was a pound, the equivalent of eight oxen, and the sale took place, like that of cattle or other goods, before proper witnesses, so that the purchaser could vouch the seller to warranty if later anyone claimed that the slave had been stolen. Toll, the king's cut, was paid on the transaction, as on any other sale. But slaves obtained certain rights by custom, including their right to earn for themselves in their free time, and Archbishop Wulfstan considered the disregard of these rights as one of the abuses that brought down on his compatriots the wrath of God, in the

70

form of the Viking invasions.

Slavery having always been a fact of life in the Mediterranean region, to the Conquistadores, veterans of their nations' struggles against Turks and Moors, it seemed only natural to apply the methods learnt over centuries of Mediterranean warfare to the peoples they conquered. When the supply of these slaves ran out, as it quickly did, largely because of the genocidal effect of smallpox and other diseases fetched by the newcomers (it was said a Spaniard had only to breathe on an Indian for the Indian to die, and towns that a band of Conquistadores merely passed through no longer existed by the time they returned) they had no qualms about replacing them with Africans, especially as no rescue missions were likely to be launched on Africans' behalf and they could be regarded as heathens.

Within fifty years of Christopher Columbus reaching what is now Haiti, half a million of the island's aboriginal Taino-Arawak Indians had perished in the Spaniards' gold mines, and pre-Columbian culture had vanished. A missionary philanthropist named Bartolomé de las Casas, in his book *A Brief Account of the Destruction of the Indies* (1542), offered such a powerful indictment of Taino-Arawak slavery that it achieved its abolition. As an alternative to the cruelty of submitting Caribbean Indians to physical labour (for which they were 'constitutionally unsuited'), he suggested the importation of physically resilient Africans. Thus began the shipment of African slaves to the Americas (provided by Arab traders). When, in due course, it became the turn of the English and French to establish colonies in the New World, they logically copied the Portuguese and Spaniards.

The stroke of fortune that deprived the first Portuguese in Africa of the chance to see the great Mali civilisation at the height of its glory in the fourteenth century seems, in retrospect, one of the most tragic ironies of history. By the 1430s Mali was so reduced and weakened that Tuaregs from the desert were able to seize its major cities of Walata and Timbuktu. Two decades later, when Portuguese expeditions, pushing up the River Gambia, made the first recorded direct contact between outposts of Mali and European explorers, the former great civilisation had drastically declined. Had the first encounter with an important black polity happened a century earlier, when the grandeur of Mali was at its height, the whole subsequent history of relations between the two races might have been different.

As it was, when Africans' heartlands and home societies first became exposed to European explorers they were classified in a category close to that of the apes. Europeans seeing both Africans and apes for the first time reported a facial similarity and reached misguided conclusions.

The tradition that the descendants of Noah's son Ham were cursed with blackness - as well as, in Genesis, being condemned by Noah to slavery - reinforced the mental associations evoked by a 'diabolical' colour, generally preferred for depicting demons and signifying sin as well as being used in such phrases as 'black day', 'black mood' and 'black look'. Portuguese chronicler Zurara found the first slaves directly shipped from Africa 'so deformed in their faces and bodies as almost to resemble shadows from the nether world'.

Images like these, reinforced by the sacred text of Genesis, were hard to dispel. The Portuguese interlopers conceived a pejorative image of their hosts and spread it back home.

It was, in a way, an accident of history. You can appreciate today's blacks exclaiming, 'Some accident! Some history!' but, to quote sacred text again, the sins of the fathers are only supposed to be visited on the children 'unto the third and fourth generation' or at most the seventh; anyway not in perpetuity. Each new generation is a new people. We, however, are still paying and apologising for slavery ('atoning').

In 2006 Atoning Blair expressed his 'deep sorrow' for Britain's part in the slave trade.

This followed well-funded campaigns by organisations like English Heritage, who wanted to feel guilty that many of the houses in their charge were partly financed by money from slave labour, and academics and politicians from former slave trade ports like Bristol and Liverpool.

The agitation to compel never-ending atonement for slavery is part of a sinister ethnic power-play, a decades-long attempt to demoralise Britain's indigenous inhabitants so as to grant legitimacy to newcomers.

The first notable anti-slavery victory, the freeing of James Somerset in 1772, concerned the right of a slave who had been brought to England not to be forcibly returned to servitude in America, celebrated at a Westminster pub a few days later by two hundred Africans who drank to the health of the Lord Chief Justice. 'The evening was concluded with a ball,' reported the *London Chronicle*. 'The tickets to this Black assembly were 5s.'

Once launched, the crusade against slavery followed a logical course. The slave trade, because of its peculiar horrors and because the regulation of trade was an accepted function of government, was the obvious first target, and, with tens of thousands of Britons demanding an end to it, fifteen years after the Somerset case the London-based Society for the Abolition of the Slave Trade was formed, achieving its objective in 1807.

Dealing with slavery itself, which could be represented as an assault on the rights of property holders, presented more of a problem. It was one that Britain, thanks to its strong centralised government, was able to solve, but only at the staggering cost of £20m. The British effectively bought the slaves, buying off their owners. An Irishman named James Blair (no relation to Atoning) got the most compensation, in 1833 receiving £83,530 for 1,598 slaves.

Those urging endless atonement for our ancestors' involvement in human trafficking fail to recognise the Victorians' achievement in abolishing it. It is astonishing that the first countries that abolished slavery, even though it had remained immensely profitable, are now the only ones to be the object of accusations and demands for reparations.

Why is only the West blamed, while Asia (seventeen million captives since the seventh century) and Africa (fourteen million), which have never publicly apologised for it, are exonerated of all responsibility? Is it because so many Westerners are hyper-sensitive to moral arguments? We have become a race of Uriah Heeps, forever wringing our hands while making grovelling apologies for existing.

Our masochists are like Huckleberry Finn in Mark Twain's classic novel, in which the boys Huck and his friend Tom Sawyer set off on a raft down the Mississippi with a runaway slave, in a daring bid for freedom, knowing he was already free. When reprimanded by his aunt at the end of the book, he tells her, 'He ain't no slave; he's as free as any cretur that walks this earth!'

'What does the child mean?'

'Old Miss Watson died two months ago, and she set him free in her will.'

'Then what on earth did you want to set him free for, seeing he was already free?'

'I wanted the adventure of it.'

So it is with today's atoners. Slavery is ended but they want the adventure of it.

The atoners also fail to condemn Africa's current extensive slave trade. Slave girls remain on sale even now in Sudan, Mozambique and the Ivory Coast for as little as £5 each. It is as if the do-gooders are saying that we only expect humane behaviour of ourselves, as though they are condoning African slavery practised by Africans, a message that surely has racist connotations.

British Black History Month is untruthful in another way also. One London event during the October shenanigans of 2009 was entitled Black

Britain: From Roman Times to Today. Claims that a country has always been a 'country of immigrants' can be heard throughout Western Europe. You hear it even in Sweden, the evidence being a handful of Hanseatic trading outposts and reindeer-meat entrepôts in Lapland. In the case of Britain, it is like Red Indians claiming to be part of our history because of the visit of Pocahontas.

Contrary to these assertions, there have been only two groups of immigrants to Britain since the Norman conquest, the Huguenots and Jews, and even these were numerically insignificant. Britain has become a country of immigrants only in the last fifty years, not over the previous millennium. And even the Normans, though of course culturally important, were insignificant demographically. To claim Britain has always been multi-cultural is too disingenuous - or, more likely, too ignorant. The 1938 census showed there were then only 30,000 non-Europeans in the United Kingdom, and in 1951 the country still had only 50,000 Caribbeans and South Asians, most of them living in a handful of towns and ports. And even if you double or treble these figures, that still does not add up to mass immigration.

Much is made in Black History Month of Mary Seacole, the Jamaican nurse of the Crimean War. Her story can indeed rival that of Florence Nightingale, and she was probably a better person than arrogant Flo - but her father was Scottish and one mixed-race nurse does not add up to a country of immigrants. One columnist in the *Voice* objected to the eulogising of her because she 'never thought to go to Africa and help take care of the Zulu warriors with their war against the British'. At the time of the Zulu war Mary Seacole was aged seventy-two. To expect a half-Scottish seventy-two-year-old woman from Jamaica to go to Africa in Victorian times to nurse Zulu warriors wounded in the war with the British is about as unreasonable as it gets.

But then the *Voice* is consistently that unreasonable. Reeking of double standards, with poor journalism and lack of logic, its racist digs at Whitey are an insult to indigenous people and to intelligence. I do not know if any of its articles or editorials violate the race relations laws but it is certainly full of unremitting racial hatred. Shallow and crude, it lumps together writers and readers who have nothing in common other than their negritude. Africans and West Indians do not share a language or a culture. Their only bond is their skin colour, which, in other contexts, when it suits them, they maintain is irrelevant. In reality, they can no longer pretend they are soul brothers. But the *Voice* tries to keep up the pretence. Often the columnists' writings are disjointed and illogical. They write as though they were on drugs.

All the faults of the *Voice* were encapsulated in one long article in December 2009 by Lee Jasper, whining about a blog by *Spectator* journalist Rod Liddle that no one would have noticed if Jasper had not drawn attention to it, in which Liddle wrote: 'The overwhelming majority of street crime, knife crime, gun crime, robbery and crimes of sexual violence in London is carried out by young men from the African-Caribbean community. Of course, in return, we have rap music, goat curry and a far more vibrant and diverse understanding of cultures which were once alien to us. For which, many thanks.'

Under the big headline '"Freedom of speech" does not justify this vile ranting' Jasper writes that Liddle's readers are 'inbred bigots, demented fascists and assorted lunatics'. If that is not vile ranting, what is?

He concludes, 'We all know that Britain has always been multicultural, at least since it was a province of the Roman Empire 2,000 years ago and then went on to rule two thirds of the globe under colonialism.

'Britain will never again be exclusively a "white man's country", and is much improved as a consequence. Get over it. ['Get over it', indeed! Damned cheek! Jasper does not appreciate that the likes of me never invited the likes of him and we can remember when they were not here. How does he know Britain is 'much improved' when he was not here before the ethnic invasion?] No doubt as the government begins to slash public spending we will see many more such articles.

'Muslims and black youths, among others, will be blamed for ruining England's "green and pleasant" landscape. [Note the inverted commas.]

'Riddle is a troublemaker no doubt but I think it's time we asked some uncomfortable questions about our long term future, safety and prosperity here in the UK. Given the bleak outlook of a country in decline, maybe it's time for a sensible discussion about whether or not we have a sustainable future here.'

This article has it all - racism, insulting Whitey, perpetuating the untrue claim that Britain has always been multi-cultural, blaming mass immigration on Britain's colonial past... Jasper, chairman of the National Assembly Against Racism, was an adviser to the mayor of London, presumably on the basis that it is acceptable for blacks to be racist.

In reality, just being black does not qualify you to understand the race situation any more than being ill makes you an expert on medicine. Blacks' feeling of victimhood is a disease, an itch they cannot stop scratching. They are like hypochondriacs, over-reacting to the slightest discomfort and every pimple. The dormant bacilli of slavery are like shingles, always ripe for resuscitation.

Everyone has ancestral grievances to exploit. Should the likes of me demand that capitalists pay damages, with interest, for their shameless exploitation of workers over two hundred years? Will the common folk of England one day seek revenge on aristocrats for the lords' repeated false promises and mass murders as they combated the many rebellions against their rule since the great Peasants' Revolt of 1381? Should not Anglo-Saxons demand an apology from Denmark for the depredations of the Vikings? Surely the descendants of all the tribes such as the Iceni and the Trinobantes massacred by the Romans have a case for reparation from the Italian government? And who killed our peaceful, innocent ancestor Cheddar Man and, no doubt, thousands like him, with a violent blow to the head, possibly in order to eat him, in 7150BC? We do not know but if ever we find out woe to those descended from the murderers!

If the politically-correct encouragement of ethnics' self-pity continues, blacks, Arabs and Muslims will still be wallowing in it centuries from now, becoming with every passing year more and more absurd and pathetic. Already the Western colonialism and transatlantic slavery that they still blame for nearly everything were several generations ago. It is hard now to see events that long ago as causally related. For how long can ethnics continue to maintain that everyone in the West is born into guilt while everyone else is born into innocence? And for how long can we continue our self-flagellation? As Jeremy Paxman said in February 2012: 'Apologising for things your great, great, great-grandfather did seems a complete exercise in moral vacuousness.'

The likes of Jasper complain endlessly about not being integrated into British society at the same time as proudly accentuating their difference to indigenous Britons. In the January 18th-24th 2010 issue of the *Voice*, one of them, Patrick Vernon, in a full-page article, actually called for a 'Windrush Day' to be a public holiday (typically citing an American example - Martin Luther King Day.) He initiated a campaign for it with a petition for readers to sign.

Vernon's call followed a call by Muslims to institute British public holidays to mark Islamic festivals. This is not fair! Why should blacks and Muslims get special treatment? Let everyone also have a day off every year to celebrate *diwali*, the Hindu and Sikh festival of lamps held every October or November, especially as the Sikhs feel aggrieved so easily and are allowed to carry knives! And what about the neglected Parsees? Surely their annual Peteti Day deserves celebrating in Britain. We could hold supplementary tributes on this day to Britain's most famous Parsee, the late singer Freddie Mercury. What fun! How jolly we will all be, all the time! As there are so many Nigerians in Britain now, let us also celebrate with them Nigeria's Independence Day as a British national holiday! So what that the independence being celebrated is independence from Britain! We are almost in that absurd position now already, with US Independence Day, every July 4th being celebrated here in articles and programmes despite the obvious irony.

A country that annually celebrates a defeat has clearly lost any sense of identity. Any excuse will do for a holiday. Life is never better than in a demoralised, declining rich country, when a people's fading vitality increases the attractions of modern versions of the Roman bread and circuses. To satisfy this insatiable desire for amusement, we have already imported foreign festivities such as Gay Pride and Halloween. Why stop at homosexuals and witches? Surely there are Buddhist festivals we can honour every year also, naturally letting Buddhists have the day off! And as January 1st is a public holiday surely it is only fair to proclaim the Chinese New Year, the first day of the Year of the Toad or whatever, also a holiday! Surely there are enough Mexicans in Britain to warrant a fiesta each November, adults knocking back tequila, children eating chocolate skulls, on the Day of the Dead! Let no one in Albion work any more, let the whole of life be a great big celebration of diversity! The possibilities are endless. Special months, weeks and days already now disfigure the calendar like the pimples and rashes of a skin disease. My favourite, which I would support, is one of Venezuela's - Indigenous Resistance Day.

The only problem is a saturation of atonement days. A feeling exists among ethnics that the Jews have monopolised all the suffering in the world, a jealousy resulting in an unseemly competition in victimhood. One adviser to Tony Blair, Tariq Ramadan, said that today's Muslims are comparable to the Jews of the 1930s, meaning that anyone who criticises Islam is no better than a Nazi, and the secretary of the Muslim Council of Britain, Sir Iqbal Sacranie, has proposed the replacement of Holocaust Memorial Day by Genocide Day because 'Muslims feel hurt and excluded that their lives are not equally valuable to those lives lost in the Holocaust time'.

That issue of the *Voice* calling for a Windrush Day also contained the word indigenous for once without the contemptuous inverted commas reserved for the English. It was in a film review and referred to the Blue People of the planet Pandora in the science fiction fantasy *Avatar*. Blues and Blacks can be indigenous but not poor old Whitey.

Also in the same issue, Darcus Howe wrote, of the time before the ethnic invasion, 'British culture, whatever that was'. He can get away with laughing at the very idea of British culture, but laugh at the idea that such a thing as 'African' or 'black' culture exists and you would be thought not merely ignorant but racist. It is only we who do not have a past, only we who lack an identity.

The masthead for Howe's column says he is angry. The likes of me are also angry. Add all the angry Muslims, and a miasma of anger seems to hang over Albion. (The Muslims, typically, ask for more government funding on Islamic youth projects to alleviate *their* anger, when, from 2007 to 2010, £53m had already been spent on such projects in a vain bid to stop young Muslims attempting mass murder.)

All those ethnics of distant immigrant origin like Howe and all those second-generation English Muslims who hate England but have nowhere else to go make us think of dysfunctional marriages in which the partners detest each other but cannot make up their minds to separate and end up cohabiting in mutual antipathy.

As the great Igbo author Chinua Achebe, a writer of major historical importance who should have won the Nobel Prize for Literature, showed in all his novels, a society as divided as this cannot survive. Okonkwo's suicide in the stunning ending of the classic *Things Fall Apart*, Ezeulu's banishment in *Arrow of God*, and the various morally compromising expressions of greed and obsession with power in *No Longer at Ease*, *A Man of the People* and *Anthills of the Savannah* betoken Achebe's unequivocal commitment to the notion that a society which does not work together is a society doomed to failure. One assumes the editors of the *Voice* have read Achebe's famous novels. It is a shame they have not learnt anything from them.

Howe also uses the phrase, 'We in the black and Asian community', lumping together all blacks and all Asians of whatever origin.

This ethnic ganging up is a new phenomenon becoming ever more prevalent. Even the London Jewish Cultural Centre has hosted a series of women's workshops 'raising awareness of racist experiences shared by all immigrant communities'. The Black and Minority Ethnic movement is a vast segregationist network embracing all aspects of human life, the services of its many branches available to anyone who is not white.

Councils also now routinely do this. Their Black History Months have expanded to include 'celebrations of the talent, achievements and contri-butions' of all ethnics, not just blacks. Naturally, grants are available to ethnic groups wishing to participate, Lewisham Council offering £800 each. Every year for a whole month there is a subsidised nationwide jamboree for everyone in Britain except Whitey.

Such dubious thinking has become politicised, with alliances being formed on the basis that all settlers and their descendants regard Whitey not only as an outsider but a hostile one.

This mentality is extremely dangerous.

Does anyone really need rags like the *Voice* that tediously repeat in every issue a litany of grievances and alleged injustices endured by blacks and other settlers ever since the arrival of the *Empire Windrush*? These exaggerations and lies matter because, uncorrected and unchallenged, they get perpetuated and acquire orthodoxy.

And this repetition has led to the idea of an unending cycle of repentance for past wrongs. In 2007, the 200th anniversary of the abolition of the slave trade, many supported a plan that Britain should make a formal apology for its role in the trade, in the person of the queen or the prime minister. A black commentator in the *Guardian* suggested a version of such a grovelling speech. Others more sensibly argued that apologising for something your ancestors did centuries ago is a cheap gesture that strips the word 'apology' of any meaning (not that debasing words has ever bothered the race relations industry).

It is too easy to say sorry for a sin committed by people long dead, and achieves nothing, not even any genuine feeling of satisfaction for the victims' descendants, as they will remain determinedly vengeful. It seems that vengeance for a sin of more than two hundred years ago is all some of them live for. Their ideal is to acquire the title of pariah without having actually endured anything. Grovelling platitudes lack any redemptive power or lessons.

Campaigning blacks exploit Primo Levi's expression 'the duty of memory', coined by him when he called on the survivors of the Nazi concentration camps to remind contemporaries of a horror that was close to being forgotten. This simple injunction to remember a specific evil has since been developed to become a call to remember all past evil and for eternal vigilance lest such horrors return. It is useless knowledge. 'The duty of memory' has never prevented current evils. As French philosopher Pascal Bruckner writes in his groundbreaking book *The Tyranny of Guilt*:

The memory of old persecutions serves chiefly to open up wounds, to begin an endless prosecution of the West. In this case, what is 'the duty of memory' is usually the imposition of an official history in which the roles are assigned in advance, a coagulated knowledge that resembles propaganda, paralyses research and impedes investigation.

The period of imperialism is frozen in an eternity of bitterness... the centuries form one long saga of reprisals and bloody torments. The duty of memory is brandished by some only in order to arouse the duty of penitence in others.

The organisers of such events as Black History Month and all those discriminatory awards, and the participants, want it both ways - they want to emphasise their difference at the same time as complain of lack of integration.

Double standards permeate the country. Politically-correct beliefs are upheld in many ways. Draconian codes of conduct are used.

Newspapers omit the race of an ethnic if it is a negative story but glory in the 'irrelevant' fact of race when it comes to such events as the MOBOs, the Asian business awards, Black History Month, Halle Berry winning an Oscar or Barack Obama becoming US president. The National Union of Journalists' guidelines state forcibly, with Stalinist fervour, that journalists must promote immigration and diversity.

(These guidelines were drawn up by a man sacked by the BBC for gross dishonesty, who then became a corrupt politician - see essay 'Denis MacShane'.)

All over the country now are ethnics asserting themselves racistly - staging discriminatory events and forming racist organisations, getting laws changed to suit only them and pressing for new laws that benefit no one else, violating history, messing about with the language, forming illogical and potentially dangerous alliances - while Whitey looks on bemused, worried and indignant. As Bruckner writes:

The first duty of a democracy is not to ruminate on old evils, it is to relentlessly denounce its present crimes and failures. This requires reciprocity, with everyone applying the same rule. We must have done with the blackmail of culpability, cease to sacrifice ourselves to our persecutors.

Following the hard-done-by Caribbeans, the custom of placating settlers claiming eternal victimhood was to have catastrophic consequences when the next tsunami of disgruntled ethnics swamped our shores and oozed among us - the Muslims. Now Muslims too clamour for this convenient status, leading to today's contest, with Jews resented because they have the Holocaust.

Throughout England now workshops, meetings and conferences are held where, as long as someone abuses the English, all goes well, everyone is fulfilled. Our masochists, accustomed to acquiescing in everything poor persecuted settlers claimed, eagerly took from the Muslims the proffered new instruments with which to torture themselves.

DEMONIC DEMOGRAPHY
Eurabian Nights

THE famous Muslim mantra begins, 'There is no god...' If only they would leave it at that and let us live in peace. All our problems with Islam stem from the fact that all religion is taken seriously. It is only because vestiges of religiosity remain in otherwise enlightened England that Muslims' beliefs and practices are treated with respect instead of being ridiculed and derided for the nonsense they are. If ALL believers in the power of an imaginary supernatural being were regarded as being simply like fans of that other doughty fighter in an eternal celestial war between good and evil, Harry Potter, the problems would vanish.

Let there be NO state-funded religious schools, NO laws against inciting religious hatred or insulting religion, NO special dispensation for religious dress or ornamentation in jobs or schools that require a uniform. As Richard Dawkins wrote: 'As long as we accept the principle that religious faith must be respected simply because it is religious faith, it is hard to withhold respect from the faith of Osama Bin Laden and the suicide bombers. The alternative... is to abandon the principle of automatic respect for religious faith.'

Religious claims, withering under rational scrutiny, deserve no special place in public life. Religion is a private matter and should be kept that way. Millions have died in its ongoing campaign to force its beliefs on its victims. Socially divisive by design, it is mostly about the desire of competing religious hierarchies to control people's minds, just like secular ideologies. It seems to have an amazing immunity from normal laws. If anyone advertised that by taking a certain medicine one would live for ever and go to heaven, the product would be banned under the trades description act. Yet religion can publicly make its totally unprovable claims and get away with it. When faith rules over facts, magical thinking becomes deeply ingrained and warps all areas of life. It produces a frame of mind in which concepts are formulated with deep passion but without the slightest attention paid to the evidence.

We owe it to ourselves to push back against this tide of intolerance. The problem lies not with people obtaining quiet comfort from their belief, but with vehement modern crusaders who would have us live by medieval standards or teach our children that the world was created a ridiculous 6,000 years ago, as famously calculated by Bishop James Ussher in the seventeenth century, who deduced from biblical chronology traced back to Genesis that the first day of creation began at dusk preceding Sunday, October 23rd 4004 BC.

You would have assumed that once facts about the natural world had become known, as they have done during the Enlightenment, it would not be possible for a civilisation to cease knowing them. But that is what is happening. Great philosophers such as Bacon, Descartes, Hobbes, Spinoza, Locke, Bayle and Leibniz changed the history of Europe for two centuries, all the radical reforms of the Enlightenment built on freedom of thought, tolerance and humanism. Now we are returning to darkness. Gradually we sink into the greyness that exists just before the dark. Macabre shadows lengthen. Minds, having become more open than any previous period, are closing down again. Facts are denied, falsehoods resurrected. The Enlightenment is incomplete. In spite of all the advances of the past two centuries, magical thinking and the cultural inheritance of religion have remained widespread. And because of this we are tolerating among us believers in an alien religion that is murderously intolerant.

Religion in the abstract does not actually exist, and only politicians profess any allegiance to it. Because the creeds of the major religions are mutually contradictory, the one thing we know for certain about religion is that if any religion is true then most religions are false.

I have a sharp, cultivated sense of the ridiculous, and the absurdity of human individuals presuming to know who their deity helps or hinders seems like gratuitous impertinence. Does He help only those who believe He exists, while atheists can struggle by as best they can unaided no matter how meritorious and beneficial their lives and actions? A passage near the end of the Pentateuch seems to support this view. The Israelites are told they were chosen not for their righteousness but because other nations were wickedly following false gods. What mattered was not what you knew but Who you knew.

Most peoples have traditionally sought a supernatural explanation of every event. The irrational belief in the veracity of ancient folk tales, that we share this planet with supernatural beings, is an old one. Students of magic and religion have identified innumerable varieties of them - gods, devils, angels, pixies, elves, fairies, genies… In Russia, if some household item could not be found, this was because it had been moved by the mischievous house spirit, the *domovoi*, imagined as an old dwarf living under the threshold. If you got lost in the forest it was because you had been led astray by the *leshii*, a blue-skinned wood-goblin with bulging eyes and long hair - you had neglected to outwit him by wearing your coat back to front and putting your left shoe on your right foot. Drowned young men were said to have been lured into the water by *rusalki*, beautiful wanton mermaids, who may have tickled them to death.

I can see no distinction between believing in all this and adhering to a belief system handed down from Bronze Age people, with Iron Age refinements, whose lives were ravaged by their basic ignorance about the world. Even a thousand years after the Iron Age, well-educated people were still totally ignorant, their beliefs about the stars and planets, the mind and body, based on false premises and insufficient data and their ideas on religion winnowed from a thousand years of ambiguity. As late as the seventeenth century, Catholic nuns used to try to convert heretics staying at their convent by mixing tiny morsels of ground saint's bone into the heretic's gruel. But while other beliefs of the past are today known to be wrong even by children, religious ideas are still expected to be considered beyond reproach. Clerics of all denominations expect their holy books to be excluded from the profound suspicion of the past, coming out with such nonsense as 'The sacred wisdom of yesterday' (Britain's chief rabbi, Sir Jonathan Sacks). As a sports reporter I specialised in football, and in my seat in a stadium press box I scoffed to myself whenever I saw Catholic players crossing themselves when running on to the field for a match, as though God cared who won a game of football and would intervene, like Homer's gods diverting spears and arrows from their favourite warriors at Troy, or the angels fighting on the Muslims' side at the battle of Badr in 624, to which Mohammed attributed the victory. To me the idea was laughable. When a player's equally devout opponents also crossed themselves, did the gestures cancel each other out? And what if the opposing team had a Hindu player invoking his monkey god? Did the Lord, in His Almighty wisdom, weigh up the respective worth of all these supplicants before allocating the victory, make a decision as to which team should progress in the cup or gain the points in the league? What absurdity, I would think.

Then, it was harmless absurdity. But now Islam has invaded our shores. Now we are surrounded by people who not only believe such nonsense but want to kill or subdue the likes of us who do not believe it.

In this predicament, everyone is forced to choose sides, to choose the proper friends and enemies. The opponents of the Enlightenment have started to show themselves. They are many and, despite their cunning, obvious, easily able to distinguish. But who are the defenders of the Enlightenment? Are they the ones denigrated as fascists? Are all those appalled at the threat to our civilisation, the assault on our values, to be so tritely dismissed?

Even if you think European culture is no better than that of anyone else, the fact remains that millions from other cultures are desperate to cross our borders in order to get out of their societies and into ours. Peoples who drove us out now want to come and live with us. The crowd of Algerian youths greeting French president Jacques Chirac on his visit to Algiers in 2004 did not shout, 'Down with colonialism!' or some such but, 'Visas, visas!'. Europe got over the loss of its colonies much quicker than the colonies got over the loss of Europe. The trouble is, Muslims, when they come here, do not lose their contempt for the likes of us. They outdo us in greed, criminality and perjury and yet regard themselves as our superiors! This disdain was until recently camouflaged but this was purely a tactic until they felt strong and confident enough to come out openly with it, which was when there would be enough of them, which has now happened.

All settlers should be classified somewhere in the invasive species category, along with Japanese knotweed, pennywort, water primrose and Harlequin ladybirds, but Muslims, because of their birth rate, their aggressive hostility and their traditional culture of entitlement to power, should be regarded as particularly dangerous - indeed, as a mortal threat, a vindictive enemy.

And these are people who still seriously believe in several types of supernatural beings as well as their deity, including angels and genies.

Genies are defined in my Chambers dictionary as 'a class of spirits in Muslim mythology, formed of fire, living chiefly on the mountains of Kaf which encircle the world, assuming various shapes, sometimes as men of enormous size and portentous hideousness.' Genies, of course, as every child knows, come out of the magic lamp when it is rubbed in the tale about Aladdin in the *Thousand and One Nights*.

Muslims believe that humans, angels and genies make up the three sentient creations of Allah. The *Koran* mentions genies often, including the statement that Mohammed was sent as a prophet to both 'humanity and the genies'. One chapter, The Genies, is solely about them.

While Christianity maintains that Lucifer was an angel who rebelled against God's orders, Islam maintains that Iblis was a genie who had been granted special privilege to live among angels prior to his rebellion. Muslim scholars have ruled that it is apostasy to disbelieve in one of God's creations; so, as under Islam law apostasy is a capital offence, Muslims who do not believe in genies can be executed.

Surely it must be obvious that people brought up to earnestly believe, on pain of death, that spirits formed of smokeless fire exist alongside us at the fringes of perception, become incapable of reason. Brainwashed from early childhood into believing such nonsense - or else! - they must lose the ability to think, become bovine. Dealing with them is impossible, attempting a dialogue unthinkable, showing indulgence suicidal. They have as much chance of seeing sense as dustmen have of smelling clean. They cannot be reasoned with. Hence no attempt should be made to do so. Their religion should simply be ridiculed for the idiocy it is. The political mainstream should denounce cultural Islamic imperialism and refuse to give one inch to *sharia* law, saying no to oriental bigamy and all attempts to set up a parallel Islamic society.

Instead of this, with Britain's collective brain turned to multi-cultural jelly, the Labour government, in its doomed attempt to assimilate Islam, actually strengthened the enemy's position by campaigning to criminalise incitement to hatred of religion (in practice, denouncing Islam), punishable by up to seven years in prison. Remember the Aesop fable about people often giving their enemies the means for their own destruction? If Labour's planned legislation had been passed (it failed by one vote) I would be risking incarceration for the lines I write here. It could be worse. Aesop was executed by being thrown from a cliff.

The political establishment is supinely going along with the gradual Islamification of Britain. Muslim pressure groups have been elevated to pseudo-governmental status in the hope this will produce an Islam that reflects the values of Britain rather than the other way round, a policy that raises the question of who will absorb whom. Who is doing the adapting? Surely you do not imagine it is Islam? It cannot be. The *Koran* forbids it. And yet leading 'moderate' Muslims such as the head of the Muslim Council of Britain, Sir Iqbal Sacranie, get a knighthood or a peerage for not being an 'extremist'. (It was Sir Iqbal, remember, who called for Holocaust Memorial Day to be replaced with Genocide Day because Muslims feel their sufferings are not sufficiently acknowledged.)

The Muslim Council of Britain is one of many bodies with official-sounding names that have acquired prominence as journalists frantically seek individuals and organisations to use as credible sources of 'Islamic opinion'. All these people and organisations are treated as if they can speak on behalf of 'the Muslim community'. The Muslim Parliament is the one with the silliest pretentious title. All incessantly push for more concessions, rights or public money.

The Muslims are interfering more and more in the affairs of this Britain of ours. Why are they being allowed to do this? Because a fundamental irresponsibility exists at all levels, strongest precisely at the top. Those engaged in the struggle for our spiritual values are hindered by heedless political leaders blinded by political correctness.

At the highest levels of government there is a kind of conspiracy not to believe bad things about Muslims, to accept all that they say at face value as though they were basically trustworthy; the same as us, just with a slightly darker complexion.

In the past, throughout the world, leaders have employed noble rhetoric when their land was threatened, such as Winston Churchill's, 'We shall fight them on the beaches, we shall never surrender...' Numerous great battles have been fought in which the defenders were inspired by the thought that they were defending their country, the invaders in the hope of winning it. Hitherto conquest was starkly geographical. It was measured by the extent of the conquered territories. You dip into tomes such as the *Collins Encyclopedia of Military History*, with its terse references to battlefield slaughter through the ages, starting with the Battle of Megiddo, the original Armageddon, and its concise explanations of how such battles decided the fate of nations, and you realise the death of the English nation can never be described in this way. Our demise is not coming from defeat on the battlefield.

Invading Muslims are no longer the bold Moors who conquered Iberia on camels and fought with scimitars. Now they settle in their millions among us and form close ties with our television and radio channels, our publishers, our universities, our trade unions, our newspapers and magazines and our mainstream political parties. Socialists have become collaborators with their forces.

Some indigenous people are so blinded by their propaganda they become Islam's useful idiots. An article in London listings magazine *Time Out* in 2007 by someone with the English name of Michael Hodges, after comparing the virtues of Islam, 'a religion based on noble traditions and compassionate principles', with English vices, concluded that London would be a much better place if all its citizens became Muslim. Even indigenous people not fooled still hesitate to resist the invasion. If you never see the forces deployed against you in open hostility, you never rouse your will to action. Doubts and misgivings nag you, making you unable to calculate the best forms of resistance.

Are all our bearded guests and their demurely shrouded, perpetually pregnant wives really unconnected to *jihad*? They come from the poorest countries of the world, from villages where 2p is a lot of money. By what means do they end up in England? Where did they get the money for the journey? Whole extended families come. The combined fares amount to thousands of pounds. Something extremely sinister is happening here. Might it be that this money is supplied by billionaire sheikhs for the mere purpose of materialising a conquest of our territory? Maybe the settlers, in return for the price of the fares, promise to multiply prodigiously as enjoined by the Prophet. Certainly most mosques in Britain are built with Saudi cash. Islam is waging a covert *jihad*, its settlers emissaries of deceit.

How to combat such an invasion, unprecedented in world history? Military resistance is impossible. Valour counts for nothing against the infernal machinations of deceit. Our only weapon is truth. Let us cut through the Muslims' lies and the lies of our traitors.

Let us regard the Muslims among us as triffids, the plants in John Wyndham's science-fiction novel *The Day of the Triffids*, in which the triffids, monstrous stinging plants, 'mobile, and rapidly multiplying, of invasive habit and malign intent', are cultivated until they get out of control and roam everywhere, taking over the world. They dominate after mysterious bright green shooting stars have blinded most humans, and they too blind people, with poisonous stings, to render them helpless. For shooting stars and poisonous stings read political correctness and Muslim lies; for triffids read Muslims.

Nowadays England is not an amalgam of related peoples but of the most widely separated races of the world, the most divergent, including some that for centuries had ignored the fact that they inhabited the same planet and others that had waged almost incessant war on all other races. The globalisation of the last few decades is not sufficient to make up for those centuries. Just when science was supplanting superstition, vast hordes of aggressive foreigners have settled among us, aliens who seem to have come from the distant past as much as from faraway lands. The primitive hostility of Islam rises up to face us across millennia. Muslims belong to another age, another epoch. Between us is a wall of glass. We cannot understand what they are saying on the other side of the wall but we can see their incomprehensible dumb-show: and we wonder what they are doing here. They care nothing for the thousand books I have read. Despite the *Iliad* and the *Odyssey* being the two greatest epics to appear in the history of humanity, Muslims do not read them because their numerous gods are incompatible with Islam. Homer was not translated into Arabic until 1904, even though his writings were ubiquitous in the Greek-speaking lands that came under Arab rule in the seventh century. Few Muslims read Dante, Chaucer or Shakespeare either.

Muslims' ignorance is such that you wonder if they are aware the world is not flat but round and if they know the position of different countries on the map. They move in a world of ideas and customs that is not mine. They have no point of contact with my values. They are dismissive of such values, while I on my side care nothing for their habits, superstitions and ideas, which, nevertheless, form the basis for vital beliefs I am expected to regard just as valid as mine. Wherever they live, Muslims inhabit a different time zone - the Dark Ages.

Understanding the world for a human is reducing it to the human, stamping it with his or her seal. The cat's universe is not the universe of the ant. And the universe of the Muslim is not my universe. The Muslim is a creature from the past who not only believes in fairies but hates, despises and threatens all who do not share that belief.

Inviting such barbaric people to settle in England is no better than inviting the likes of the delegation of African cannibals who thanked a neighbouring chief for making them a gift of a slave girl, their lips daubed with the blood of the gift they had just eaten. These cannibals had their code of honour, their standards of behaviour. But, like those of Muslims, they are not our code or standards.

The English cultural identity is well defined. And it does not include the Muslim world, any more than it does the world of the cannibals. Our identity has not been influenced by Islam in the slightest. For historical and cultural reasons, Christianity belongs in England; Islam does not. Our entity has been based on Christianity for nearly 2,000 years, on a church called the Anglican Church. Edward the Confessor and Alfred the Great both ensured that English Common Law was founded on Judaeo-Christian principles. Without the Judaeo-Christian tradition the language, the literature, the art and even the science of our civilisation cannot be fully understood.

And acceptance of the law is deeply imprinted in the English character. In England, the pledged word, honesty, are traditionally inescapable values that admit of no discussion. During the first half of the 20th century there was an extraordinarily high level of honesty, the English probably one of the most honest races in world history. In a way, even criminals were honest. When caught, they did not rant and rave, maintain their innocence, blame society, claim the status of victim or demand their human rights. They said, 'It's a fair cop, guv,' and went quietly. When Great Train Robbery mastermind Bruce Reynolds was arrested by tenacious detective Tommy Butler in 1968, Reynolds said, '*C'est la vie*, Tom.' A remnant of this heritage survives in our unarmed police force.

Muslims clearly do not belong in this setting. It is evident that they are out of place here. Their world is a world of subterfuge, duplicity, deceit; everything there is disguise, stratagem, artifice.

No promise can bind Muslims against the interest and duty of their religion, and they can abrogate their own contracts and agreements and those of their predecessors with an easy conscience. What the likes of me would regard as endless deceit, they see as service to Allah. To Muslims, words are just another weapon of war.

Other religions have in the past practised deceit in the name of their deity. When the Provincial of the Jesuit Order in England, Father Garnet, was discovered telling lies to his examiners at his trial for treason in the seventeenth century, he alleged that he had done so in accordance with the doctrine of 'equivocation', which allowed the faithful to say one thing while holding, but not uttering, mental reservations. Equivocation, the 'double sense' of Macbeth, the lying that Macduff's son refers to, is indeed a principal mode of the operation of evil forces throughout Shakespeare's play. The Muslim 'equivocation' is called *tarquiya*. Its observance means that any falsehood is permissible if it supports Islam. As Islam permeates all aspects of Muslims' lives, *tarquiya* makes them stupendous liars. Though they eat no pork, they are forever telling porkies. In all their dealings with the infidel, whether politics or business, they seek not the truth or fairness but the advantage. Outwitting or cheating a *kafir* is regarded as no more reprehensible than fooling a dog. Muslims use the word 'dog' interchangeably with 'infidel'.

Muslim settlers will always be distrusted and disliked, despite the inexplicable acceptance and recognition that has been rendered to their deity, for they are not tractable and harmless but arrogant and preachy, the type who believe they have some spiritual precedence over the rest of the world, who know how to see to their own advantage when trading, to the point that one's self-esteem actually suffers when one deals with them.

After several decades of Islamic infiltration many indigenous people have now been cheated by Muslims, who, in all their dealings with infidels, lack qualms of conscience, being convinced that they have been given permission to purify reality on an epic scale. Indigenous people, when dealing with Muslims, suffer from the crippling disadvantage of ignorance of such profound deceit. Muslims are not bound by our conventions and moral beliefs. It requires great acuity of mind to detect and defeat the chicanery of Muslims, who labour to disguise the truth of facts and to pervert the sense of laws. You need to know beforehand that they cannot be trusted, and proceed on that basis.

In antiquity, whenever the simple and truthful Germans came among the plotting and artful Romans, and experienced their duplicity and craftiness, they immediately became more false and subtle than the Romans themselves; to their own compatriots they kept their characteristic sincerity and good faith; but, once duped and tricked by the southern schemers, as if with a fierce scorn they exulted in mastering them in their own wily statesmanship; and if reproached by the Romans for insincerity, retorted, with naïve wonder, 'You are Romans, and complain of insincerity! How otherwise can we deal with you - how be safe among you?'

Muslims who grew up here, and even those born here, remain on the other side of the glass wall. Sidique Khan, the mastermind of the July 7th 2005 London bomb plot, spoke with a thick Yorkshire accent and played football with English friends who called him 'Sid'. His mother-in-law, who worked as a council liaison officer at a school in Dewsbury, in 1998 became the first Asian woman ever to be invited to a Buckingham Palace garden party, meeting the queen and other members of the royal family and the aristocracy, in recognition for her work among Muslims. She attended another Buckingham Palace garden party in 2004, when, even as she was having a cuppa with Her Majesty, her son-in-law up the M1 was by now studying the properties of acetone to investigate how it is used in the making of bombs.

Islam cannot be accommodated. Friction exists between it and every single culture with which it is in contact. With the perverted reasoning typical of Muslims (for, as is well known, habitual liars come to believe their own lies), they would have us believe that by an incredible coincidence a wide variety of non-Muslim cultures has developed exactly the same unjust malevolence towards Islam.

The Christian religions were bloodthirsty and murderous by deviating from their texts, whereas Islam is the same by following its text closely. Talk of 'moderates' and 'fundamentalists' is valid in connection with Christianity but not with Islam. Moderate Islam does not exist. There is no such thing as good, peaceful Islam or bad, violent Islam. There is simply Islam. And Islam is the *Koran*, the *Mein Kampf* of a religion that has always aimed not only at eliminating all other religions but to eliminate secularism as well. It identifies itself with politics, with governance.

To see just how intolerant Islam is, you have only to open the *Koran* at almost any page. Even the most cursory glance shows it.

I open my Penguin Classics edition at random. On page 88 we have, 'You see many among them ['Israelites'] making friends with unbelievers. Evil is that to which their souls prompt them. They have incurred the wrath of God and shall endure eternal torment... Those who disbelieve and deny Our revelations shall become the inmates of Hell.'

On page 130: 'If you could see the angels when they carry off the souls of the unbelievers! They shall strike them on their faces and their backs, saying: "Taste the torment of the Conflagration!"'

On page 133: 'When the sacred months are over slay the idolaters wherever you find them. Arrest them, besiege, them, and lie in ambush everywhere for them... Make war on them... Fight against them until they pay tribute out of hand and are utterly subdued... The day will surely come when their treasures shall be heated in the fire of Hell, and their foreheads, sides and backs branded with them.'

On page 178: 'Punishment awaits them [unbelievers] in this nether life: but more grievous is the punishment of the life to come... the Fire shall be the end of the unbelievers.'

Flicking through the holy book again, I come across more vituperation.

'Let not believers make friends with infidels' (3:28).

'He that chooses a religion other than Islam, it will not be accepted from him and in the world to come he will surely be among the losers' (3:85).

'Those that criticise Islam shall be slain or crucified or have their hands and feet cut off on alternate sides' (5:33).

'Allah revealed His will to the angels, saying, "Give courage to the believers. I shall cast terror into the hearts of the infidels. Strike off their heads, strike off the very tips of their fingers!"' (8:12).

'Muster against the unbelievers all the men and cavalry at your command, so that you may strike terror into the enemy of Allah and your enemy' (8:59).

'If there are twenty steadfast men among you, they shall vanquish two hundred; and if there are a hundred, they shall rout a thousand infidels, for they are stupid' (8:65).

'The infidels are unclean. Do not let them approach a mosque' (9:28).

'Believers, make war on the infidels who dwell around you' (9:123).

'Garments of fire have been prepared for the unbelievers. Scalding water shall be poured upon their heads, melting their skins and that which is in their bellies. They shall be lashed with rods of iron' (22:19).

And so it goes on throughout. This repetition makes the *Koran* an extremely boring book. It is little more than a hundred verses ordering the murder of infidels. Reading it, you are initially appalled, and soon bored. The incessant self-righteous barrage of hate consigning all infidels to the fiery pit quickly becomes wearisome. 'Moderate Islam' is an oxymoron.

Why should we respect silly beliefs, just because their adherents call it religion? Children can be indulged, and respected for other reasons, but not because they believe in mythical beings such as Father Christmas and fairies. The great religious prophets occupy a special place in the realm of ignorance. The myths that are called religion developed over the years roughly in the same way as other, secular myths. King Arthur was a petty chieftain of the early sixth century who fought bravely in twelve battles against the invading Saxons. His knights, the round table and Merlin were later accretions as he became the splendid personage celebrated for many centuries in countless songs, romances and stories. (This development is traced by Richard Barber in his fascinating book *King Arthur in Legend and History*.) The case is the same with Robin Hood, a medieval mugger. Again, his companions - Maid Marian, Friar Tuck, Little John - were added later as the myth developed.

The only difference with Mohammed is that a few more facts are known about him and that he himself deliberately added to his myth. It was he, and not future bards, who invented his mythological allies, including the Angel Gabriel, who fluttered down from heaven for chats. In reality, his visions, like those of many other visionaries, were probably caused by epilepsy. Grandiose ideas are also often associated with cerebral syphilis. Herod the Great, with his multiple building projects, is a possible example of this. And it is now known that most prophets and other messianic leaders suffered, if not from epilepsy or syphilis, then from a personality disorder called manic episodes. Napoleon was one such. The authoritative book about psychiatric therapy, the *American Psychiatric Association's Diagnostic and Statistical Manual of Mental Disorders*, devotes several pages to this malady. Those suffering from it set themselves up as experts on subjects they know nothing about, take excessive risks and claim a special relationship with God. It is caused by a lithium deficiency. A lot of trouble in world history could have been prevented by a dose of lithium.

We cannot blame the Great Men of the past for their delusions of grandeur. They were ill. Nor can we blame those who lived in those realms of ignorance for being deceived. But we can, and should, blame those among us now who continue to revere such people.

Humankind would have been happier if most Great Men had never been born. Bullying, brutal, dogmatic and noisy, they have always been a curse. People who love to talk about a concept brought out by a Great Man and forget to go deeper into it are mentally asleep, more bovine than human. One of the tragedies of the human condition is the tendency of too many people to judge the truth of an opinion by the vehemence with which it is expressed.

Falsehoods remain falsehoods, no matter how forcefully expressed or how pious. I do not see why, because other people are simple-minded, I should respect a pack of lies. The ancient Greeks had a moral code for a thousand years with no moralistic religion. History shows that the moral and ethical guides that most of us live by did not originate with the monotheistic religions, as proponents of those religions would have us believe. Instead, moral behaviour appears to have evolved socially. And those who believe religion is a force for good have to explain the paradox that the countries where religion is most closely tied to the state - Russia, Italy, of course the Islamic countries - are also the most corrupt.

Nietzsche said that any effort to cast off the Christian faith while keeping the best elements of Christian morality is doomed to failure but I do not see why. There is the Greek precedent of a code of behaviour without any reference to a deity, and Britain today does indeed have Christian values while preserving our Bible largely because of a certain poetic quality it possesses. And this is fair enough. This is sufficient.

Islam is intolerable because of its ideology. The *imams* really do plot to take over the Western world.

Oriana Fallaci described in her best-selling book *The Rage and the Pride* how during a synod that the Vatican held in 1999 to discuss areas of co-operation between Christians and Muslims, an eminent Islam scholar stunned the audience by declaring with placid effrontery, 'By means of your democracy we shall invade you, by means of our religion we shall dominate you.'

Muslims' first allegiance is to the *umma*, worldwide Islam, the 'Community of the Believers', not to the country they live in. An Egyptian, Mahdi Akef, former General Guide of the Muslim Brothers, recently declared he would prefer a Malaysian Muslim as president of Egypt to a Christian Egyptian. This allegiance is inculcated as early as primary school. In an investigation of schools by the French ministry of education, teachers said that many pupils, when asked what their nationality is, reply, 'Muslim.' When the pupils are informed they are French, they reply that it is impossible, because they are Muslims.

This allegiance makes Muslims unreliable citizens, who, in any future conflict, could not be trusted. They are inherently traitors. They therefore have no claim to civil liberties.

And yet, in their intolerable self-righteousness, they vociferously demand more and more as citizens, including changes to the law to suit them. If we remain inert they will boss us around more and more and vex us more and more, until they subdue us; and, as Oriana Fallaci wrote, 'Anyone who believes the contrary is a fool.'

She cites the case of the Barbican Theatre in central London cutting the scene in Christopher Marlowe's play *Tamburlaine the Great* in which Tamburlaine scornfully burns a copy of the *Koran* and challenges the Prophet: 'Now, if you have the power, come down and make a miracle!' She writes that the scene infuriated local Muslims but it is more likely the theatre pre-empted their protests with protective self-censorship, even though the scene comes near the end of the play and is vital to the theme and Tamburlaine's fatal illness strikes him immediately afterwards, suggesting divine retribution, and to stage the play without it is pointless.

The clash between us and Muslims is not a military one but a demographic one - while we are being responsible on an already overcrowded planet by not having too many children, they, already in their billions, are having babies deliberately and consciously in order to populate the world. As Algerian leader Houari Boumediene said to the General Assembly of the United Nations in 1974 with startling frankness, 'One day, millions will leave the southern hemisphere to go to the northern one. But not as friends. Because they will go there to conquer it; and they will conquer it by populating your territory with our children. The wombs of our women will give us victory...

'No amount of atomic bombs will be able to dam up the tidal wave comprising human beings in their millions that one day will leave the southernmost and poor part of the world, to engulf the relatively open spaces of the wealthier northern hemisphere.'

In that very same year, the Islamic Conference in Lahore concluded its meeting with a resolution that included the precept to increase the then modest flow of immigrants to Europe and to dominate the continent through 'demographic preponderance'. This is logical (one of the few things about Islam that is logical). If you desired to challenge the supremacy of a society that was secure and had powerful weapons, what would you do? Would you meet it on its own terms by launching a costly and destructive assault or, if time was unimportant, would you prefer to employ a version of a more subtle attack? Would you, in fact, seek to infiltrate it in order to attack it from within? The main point of Carl von Clausewitz's classic *On War* is the vital importance of outnumbering your enemy in the right place at the right time. What better tactic can there be then, if time is on your side and the enemy stupidly allows it, than gradually building up your forces in his own country? All the old battle terms such as front line and outflanking cease to have any meaning but the same aim, victory, is achieved.

Eventually, though it is already too late, Britain's leaders will realise the problem was more serious than they thought. If the intruders remain, they shall dominate us - that, by then, will be clear and inevitable. Will we agree to be superseded, and start on the way to extinction without a struggle? By then we may be so decadent this is indeed possible. Politically, the question will be, can any state, however tolerant, afford to harbour increasingly powerful foreigners over whom it has no control? Obviously the answer is no.

So what will the politicians do? The intruders will probably remain safe while the waffling continues among the politicians, who, glowing with righteousness on our behalf, will continue to defend the intruders' human rights. The politicians will claim, still without a referendum, to be representing justice, compassion and the great heart of the British people. Before, as members of a securely dominant race, they could afford to lose touch with reality, and amuse themselves with abstractions. 'Live and let live' is a piece of patronage that can be afforded by the consciously secure. But reality is encroaching. Politicians are already petrified of saying anything meaningful about either the steady encroachment of Islam into Britain's public space or the linked phenomenon of mass immigration, as the problem becomes not just by far the most important in British politics but the defining issue of our age. But it already appears insoluble and we could easily have a curious epoch when deeply demoralised politicians are fighting to keep out of office rather than be the one who has to take action on it. Britain has lost all sense of belief in itself and, because of this, has lost the will to defend itself, allowing the country to be taken over by settlers full of a sense of injury and entitlement.

Religion is all right as long as it is not taken too seriously. Most English people correctly regard it not as a source of solace but rather as a creator of division and tension. Words such as 'massacre', 'assassin' and 'thug' have their origins in religion. Without the work of theologians we would not have had the Crusades, the Inquisition, the destruction of the World Trade Centre. In spite of this, and the obvious dangers in encouraging the brainwashing of future generations, Labour doled out state funds (taxpayers' money) to Islamic faith schools, presumably hoping that once these schools were thus funded they might stop being quite so Islamic. The term 'faith school' was introduced in 1990 following demands by Muslims for institutions comparable to the existing Church schools.

'Faith' has become the new word for religion. I do not know why but there is always a reason for this sort of thing and it may be the users of 'faith' feel deep down, really deep down so they are not aware of it themselves, that 'religion' no longer applies in this country. It derives from the Latin *religare*, to bind. The nation that prays together stays together. Religion, with its belief in watchful gods and its extravagant rituals and practices, has been a social glue for much of human history. But recently some societies have succeeded in sustaining co-operation with secular institutions such as courts, police and mechanisms for enforcing contracts. In northern Europe, these institutions have precipitated religion's decline by usurping its society-building functions. These societies with atheist majorities are some of the most co-operative, peaceful and prosperous in the world.

Subtle reminders of secular moral authority, words such as civic, jury and police, have the same fairness-promoting effect as reminders of God in totalitarian theocracies. People have discovered new ways to be nice to each other without a watchful deity. Society has been gradually learning to live without religion by replicating its success at binding people together. And now this process of the Enlightenment has been disrupted by having hundreds of thousands among us who not only pray five times a day but pray to the alien god of an aggressively proselytising religion. 'Proselytise' comes from the Greek *proselytos*, which means a newcomer, resident foreigner.

The Jesuits are not the only people to have realised that children thoroughly indoctrinated before the age of seven remain imprisoned in faith for the rest of their lives. The *mullahs* know it too, which is why they apply themselves before all else to getting these tender years into their possession. Ducklings and chicks will follow a trailed old boot if that was the first thing they saw on hatching, taking it for their mother. So Muslim toddlers follow Islam, not knowing any better. They are then reared not to question but to obey, so that in adulthood their reasoning faculties remain undeveloped.

In this dull condition, there is nothing so absurd or revolting they will not firmly believe in. When the killing of a heretic, an unbeliever or an apostate is declared to be praiseworthy and promoting their eternal salvation, they make doing so a main objective. All devout Muslims consider murdering unbelievers a most pious act. As it says in the *Koran*, many times, with variations, 'Believers, make war on the infidels who dwell around you. Deal firmly with them.'

They want to kill the likes of me! Unfortunately for us, this awareness is not shared by our leaders, who give our money to organisations that use it to fund Holy War.

Research in public records reveals that many bodies closely linked to Islamic extremism enjoy an enormous amount of public funding. In 2011 East London mosque was paid at least £256,000 and the Osmani Trust received almost £600,000. The Islamic Forum of Europe controls both of these organisations, who openly work to change the 'very infrastructure of society, its institutions, its culture, its political order'. Many terrorist *imams* have been guests at the mosque.

And more than £113,000 in government school grants is given every year to leading members of Hizb ut-Tahrir, a militant Islamic group that Tony Blair promised to ban after the 2005 bomb attacks on London but never got round to doing. Gordon Brown later said it could not be banned as there was no proof it was a terrorist organisation, though it is banned in other countries, and it continues to receive six-figure sums from the taxpayer, despite its website promoting racism and anti-Semitic hatred. The website calls suicide bombers 'martyrs', and urges Muslims to kill Jewish people. The Tories too pledged to ban it but have not done so.

Hizb ut-Tahrir declares *fatwas* against things like promoting religious tolerance and watching football matches. It has said that British Muslims should fight assimilation into British society as taking part in it contradicts Muslim belief.

The public money given to Hizb ut-Tahrir helps the running of two Islamic primary schools in Tottenham and Slough where children are taught key elements of the group's ideology from the age of five.

The two schools are run by the Islamic Shakhsiyah Foundation, a registered charity. Three of the four trustees are Hizb ut-Tahrir activists, and one of the school heads, a young lady named Farah Ahmed, is a former member who has attacked the national curriculum in a Hizb ut-Tahrir pamphlet for 'pushing the idea of religious tolerance', saying English is 'one of the most damaging subjects' a school can teach and criticising attempts to integrate Muslim children into British society.

Another Ahmed, a male one this time, named Iftikhar Ahmed, of the London School of Islamics Trust, writing elsewhere, demanded both that Muslims live outside British society AND that they receive state funds for their schools!

'State schools with monolingual teachers are not capable of teaching English to bilingual Muslim children, who need state-funded Muslim schools with bilingual Muslim teachers as role models,' he wrote. 'Muslims have the right to educate their children in an environment that suits their culture. British schooling and the British society is the home of institutional racism. The result is that Muslim children are unable to develop self-confidence and self-esteem, therefore, most of them leave school with low grades.'

He then wrote two such grossly unfair sentences that I want to hit him: 'Racism is deeply rooted in British society. Every native child is born with a gene or virus of racism.'

This is truly evil. And, by any definition, truly racist. Why do such people think they are entitled to use such offensive, insulting language and deny it to others? The man must be as thick as a plank and as nasty as a snake.

'Therefore,' he continues, 'no law could change the attitudes of racism towards those who are different. There are hundreds of state schools where Muslim pupils are in the majority. In my opinion, all such schools may be designated as Muslim community schools with bilingual Muslim teachers. There is no place for a non-Muslim child or teacher in a Muslim school.'

Five weeks later it was reported that a Christian nurse was facing the sack for wearing a cross while she cared for patients. But though the Royal Devon and Exeter Hospital had banned the crucifix in its wards, it made concessions for other religions, including allowing Muslim nurses to wear headscarves on duty.

Religions have been re-defined as race, which they are not, and opposition to religion re-defined as race hatred, which it is not. Although the law now treats Sikhs and Jews as racial as well as religious groups, any religion remains a system of ideas no different to any other ideology, and, as with all ideas, religion must be open to criticism, even that deemed unfair or hateful.

A distinction is usually made between religion and ideology but it is not a hard and fast one as they share many aspects, and, as each mutates, it takes on the characteristics of the other. Islamism should be treated as an ideology as well as a religion.

Outlawing the incitement of religious hatred, which the last Labour government pressed for, strengthens the very nutters who want to murder us. When society decides that people's religion, rather than their class or gender, is the cultural fact that matters, power inevitably passes to religious fanatics who take offence at the smallest thing and who believe religion justifies any crime.

Religion should be made utterly unimportant in the public sphere, not elevated to supreme importance. When such elevation has happened in the past it has invariably led to the most horrific bloodbaths. During and after Partition, when Pakistan was created on the basis of religion, the peace-loving adherents of Islam, Hinduism and Sikhism took it in turns to slaughter each other in their tens of thousands. Long after Partition, massacres have continued: in 1984, more than 3,000 Sikhs; in 1993, 2,000 killed after the destruction of a mosque by Hindus planning to build a temple in its place; in 2002, more than 2,000, mostly Muslims.

Turning religion into an equal opportunities cause results not in equality but in the social fragmentation that goes with special treatment. The state should be committing itself to secularism, the only ideology that can make a multi-religious society successful. It should diminish the importance of religion, not increase it.

The alternative is a future of competitive religious grievance, incessant vexatious litigation and, eventually, domination by Islam.

The liberal freedoms that British citizens have won over decades of struggle are useful to Muslims to organise politically, even as they hope to reject these very freedoms that they exploit.

Recently there have been many calls for Parliament to acknowledge a limited code of *sharia* law as a parallel system in Britain, allowing Muslims to manage their personal and family affairs according to the demands of the *Koran*, its ancillary texts and the body of jurisprudence that has been built up by Muslim scholars over many centuries.

This tradition allows for no deviation even when it becomes irrelevant to real life. Innovation (*bida*) is widely considered a form of heresy or outright unbelief. The Prophet is recorded as saying, 'Every new matter is an innovation, every innovation is misguidance, and every misguidance is in the Fire' [of Hell]. This doctrine has had a severe dampening effect on attempts at legal reform. At its worst, it can lead to an insistence on a return to the state of law that is supposed to have existed in the time of the Prophet and his companions. By thus idealising a mythic perfect state of government and legislation, it becomes all too easy to dismiss or condemn anything that does not match up to these impossible standards.

In August 2006 the head of the Union of Muslim Organisations of the UK and Ireland, Dr Sayed Pasha, as well as calling on the Secretary of State for Communities to institute public holidays to mark Muslim festivals, something that has never been done for any other religious group, called for the introduction of elements of this unreasonable medieval law to cover family matters.

Such calls have generally been made by Muslims but in February 2008 the Archbishop of Canterbury, Rowan Williams, made his infamous speech in which he called for the limited application of Islamic law in Britain. He said, 'There are ways of looking at marital disputes, for example, which provide an alternative to the divorce courts as we understand them. In some cultural and religious settings they would seem more appropriate.'

Reports then revealed that *sharia* courts were already operating in Britain. The think tank Civitas estimated that there were eighty-five *sharia* councils, and several bodies like the Islamic Sharia Council have seen a big increase in their cases in the past five years, with thousands of Muslims using them. Their arbitration decisions are enforced by the state courts even though *sharia* judgments on marital disputes, so far their main field of activity, contravenes the same Human Rights Act that in other contexts is invoked so often and with so much reverence. For of course in these cases the woman always loses. Wives are also usually unable to escape domestic violence or abusive husbands because *imams* are reluctant to allow them to initiate divorce.

'One law for all' is the principle that should guide our lawmakers, but as in so many other respects in recent years Parliament has lost its way, bemused and intimidated by aggressive self-righteous Muslims amply funded by oil money from the puritan regime in Saudi Arabia, even though *sharia* often blatantly contradicts British law codes.

In March 2012 Baroness Cox told a House of Lords conference that the growing number of *sharia* courts could bring about the destruction of democracy. She said: 'We do not at the moment have the most brutal punishments but there are those in this country who would like to bring them in. Many *sharia* courts are an institutional means of intimidation backed by death threats.' Under *sharia* homosexuality, adultery and criticism of Islam are all punishable by death. Methods of execution include beheading, stoning, firing squad and hanging. Theft is often punished by amputating the accused's hand. Drinking alcohol is frequently punished by flogging.

Britain's Muslim population is estimated at 3m, five per cent of the total population, and an increase of about 75 per cent in the last decade.

The continued levels of Muslim immigration make the state implementation of *sharia* law unavoidable. Applying *sharia* law only to marital issues is just the beginning. Islamic clerics insist on the absolute integrity of the system. To remove one part of it invites its total dissolution. This is similar to (and linked to) the view that to alter even one letter of the *Koran* or the supplementary *hadith* literature invites a more wholesale challenge to the texts and the authority they exercise.

For centuries, *sharia* was applied with the assumption that Muslims were in the majority and ruled the country. This situation has changed dramatically with the migration of millions of Muslims to Europe and their clerics refusing to adapt Islamic law to European societies, insisting that Muslims are bound by all of *sharia* regardless of where they may be. Not only that, but the *Koran* is to be accepted 'as a whole, not partially'.

Some online *fatwa* sites carry statements to the effect that properly-instituted *sharia* law compels the execution of adulterers by stoning. As Islamic law is deemed immutable, and communal pressures are linked to the idea that its barbaric punishments are decreed by Allah or the Prophet, British society faces a crisis. Modern secular legal systems are built on rationality, not on arbitrary pronouncements of presumed divine or traditional origin. (Stoning cannot be dismissed as a perversion of Islam. Mohammed himself decreed, in a test case, that an adulterous couple should be stoned to death. It is recorded that the man tried to shield the woman with his body.) We are in an undeclared war of legal systems, in which one will eventually prevail and the other defeated. The enemy, having successfully infiltrated our society in vast numbers, has now embarked on its destruction.

In Islamic writings, this process is called gradualism. It is the doctrine that Islamic law must be introduced into Western systems in a piecemeal fashion. The influential leader of the European Council for Fatwa and Research, Yusuf al-Qaradawi, wrote in *IslamOnline* on April 26th 2005:

> Gradualism is to be observed when it comes to applying the rulings of the Shari'ah in today's life when Muslims have been socially, legislatively and culturally invaded... It here refers to preparing people ideologically, psychologically, morally and socially to accept and adopt the application of the Shari'ah in all aspects of life... It does not mean we are to procrastinate and put off applying the Shari'ah. It is not to be taken as a pretext for discouraging people and foiling their pressing demands to establish Allah's laws.

One of these pressing demands was made in Britain in January 2007 when a professor in the Division of Community Health Services at Edinburgh University named Aziz Shaykh published an article in the *British Medical*

Journal in which he demanded that Muslims have entirely separate health services from everyone else.

Demands will continue to be made for preferential treatment for Muslims in all areas of life. The danger is that they will become the only group to receive preferential treatment on purely religious grounds, at a time when religion should be forced to remain a private affair, not become ever more public.

The next demand will be that of a Muslim girl for permission to wear a *burka* in school, so that not the smallest portion of her provocative body can be seen, not even her eyes, as in Taliban areas of the world; or to be excluded from lessons taught by men; or to miss lessons that contradict the *Koran*, such as studying Shakespeare (Romeo and Juliet had pre-marital sex, and none of the protagonists in the history plays, those scheming megalomaniac aristocrats and monarchs, accepted that all was *quadaa*, fate, the will of Allah). This could be followed by the need to be excused from class five times a day, as though she had a problem with her bladder.

If her demands are not met, two recently discovered phobias will be used to explain her plight, that of 'school phobia' to describe a child who hates going to school, and 'Islamophobia'.

'Islamophobia' was invented by Muslims in the 1970s, first used against an American feminist who they claimed was guilty of it when she called on Iranian women to wear normal clothes. A cunning invention, it makes Islam a subject that no one can criticise without being accused of suffering from a personality disorder. (The traditional accusation of racism was inconveniently used too often by other victim cultures, notably that of despised blacks.) Although churches are banned and Christians persecuted and murdered in many Muslim countries, the corresponding disorder 'Christianophobia' does not exist. Islamophobia serves the purpose of denying the reality of a global Islamist offensive. The aggressors are demanding that they themselves not be attacked.

Are we to re-establish the archaic crime of blasphemy, just because Muslims demand it? We have every right to reject all religions, to regard them all as mendacious, retrograde and mindless. Muslims in Britain are in an awkward position, living in an environment that is not religious, confronted everywhere by advertising hoardings that offend their sense of modesty, customs that contradict their prejudices, a freedom of style, tone and discussion that is far from their dogmas. But if this environment disturbs them so much, why do they stay here? Why do none of them ever go to live in an Islamist country? British Communists used to be told, 'Why don't you go and live in the Soviet Union?' but it is not a fair comparison. British subjects could not get visas to live and work in the Soviet Union and there were language problems. None of this applies to Muslims in Britain. Nothing is stopping them buying a one-way ticket to the land of their fathers, whether it is Pakistan, Bangladesh or anywhere else where Islamic customs and laws such as banning blasphemy predominate.

'Islamophobia' is now routinely used to describe anyone who does not wish a cruel, unjust, barbaric, alien, intolerant and downright silly religion to be favoured with government support.

But encouraging Islam is too risky. Justice does not require that we stand idly by while others destroy the basis of our existence. (Churchill was called a Naziphobe.)

When religion invades the public domain as Islam has done in Britain it becomes an ideology like any other, and when it gains control that country becomes a theocracy. Oliver Cromwell was the last theocrat to rule Britain. A regression to a puritanical theocracy in the 21st century would be a farcical disaster. As Bruckner writes:

> Islam is convinced that it is the last revealed religion and hence the only authentic one, with its book directly dictated by God to his Prophet. It considers itself not the heir of earlier faiths but rather a successor that invalidates them forever. The day when its highest authorities recognise the conquering, aggressive nature of their faith, when they ask to be pardoned for the holy wars waged in the name of the *Koran* and the infamies committed against infidels, apostates, unbelievers and women, when they apologise for the terrorist attacks that profane the name of God - that will be a day of progress and will help dissipate the suspicion that many people legitimately harbour regarding this sacrificial monotheism.

Throughout our lives, the likes of me have been urged to respect difference. Up until the late 1990s this mainly meant accepting blacks. Since then we have been asked to avoid evaluating an alien religion in terms of our Western culture. Our values were increasingly called prejudices. The thoughts of a medieval Middle East fanatic who believed that God had spoken to him through an angel were declared sacrosanct, the most innocuous criticism forbidden.

During my lifetime England has become afflicted with a condition from which it will probably never recover - a suicidal condition. I have seen in the country over the years self-criticism change to self-distrust, then into a form of self-flagellation. A time has now emerged when we are taught we were born into guilt while everyone from the South and the East was born into innocence. Our civilisation has become obsessively preoccupied with drawing up a list of its crimes and creating an image of itself as torturer. Diagnosing an infuriating disease, Bruckner writes: 'When doubt becomes our only faith, it begins to denigrate all the energy that faith used to put into veneration. Then we refuse to defend our societies: we would rather abolish ourselves than show even a tiny bit of attachment to them... with a suicidal blindness, our continent kneels down before Allah's madmen.'

SI FUERIS ROMAE...
or, v chuzhoi monastyr so svoim ustavom ne khodyat

THE very word 'multiculturalism' is ugly and awkward, which is why I break it up with a hyphen. It seems to have been coined some time in the 1980s, for it is not in the 1984 Oxford dictionary but is in the Chambers dictionary of four years later.

The idea of multi-culturalism has been stealthily advanced since then by politicians, civil servants and council officials, its doctrine spread in schools and teacher-training colleges. 'Celebrating diversity' is the political orthodoxy of modern Britain, just as 'Long live Stalin' was in the Soviet Union. The indoctrination begins in primary schools, with the study of the Roman occupation. In the national curriculum's history books the pain of being invaded is swiftly superseded by a 'celebration of social, cultural, religious and ethnic diversity'.

Academics spread such a distorted interpretation of our history that it amounts to outright lies. Dr Gavin Schaffer, Senior Lecturer in History of Race and Ethnicity at the University of Birmingham, had the gall to write in the *Sun*, 'We are a country built on foundations of cultural difference. Our food, language, music and TV remind us at every turn of this history of rich mixture. In Britain multi-cultural society is not a good or bad thing. It is simply what we are, and always have been.'

If this were true, a word to describe the phenomenon would have been coined long before the 1980s.

Such commentators claim that all cultures are equal, not as a human response to a particular climate, history or place, but equal in all respects everywhere. As a consequence of this encouragement not to adapt to their new country, millions of southern and eastern peoples settled in Britain have kept the traditions and habits of their villages, oases, temples, bazaars and mosques. This shows itself in many big and small ways that together are actually changing the way things are done in this country.

I have a Christian friend whose grandparents came to England from the Caribbean in the 1950s, so he and his parents were born here and he had a very English upbringing. When you are with him you forget he is black, it ceases to register, his dusky skin, brown eyes and dark hair no more important than his height. But his attitudes and outlook on life are still very West Indian. While they are not overtly detrimental to our way of life, it is the seemingly insignificant differences that, if there are many such settlers, over decades undermine our whole culture. What seem to be small and harmless changes to our ways actually end in its destruction.

This would still be so even if all the settlers were Christian like him. For a start, many Caribbean and African Christians celebrate their religion in a very un-English manner - loudly and flamboyantly, with much yelling, rhythmic clapping and rattling of tambourines. The Anglican church hall near me has been taken over by noisy Africans belonging to some Christian sect with a silly pretentious name.

Their loud services are so frequent that they have changed the nature of the neighbourhood. The few remaining indigenous people, no lovers of hubbub and jangle, have had to learn to be tolerant. (It is always us who are urged to be tolerant, never the settlers.) The hall is no longer Anglican but African. The profound peace of Anglican prayer has been replaced by African worship that is like a swimming pool in which all the noise comes from the shallow end.

The sheer number of ethnics here means our whole way of life is being undermined, as they stick to their way of doing things. They behave in this manner because this is how they behave back home and they see no reason to change - to adjust to local customs.

Nobel prize-winning author V S Naipaul, who was born in Trinidad to Indian parents, once said, 'A person can't say, "I want the country, I want the protection, but I want to live in my own way." It's wrong. It's become some kind of racket, this multi-culturalism. Jobs for the boys.'

St Ambrose advised St Augustine in the fourth century, '*Si fueris Romae, Romano vivito more*' - 'When in Rome, do as the Romans do.'

The same sentiment is expressed in Russian as, '*V chuzhoi monastyr so svoim ustavom ne khodyat*' - 'Don't bring your rules to our monastery.'

In this country now is a vast and expensive bureaucracy ('jobs for the boys') whose reason for existence is to guarantee that migrants share in the benefits of British nationality, no matter what, without them making the slightest effort to adjust, often at the expense of the indigenous people. An army of anti-discrimination officers and equal opportunity consultants generates tribunals, political correctness rules and other devices for enforcing on the likes of me the virtue we were always famous for and was largely the reason many ethnics came here - tolerance.

The pathology of multi-culturalism is in its insistence that the local people must not think their language, religion, laws and customs in any way superior to those of the settlers who, for some mysterious reason, have come to live among us rather than stay at home.

The result has been that in any conflict between the settlers and local custom, it is the settlers who prevail.

Settlers have to be supplied with official materials in their own language rather than being required to understand English.

Information about free travel in London for over-sixties is available in FORTY languages! And 'Additional languages will be included when they become available.' Where will this lunacy end? Njerep, a language in Cameroon, reportedly has only four speakers left. They are all aged over sixty, and so if they decided to spend the autumn of their years in London would be entitled to free travel. Would they be informed of their right to a Freedom Pass, and how to apply, in Njerep?

Religious holidays of the alien cultures have to be accommodated by employers, and legislation has to be adapted to migrant customs.

College calendars have a section called 'notable diary dates' that includes the religion and date for events such as *Al Hijra*, *Baisakhi* and *Saka* but Christian holidays such as Christmas are not even mentioned. The most important festival in all Christian countries has simply been downgraded to a mere 'public holiday' with no mention of the religion or even the name of the day! Schools with many ethnic pupils exclude Christmas festivities, and local councils use some word other than Christmas on their seasonal cards. Stoke City Council celebrates 'Winterfest', while Oakengates Town Council in Telford, Shropshire, has its 'Winter Celebrations' - all in the cause of 'not offending other cultures'.

Birmingham City Council meanwhile is an avid supporter of the annual Islamic Awareness Week (funded with taxpayers' money, of course) and in 2010 the Department of Health announced that female Muslim staff would be permitted to cover their arms in hospital wards despite strict dress codes introduced in 2007 to prevent the spread of deadly hospital superbugs, blamed on long sleeves. Several universities had reported that Muslim medical students objected to the rules, including one who refused to 'scrub' as this left her forearms exposed.

Even the food served at UK colleges is *halal*. It is not labelled as *halal* and the indigenous students are not aware they are eating it.

And the really sad, stupid thing is that, generally, on any world or historical scale, the English are not racist at all. Like all people everywhere we would prefer to live among our own kind, people we can recognise and trust, but that does not make us racist. The vast majority of us would never condone hurting anyone of another group, unlike the Tamils and Sinhalese in Sri Lanka, the Muslims, Hindus and Sikhs in India, the Sunnis and the Shiites in the Middle East, all the different peoples of the former Yugoslavia, the peoples of the Caucasus, who all hate each other but who outsiders cannot tell apart, the African tribes slaughtering each other to the point of genocide...

The nineteenth century philosopher John Stuart Mill wrote that every age has held many opinions 'which subsequent ages have deemed not only false but absurd'. Every age has its madness. Throughout most of the world throughout history this has of course usually been religion. The mental illness of our modern age is multi-culturalism, the obsession with diversity, the eagerness to abandon English customs.

And so the virtue of tolerance has become a threatening disease. Recently I read of a family of Roma settlers who had broken the law by arranging a marriage between two five-year-olds, and one of these criminals said defiantly, 'Why should we change our customs just because we live here?'

In 2005 the High Court granted a fifteen-year-old Muslim girl from Luton, where Islam is rife, the right to wear in school a *jilbab*, the full-length gown that covers all the body except the face and hands, ruling that she had the right to education 'and to manifest her religious beliefs' even though her school had a uniform.

And a Sikh pupil in 2008 won the right to wear a religious bracelet at the Aberdare Girls' School in South Wales, though teachers can still send home pupils who want to wear bracelets because they think they look pretty, as this contravenes the school's uniform dress code.

The judge did not rule that all the girls at Aberdare School had the right to wear bracelets, only the Sikh girl. Sarika Singh won a High Court case against the school after it excluded her for breaking its 'no jewellery' rule by wearing a steel bangle, a *kara*, which is one of five symbols of Sikh faith. The school was found guilty of indirect discrimination under the race and equality laws.

An elderly Sikh who was Britain's first South Asian judge, Sir Mota

Singh QC, said in February 2010 (by then retired) on the BBC's Asian Network, 'The girl not allowed to wear the *kara* is a petty thing for the administrators to have done and it doesn't do them any good.'

It does not seem to have occurred to the likes of Sir Mota that the authority of the school has been badly undermined by the successful challenge of this fourteen-year-old child.

Or maybe it has occurred to him but he does not care. All he cares about is his Sikhness. He admitted this when, in the same broadcast, he said, 'The fact that I'm a Sikh matters more to me than anything else.' Like Muslims, the fact that he is a citizen of Britain is of secondary concern.

He also defended the custom of practising Sikhs wearing their ceremonial daggers, *kirpans*, at school and other public places, after another fourteen-year-old Sikh pupil was banned from school, this time for wearing his knife. Although Sikhs carrying the *kirpan* are exempt from prosecution under the offensive weapons act, governors at a north London school ruled that in school it was a health and safety risk. This may seem a reasonable ruling, especially as they tried to find a compromise by proposing he wear a smaller version welded in to a sheath, but his family said the miniature dagger was a replica and not a genuine *kirpan*, and refused. Naturally, pressure groups such as United Sikhs and the Sikh Federation UK piped up, welcoming Sir Mota's comments and condemning the bans.

And Sikh Plods insisting that their oriental turban, a towel to keep off the sun - hardly essential in Britain - becomes part of the uniform of the British bobby have added their rupee-worth to this controversy. In 2002 a Sikh policeman ordered to remove his turban to do riot training was awarded £10,000 compensation by an employment tribunal. PC Gurmeal Singh claimed religious and racial discrimination after being told he must take off his turban to don a helmet to do the course. The officer said that as a baptised and practising Sikh it was against his religion to remove his turban in public. After a three-week hearing he was awarded £3,500 for indirect discrimination and £6,500 for harassment after suffering psychological damage, injury to feelings and personal injury.

In a meeting with a sergeant to discuss the riot training he was asked, 'Can't you take that thing off... this is what you signed up for.'

The tribunal asked the Sikh if he could not modify his turban but he replied he feared he would be made to look like a comic character from the BBC television sitcom based in Peckham, *Only Fools and Horses*, where in one episode the spiv Del Boy Trotter tries to sell two hundred 'crash turbans' for fashion-conscious motorbike-riding Sikhs - the motorcycle helmets had cloth wrapped around them.

PC Singh said that because of the long-running dispute he had to take time off work, suffering panic attacks, stress and palpitations.

The tribunal rejected thirteen of his fifteen allegations but found he suffered a single case of indirect racial and religious discrimination, after he was included on a group e-mail on February 8th 2008 telling officers riot training was mandatory and he would therefore have to remove his turban. PC Singh had already told superiors he was unhappy about the situation because of his religion.

Two months later he had the 'unpleasant' meeting with the sergeant and the next day took Sikh leave.

The Sikh turban is not even one of the 'articles of faith' of Sikhism. They are the *kirpan*, the *kara*, *kesh* (uncut hair), *kanga* (comb) and *kacha* (special underwear). The tenth Sikh guru decreed in 1699 that baptised Sikhs should wear these 'articles of faith', a pompous phrase for a whimsy dreamed up off the top of his turbaned head. Imagine that the guru had chosen to be even more whimsical and decreed, 'Thou shalt every Tuesday afternoon don a bottle-green shirt with pink stripes and, thus attired, walk backwards up a hill.' Could we then expect to see every Tuesday from our ethnic-packed 108 bus in Westcombe Hill orientals dressed in green walking backwards like a scene in a sketch from Monty Python or *The Goon Show*?

Fashioning law around religion and culture has set worrying precedents. Some judgments taking into account the offender's beliefs have been bizarre. In January 2001 a Rastafarian who offered marijuana to an undercover policeman was spared a prison sentence when a judge said his consumption of the drug was 'very much bound up' with his beliefs. Rasta Brown [*sic*] was given a diminished sentence of community service after he explained that his religious and cultural beliefs permitted him to smoke and sell cannabis.

And nine years later, by which time you might have expected that some lessons had been learned, Cherie Blair, sitting as a judge at Inner London crown court, spared a violent offender jail because he was 'a religious man'. Devout Muslim Shamso Miah broke a man's jaw in a queue. Mrs Blair suspended his six-month sentence for two years, saying, 'I am going to suspend this sentence based on the fact you are a religious person and have not been in trouble before. You are a religious man and you know this is not acceptable behaviour.'

Atheists are fully aware that breaking someone's jaw is unacceptable. What has religion got to do with it? The National Secular Society complained to the Office for Judicial Complaints, saying her attitude was 'discriminatory'.

Judgments that forgive ethnic criminals because they call themselves religious, and policies that encourage settlers to maintain their own identity, culture, language, religion and customs, have fomented hostility and created even more division than there was before.

Councillors in Bradford, in an attempt to placate its *imams*, in 1981 helped to establish and fund the Bradford Council of Mosques. In order to deflect accusations of favouritism, three years later it set up the Federation of Sikh Organisations and the Vishwa Hindu Parishad [*sic*]. The inevitable consequence was that division and tensions developed between the hordes as they jostled for a bigger share of the funding. Bradford, which had been segregated along racial lines, now fragmented along religious lines (the religions being oriental and the funding British). Hindus, Muslims and Sikhs began to live in separate districts, attend separate schools and work in separate business.

The council, which had caused the rift in the first place, seemed unable to learn from its mistakes and now accentuated the trend by establishing community organisations and youth centres to cater for different ethnic and religious affiliations. Oldham and Burnley had similar problems and, making the same mistake as Bradford of assigning state funds on the basis of ethnic background, are now also fissured along sectarian lines, full of South Asians hating each other.

Who needs these problems? What is it to us whether these people worship Allah, a monkey god or some silly sanctimonious Singh?

They have also brought to these shores another charming practice - honour killing. The victim in these crimes is usually a wife suspected of infidelity or a daughter who had become the girlfriend of a boy disapproved of by her family. The manner of the killings is often brutal. In June 1995, Tasleem Begum, aged twenty, was killed by her brother-in-law, Shabir Hussain. He ran her over in his car, reversed over her and sped forward once more, crushing her three times. His plea in court that the balance of his mind had been altered by the great shame she had brought to the family was accepted and he was jailed for just three years, for manslaughter.

Culture has become an excuse for many crimes, including murder. If Aztecs had survived the Spanish invasion and some of them were now in Britain, we would no doubt be hearing justifications of the ritual essential to their 'faith', that of human sacrifice.

RAISING RACIST ROSE
Rhyme but no reason

I KNOW a Geordie woman, Rose, who came from Newcastle to Greenwich to work as a primary school teacher. One day she had to quickly choose someone to take a class swimming. The pupils were already in the coach waiting restlessly to be driven to the municipal pool for the booked session, which was only for an hour, ten minutes of which had already passed, and she also had her own class waiting. None of her four available colleagues, all South Asian women, would volunteer, so, in desperation, haste and innocence, she mumbled the old childhood choosing rhyme:

> Eenie meenie miney mo,
> Catch a nigger by the toe,
> If he hollers let him go,
> Eenie meenie miney mo.

The person being pointed at on the final 'mo' was the designated one. Rose has a thick Geordie accent, and the South Asian women were used to not understanding her, so they were all giggling and not paying any attention. None of them knew the rhyme or the offending word. One could not repeat it later because, she said, 'I closed my ears as I thought she would choose me.' But another South Asian woman in the room, named Deepthi Ghosh, overheard it, said to Rose, 'Slander' - and reported her for making a racist remark.

What followed was Kafkaesque. The procedure to judge and punish Rose was lengthy and involved many people. The official allegation of misconduct read, 'In that you made a racist comment in the presence of members of staff.' Rose had to write a response and contact the regional branch of the National Union of Teachers for someone to represent her; the four colleagues all had to write a witness statement; she had to attend a preliminary meeting.

And then came the disciplinary hearing. Also in attendance at this inquisition were a 'Personal Adviser for the London Borough of Greenwich', a council officer described as 'assistant director of access, inclusion and education', a council adviser on equalities [*sic*] and diversity, an official note-taker, the union official, the four colleagues who had not understood a word of what she said, Mrs Ghosh and the headmistress.

Unluckily for Rose the headmistress was black, who said *she* found it offensive. A thick dossier was compiled. The Investigation Report alone covered thirty-seven pages; and Rose was forced to make a humiliating public apology as well as a grovelling written one.

At the end of it all Rose was suspended and nearly lost her job. She had a mortgage. The stress made her ill.

Political correctness encourages such witch-hunts. In Stalin's Soviet Union an unwise utterance was often reported by a neighbour or a colleague who wanted the victim's flat or job. Thousands were in the Gulag because of a covetous neighbour or colleague. After a hard day at the office and a couple of vodkas someone might mutter, 'That pockmarked rascal in the Kremlin' and within a few weeks would be chopping logs in the freezing *taiga*, the informer who sent him there ensconced in his flat or seated at his desk, objective achieved. (Like many innocent victims in Stalin's show trials, Rose too said she felt she 'deserved to be punished'.)

Are Britons to eradicate from memory the old childhood rhymes? Rose had simply forgotten herself in her desperation and haste and used a jingle that, however offensive it might sound now, was once commonplace among children. Versions of the 'Eenie meenie' rhyme, all meaningless, have been chanted by British children for generations. The Scottish one goes:

Eenie meenie macka racka,
Rair roe dominacka,
Soominacka noominacka,
Rum tum scum scoosh!

Another choosing rhyme, also nonsense but making a mysterious appeal to the tongue, goes:

Winnery, ory, accory, han,
Phillisy, phollisi, Nicholas, jam,
Queby, quorby, Irish Mary,
Sink, sank, sock!

What Rose chanted as a child was as meaningless as these. 'Nigger' was not then a derogatory word and she had never seen a negro. In this cruel world, there are many rhymes involving ethnic difference, including the familiar 'Chin Chang Chinaman'. 'Nigger' is only a word. Another old childhood rhyme, which was sung when taunted, and presumably still is, goes:

> Sticks and stones
> May break my bones
> But words will never hurt me.

This was not true under Stalin and is not true in today's Britain.

After Rose had left the room, Mrs Ghosh asked the others, 'Do you all understand what she said?' Because none of them had, she obligingly told them. In her report she wrote that Rose had 'called them "nigger".' In reality of course Rose did not 'call' them anything, it was not directed at them, it was just a word in a children's rhyme, and anyway 'nigger' means negro, not South Asian. This is typical of political correctness. In the desperation to find offence, a word once specific to one group expands to include all of them.

Everyone knows that the sensitivity about the n-word derives from its association with the enslavement of negroes. Apparently American slang once had no fewer than ninety-five compounds and phrases formed from the 'nigger' root, including 'niggeritis', the urge to lie down and take a nap after a heavy meal, a condition I too suffer from. A vast verbal constellation of nastiness was built around that single word. When politician George Wallace lost the state of Alabama to a more nakedly racist opponent he vowed he would 'never be outniggered again'. No wonder it provokes such strong feelings. It is a key word in the lexicon of race relations.

But the fact that it is now actually being expanded in meaning suggests sinister forces at work. To confuse the issue further, while it is forbidden for a white person to call anyone a nigger, even South Asians who do not know or understand the word and could not care less what it means or does not mean, an orthodoxy has developed that dictates it is acceptable for blacks to use it. People who eff and blind constantly with no regard for others' feelings are outraged at hearing the en word - unless it is said by one en to another en. That makes it all right. Whites have forfeited their linguistic rights because of the way their ancestors deprived blacks of much more basic rights two hundred years ago but if the person committing the niggering is a black it is meant and taken as an affectionate soubriquet signifying ironic solidarity. When written down, it is often spelt 'nigga', with the plural taking a 'z'.

Meanwhile, *The Adventures of Huckleberry Finn* is now published in

America with the word removed, including hundreds of instances in direct speech, making the characters' talk unrealistic, and British liberal newspapers that happily spell out swear words in full for children to read now print 'n*****', with the implication that 'nigger' is now not only a swear word but worse than a swear word.

Rose was lucky. Many have lost their jobs for saying the n-word. No doubt some deserved to, if it was delivered aggressively and specifically. But one white Washington bureaucrat was sacked for using the word 'niggardly' in a meeting. One of those present, the Mrs Ghosh in the case, is said to have asked, 'Do you really think he didn't notice he had to pass "nigger" before he could get to the "dly"?'

And Rose had always been discerning, sensitive and tender. One black pupil was especially disruptive, and when his mother was called in Rose noticed she would never touch him. From then on Rose gave him a cuddle every morning - and his behaviour improved. Before the allegation of racism, she was not racist. Now she is. It was precisely because she was not racist that in a stressful moment she could unthinkingly dredge up a nonsensical childhood rhyme. The contrived outrage, the time-consuming, enervating fuss, had the opposite effect to its ostensible aim. Instead of eradicating racism, it created it. Her South Asian colleagues were also rendered racist. Before, they had hardly been aware that the headmistress was black. It had barely registered. Now it had become her defining characteristic.

The 2000 Race Relations (Amendment) Act, the fourth anti-racism law, since followed by another three, introduced a duty on public authorities to promote 'good relations' between different groups. It requires schools to refer all 'racist incidents' to local authorities, resulting in an estimated 250,000 reports between 2002 and 2009. Presumably each of those 250,000 cases and the thousands last year required the same vast expenditure of time, energy and pieces of paper as Rose's case. And other workplaces such as fire stations, hospitals, councils and government departments are also subject to the same law, creating an industry of behaviour management and control.

Political correctness has fertilised the soil for the proliferation of pressure groups that support and promote the politically correct view. They are often funded by the taxpayers, or charities subsidised by tax relief, and can campaign for public funds with no opposition.

The Labour Party pressure group Liberty is headed by one Shami Chakrabarti. Smoothly full of herself, she sits in front of television cameras smugly airing her point of view, her preening self-regard having been pandered to by being introduced as a 'human rights campaigner'. She believes in 'zero tolerance to any form of discrimination'. In fact the 2010 Equality Act makes 'positive discrimination' lawful in the area of recruitment and promotion. If there are two candidates of equal merit the employers should choose the one belonging to the less well represented minority. This is also discrimination, and should thus, logically, be worthy of Chakrabarti's 'zero tolerance'. But of course she champions this particular type of discrimination.

'Discrimination' is one of many words that have changed in meaning or, like 'community', become utterly meaningless under the weight of political correctness. Originally discrimination denoted a positive attribute. Possessing it enabled one to discriminate between good and bad. Discerning people tried to foster discrimination in themselves. It was a by-word for sound judgment. Now it usually has negative connotations. The European Court of Human Rights has become so bewitched by the idea of discrimination it has declared invalid, as discriminatory, the cheaper car insurance young women get because they have fewer serious accidents than young men.

In my lifetime the meaning of the word racism has also changed. When I was a child, still surprised to hear a black child speaking in the same accent as me, it was a simple expression of the races' inability, or reluctance, to mingle. Now it represents a crime against humanity. To be called a racist now is an accusation that carries the same weight as the crime of heresy under theocracies.

Some words and phrases remain in common use, indeed have become clichés, despite having nasty connotations, an etymological pedigree that rivals the taboo words and phrases. One such phrase, in which the original meaning lies dormant, is 'beyond the pale'. The original 'pale' was a safe area enclosed by a paling fence. The part of Ireland under English rule in the Middle Ages was called the Pale. In Russia, Jews came to be rigorously restricted to residence in the 'Pale of Jewish Settlement' in a western border region where they had always lived, turning it into a vast ghetto. Now the vast majority were not allowed to leave it. Educated or otherwise prominent Jews could usually surmount these restrictions and leave their homeland - they went 'beyond the pale'. So the expression has its roots in the great crime and enormous suffering of anti-Semitism. In 1648 the Cossacks slit the throats of 6,000 Jews. Zionism emerged after the pogroms of 1881. In the pogroms of 1905, the Tsar was an honorary member of the Black Hundreds, whose slogan was 'Lynch the Jews, save Russia'. Yet the phrase is routinely used without any sense of the weight it carries, even by Jews. Jordan Finkin, in his review of *History of the Yiddish Language* in the *Times Literary Supplement*, wrote, 'The foundational texts of modern Yiddish literature enshrine a host of forms and features well beyond the pale of standard Yiddish.'

Another phrase that so far has slipped through the politically correct net is 'nitty-gritty', which has a truly awful origin in the transatlantic slave trade. (Some police forces have discovered this however and are adding it to the long list of taboo words and phrases.)

And 'blockbuster', which now denotes a success in the entertainment industry and, with a capital B, a chain of shops renting out DVDs, was coined in the Second World War to signify bombs powerful enough to destroy cities. Strictly speaking, it should invoke not box-office hits but images of the horrors of Dresden, Nagasaki and Hiroshima.

Words and phrases only become taboo if their etymology is trumpeted in indignation. If left alone they become bland clichés or change in meaning, doing no harm to anyone except the likes of me interested in words and their use. Unnoticed, they are forgotten; resentment confers status on them. And political correctness not only harms innocent people, it harms the very causes it supposedly represents, as its phrases replace genuine thought.

In a book called *The Morning After: Sex, Fear and Feminism* author Kate Roiphe finds herself caught up in what she feels to be near hysteria about rape on US college campuses in the early 1990s. At Princeton she attended a series of rallies held under the banner of the 'Take Back the Night movement', and as she listened to a procession of her contemporaries giving intensely personal accounts of abuse, all their stories began to sound the same. Patterns emerged. The same phrases floated through different voices. Almost all the girls began, 'I wasn't planning to speak out tonight but…' , even the ones who had spoken out in previous years.

The catchwords travelled across campuses, and across the boundaries between the spoken and written words, the speakers letting the approved language of the orthodoxy of the day take over their own experiences, committing the sin of surrendering to the words, and so losing the true meaning of what they have suffered. The collective mode of expression saps the individual power of the stories, which blend together, sounding automatic and programmed.

Any orthodoxy, as Orwell said, seems to demand a lifeless imitative style. In other words, in a way, people stop thinking. This is what happens in political correctness. No matter what the experience, whether shallow or deep, real or concocted, all genuine feeling for it is lost in cliché.

Modern political correctness began at Frankfurt University in the 1920s, when its Institute for Social Research started to transfer Marxist techniques from economic to cultural and social issues and to add a bit of Freud. With the rise of the Nazis many of these professors fled to the United States, where their way of thinking quickly gained influence in the US academia, which has been the stronghold, and main propagator, of political correctness ever since. Originating as a philosophy begging for greater tolerance, political correctness is now a lie, purporting to be one thing while being the opposite. In the 1960s it developed into a new and intolerant bigotry, adopting a conviction of rigid self-righteousness that has led to such absurdities today as the drivel of millionaire Irish singers being mistaken for meaningful thought and a German student in the canteen at the School of Oriental and Asian Studies in London being reprimanded for asking for white coffee because it could be construed as racist. She was told to ask for coffee with milk. Political correctness has taken hold of everything, all aspects of the law, of morality, of aesthetics, of diplomacy, of literature, of entertainment. It pervades our lives; and nearly ruined Rose's.

And it achieves nothing. You cannot force people to think kindly of others if the impulse is lacking, and dislike and fear of outsiders seem so entrenched in the human psyche it looks as though there is some evolutionary reason for it, maybe simply that for many millennia outsiders always caused trouble. Everyone was xenophobic. Political correctness does not weaken this tendency, for dislike and fear now focus not on outsiders but on xenophobes.

And the list of taboo words constantly grows. According to *Guardian* journalist Stuart James in January 2012, even the word 'negro' is now 'regarded as extremely offensive in England'. It is not, of course. England follows the United States in all matters to do with race relations, and 'negro' continues to be often heard there. But some English blacks on reading this nonsense will gleefully pick up on it, and soon we will all have to be careful about using yet another word.

Many indigenous people mistakenly believe 'coloured' is still acceptable, as it was just a few years ago. James was writing about the outbreak of racist name-calling in English football, and, while discussing this on television, experienced commentator Alan Hansen, in the middle of saying what a magnificent contribution black players make to the Premier League, made the mistake of calling them 'coloured'; a colleague sitting next to him pulled a politically correct face; a few viewers phoned to complain; and Hansen had to make the familiar humiliating apology.

Indigenous people like Rose are fed up with forever having to watch their language while ethnics freely insult them. Racism comes in two forms - that practised by Whitey, which is heinous and inexcusable whatever the motive, and that practised by ethnics, which is justified whatever its excesses, since it is the expression of a righteous revenge, and it is up to Whitey to be patient and understanding.

OUT OF AFRICA
Macabre customs, barbaric superstitions, HIV, crime, dangerous driving

AFRICAN settlers absurdly claim that they belong naturally in England because the very first people in England, the pre-Neanderthals, like everyone else everywhere in the world, came 'out of Africa'. (I once saw a male negro in Woolwich wearing a T-shirt that proclaimed, 'The Black Man - Father of the Human Race'.)

The modern Africans conveniently ignore the obvious fact that in the intervening aeons there has been a certain amount of divergence. The early inhabitants of what is now England could have mated with Neanderthals. There is much speculation about this, with anthropologists seeing no reason why they should not have except mutual repugnance. In Portugal, a child buried has been claimed to be a Neanderthal-Homo sapiens hybrid.

I think we can fairly ignore who went where and who had sex with whom hundreds of thousands of years ago and concentrate on now. And out of Africa now come crime (fraud a speciality), barbaric superstition, macabre customs, AIDS and dangerous driving.

When the *Empire Windrush* docked at Tilbury in 1948 the bank of the Thames immediately opposite was an uninhabited marsh. Forty years ago it was drained and a model 'new town' built there named Thamesmead. Its name was the winning entry in a newspaper competition. The film *A Clockwork Orange* was shot there. Now it is called 'Little Lagos' because of the large number of African criminal gangs living there.

Andrew Goodwill, director of a fraud prevention service that screens internet transactions to help retailers detect credit card fraud, said in August 2009 his company's database revealed Thamesmead's unfortunate reputation. 'Last year we indicated it was the capital in the UK for credit card fraud, and actually we went as far as to say it was probably the capital of Europe for credit card fraud as well,' he said.

Credit cards and benefit claims offer rich pickings for fraudsters with access to a genuine address and letterbox.

Resident Anne-Marie Griffin said, 'My husband gets a lot of deliveries for work, and one day the delivery company rang up and said: "I'm just checking who you are - we've got a parcel and we wanted to make sure more or less that we think you're OK".'

She said the company told her it now generally refused to deliver in Thamesmead because the African answering the door would ask who the parcel was addressed to and then sort through a stack of credit cards all under different names.

Another resident said the hallway for his apartment block looked like an Aladdin's cave of electrical goods such as mobile phones, plasma television sets and cameras. A local postman said he often had to deliver seven or eight mobile phones to the same address in the same week.

In a report by think tank Chatham House, a police officer said that convicted fraudsters tended to escape significant punishments and often absconded while on bail. Those who do not flee may have British passports or families resident in the UK, and they regard a short prison sentence as an 'occupational hazard', worth risking for the large proceeds of fraud they can enjoy when they get out.

One former fraudster from southern Africa said she had heard of Thamesmead's reputation even before she became involved with a criminal gang using stolen credit cards and cashing cheques. 'I used to hear people say if you go to Thamesmead, anything you want, you will find it,' she said.

Only sixty years after five hundred diffident blacks arrived in the *Empire Windrush*, bold African criminal gangs have seized control of a big London suburb on the opposite bank.

And Africans are not only bringing crime to Greenwich. They are also bringing AIDS. Thanks to them, the rates of HIV in the borough are among the highest in the country. A report published in November 2010 by the Health Protection Agency revealed Greenwich and Lewisham were among the thirty-seven primary care trusts in the country with high rates of infection.

But blaming Africans was taboo.

In 2005 journalist Anthony Browne pre-recorded an interview for the BBC Radio 4 *Today* programme that was never aired. It was replaced with an interview with a government minister who had a different point of view. The subject was highly sensitive - the heterosexual HIV epidemic that was being imported by African immigrants, tripling the rate of HIV. Figures from the government's Public Health Laboratory Service were being published showing a 25 per cent rise in HIV in just one year, with almost all the increase being among heterosexuals.

The government and media had been warning for years about the dangers of the new complacency among heterosexuals, ever since the number of heterosexual cases had swept past the number of homosexual ones, a well reported and much commented-on phenomenon. The government minister was responding on the *Today* programme to the latest increase with a new sexual health campaign telling people to practise safe sex. If adolescents would only wear condoms, the rise would end.

But the problem was that the increase in HIV had virtually nothing to do with indigenous people practising safe sex - it was almost entirely all the result of HIV positive people, mainly black Africans, coming to England, and being diagnosed with HIV once here.

Browne had first written about the issue in a front page article in *The Times*, announcing that African immigration had overtaken homosexual sex as the main source of new HIV cases in Britain, according to government figures. The government's epidemiologists with whom he had worked on the article had been worried about the reaction. They need not have bothered. The reaction was incredulity. Clearly, in most people's minds, the story could not be true - everyone knew the increase in HIV was because of complacent and promiscuous Whitey.

The Department of Health's spokeswoman, when Browne spoke to her about it, clearly thought he was doo-lally - they were launching this safe sex campaign because it was common knowledge that the rise in HIV was the result of unsafe sex. The only people who phoned Browne to thank him about it were HIV doctors, who lived in the real world, not the politically correct virtual one. Their patients were now mainly, and sometimes exclusively, African immigrants, and yet no one was talking about it. Doctors told Browne that when they had tried to bring it up in public with their local health authorities, they had just been shouted at.

One of the government's own medical advisers phoned Browne secretly from within the Department of Health thanking him for highlighting the issue, and urging him to carry on: Britain was facing a massive explosion in HIV but ministers and civil servants simply refused to discuss the cause of it. 'Ministers just won't listen because they think it is racist,' he said, 'but the public deserve at least honesty.' (The government eventually got round the problem of accusations of racism by employing a Kenyan epidemiologist to be their spokesman on the issue.)

Even when the truth became intellectually commonly accepted, the BBC carried on reporting dishonest accounts, presumably because they held such deeply emotional beliefs in the issue that they could not bring themselves to be honest about it.

One person told Browne that, even if it was true that the HIV epidemic was driven by African immigration, it should not be spoken about because it would just fuel racism. But the result of that conspiracy of silence was that the government followed a policy that did nothing to combat the growth of HIV in this country. Allowing African immigrants to spark an HIV explosion was government policy. Most people who contract HIV from heterosexual sex in England are catching it from having sex with HIV positive African immigrants. In the last decade thousands of people have caught HIV from infected settlers. Political correctness comes at a heavy price.

Only in March 2011 was it publicly admitted that the main carriers of HIV in England were Africans. The National Institute for Health and Clinical Excellence, in launching new guidelines for doctors in England, admitted that the 'black African community' [*sic*] living in England is a high risk group that would benefit from increased HIV testing. It revealed that in 2009 more than 2,000 black Africans were diagnosed with an HIV infection; one-third of all new diagnoses in the UK.

As well as crime and AIDS, Africans also fetch their macabre customs and barbaric superstitions. In 2008 a Liberian former warlord admitted to eating children's hearts before going into battle. Along with wearing female wigs and going naked, the practice was believed to bring victory. People with these sort of beliefs are now flooding England.

In November 2010 the disgruntled female client of a Gambian faith healer who lured him to his death in Bedfordshire was jailed for ten years for manslaughter. The body of Alfusaine Jabbi was found in a Luton car park in 2006. Rubina Maroof had consulted Jabbi, who advertised that he could 'break spells'. Prosecutors told Luton Crown Court that Jabbi was tortured to make him repay money he had charged Maroof.

Jabbi had offered to sacrifice camels in the Gambia and asked for money wrapped in clean underwear for prayers.

Maroof parted with cash, some of which Jabbi promised to return when his 'spells' were finished, but he disappeared, the court heard. The judge said Maroof became 'obsessive' about finding him and getting her money back. Eventually, with help, he was lured to her home, where he was tortured to death.

Maroof's conviction followed that of her brother Tarik Malik and a friend named Imran Khan, who had been given life sentences in 2008 for Jabbi's murder.

And the true extent to which England has fallen into a Third World nightmare was again shockingly exposed by a court case in March 2012 involving Africans who had left their homeland behind but imported their traditions and cultures.

Revealing a revolting tale of barbaric and medieval behaviour, the trial of Eric Bikubi and Magalie Bamu for the torture and murder of Magalie's 15-year-old brother Kristy in a four-day orgy of unimaginable and sickening violence. They believed he was a witch.

The reports of such cases horrify the likes of me who thought our country had progressed beyond the medieval belief in witches and the murderous persecution of those accused as such. In 1682 three Devon women became the last people in England to be hung for witchcraft. The Enlightenment, beginning later that decade, contributed to the end of a belief in witches. Empirical reason and scepticism helped defeat the superstitions of the earlier age. Now these superstitions have returned to England. Scotland Yard have investigated eighty-three similar cases over the last decade and detectives fear that there may be hundreds of other child victims of these backward beliefs and that these crimes are far more prevalent than the official figures suggest - and that the number of cases is growing, as more and more Africans come here.

Children's minister Tim Loughton said in August 2012 that political correctness was hampering investigations. He warned that a 'wall of silence' surrounded the problem.

Some commentators say that the blame for the savagery lies with Christian fundamentalist pastors who fuel the belief in witchcraft and evil spirits among immigrants and make money by offering expensive exorcisms and other 'cures'. These commentators naturally fail to mention that these 'Christian' pastors are themselves Third World immigrants and are merely using the Christian religion to perpetuate yet another scam to enrich themselves, a Third World habit that the likes of me are wearily growing accustomed to.

The Christianity practised by these pastors and their congregations has no resemblance to the religion recognised by indigenous Christians - and has nothing in common with the teachings of Christ.

The torture and murder of Kristy Bamu took place just nine days after, and only a few miles away from, the equally savage sacrificial disembowelling of a four-year-old girl by her mother Shayma Ali because she believed her daughter was possessed by evil spirits.

Ali was sentenced to be detained indefinitely in a mental hospital, joining the many other foreigners clogging up our mental health facilities, leaving no room for indigenous people who need residential care.

This problem has been made worse by families in Africa clubbing together to buy a plane ticket to England for a mentally ill relation, knowing that the NHS will take care of him or her.

This practice has been known about for decades among mental health professionals but, as usual, the authorities have ignored this blatant abuse of our state-provided services and, by letting these people into England, have ignored their duty of care to the indigenous people.

The bestial and sadistic Bikubi - an immigrant from the Congo - was at first described as a football coach but it was later revealed that he was an 'unemployed failed football agent', while his accomplice Magalie Bamu was described as a 'former shop worker' at Marks and Spencer. They tortured and killed her brother (by drowning him in the bath) in their council flat in East London, which they had recently moved into.

So the truth was again revealed that instead of the highly skilled and hard-working foreigners that we are repeatedly told we have to accept for our continued prosperity, we are faced with Third World immigrants who have no skills and do not work so are of no use to anyone, yet are given social housing and are a constant drain on our welfare system - and then commit barbaric crimes.

Because of atavistic conflicts hundreds of thousands of them are able to claim asylum. Mohammed Kendeh came from Sierra Leone in 1992 when he was six, soon after the start of a civil war that was to last eleven years, leaving 50,000 dead. His parents had already fled to England, and been given a council flat in Peckham. By adolescence he was such a vicious criminal he was denied UK citizenship. Still, in 2007 a senior immigration judge argued that he should not be deported because, having come to England at the age of six he was 'one of us'. He should be regarded as an 'integrated alien' and allowed to remain here.

'He has almost no family left in his native country,' she said. But that was because they had all come to live in Peckham!

Kendeh had committed a wide variety of nasty crimes, including arson, burglary and eleven sexual assaults. He was eventually deported five years later only because one of the victims of his sexual attacks refused to let the authorities forget all about him.

This misguided judge would recoil in horror at the suggestion that immigration from all Third World countries should cease immediately, using the argument that it would be inhumane and unfair to punish all immigrants from these countries due to the misdeeds of a few. But the tax on alcohol is continually increasing to control the excessive consumption of a few, and there are many other examples of the majority being punished in an effort to deal with the problems caused by a minority. If these problems are deemed big enough, it is often the only way to deal with them. But of course the political will has to be there to take this course of action.

Contrary to the idealistic beliefs of the supporters of mass immigration and multi-culturalism, settlers from Third World cultures do not become just like us simply by moving here. They remain exactly the same. They import their cultures, traditions and standards with them. When imported in the massive numbers that we have experienced over the decades of mass immigration, this causes our country to degenerate into the conditions of the Third World countries that they left.

Driving in London is now more hazardous than before because of the vast numbers of African drivers on the roads. The British have always been courteous, careful drivers, possibly the best in the world. But now, in London at least, where Africans suddenly are everywhere, African drivers keep causing little scenes of havoc with wild, rude, careless driving - turning and abruptly stopping without signalling, cutting up the car in front, jumping red lights, not stopping for pedestrians at, or even on, zebra crossings, etc. Africans in London drive according to the rules of their country of origin, which naturally are the rules of the jungle - and few of them have ever taken a driving test.

Throughout Africa, as in many other corrupt parts of the world, it is the custom to buy a driving licence. Africans can then come to England with this licence, acquired with a bribe, and drive on our roads ignorant of rules and laws.

This is on top of their general low level of road courtesy and care. In Africa reckless driving is the norm, signs are scarce and speed limits are routinely ignored. Driving up the wrong side of the road to beat the traffic is usual, a chassis destroyed in a nasty crash a common sight. The World Health Organisation has reported that the top three countries for road-traffic deaths are all African.

In Nigeria large families avoid travelling long distances by car together because the risk of the entire family being in a crash is too great. They go in different cars at different times, ensuring that, if tragedy strikes, the loss to the family will be minimal. Mother, father and eldest son never get in the same car, so that, even if two of the cars are involved in a tragic accident there will always be at least one parent or the eldest son left to head the family.

Kampala newspaper the *Monitor* reported that there were about 12,000 crashes a year in Uganda due to speeding and reckless driving, costing a staggering £100m. 'In Uganda,' the newspaper said, 'the level of initial driver training is poor, with incorrect information often given to the learner. For instance a student may be told to put the vehicle into neutral and coast down a hill. The reason for this, apparently, is to save fuel! When approaching a roundabout another student asked, "Which lane should I be in?" The instructor answered, we don't bother with lanes here in Uganda! These are just a few examples of many.

'Most learner vehicles are in poor, if not unroadworthy, condition. You see some with the wheels wobbling looking as if they are just about to fall off. Some with clouds of exhaust smoke coming out the back. You think to yourself, he must be using more oil than petrol! Some don't have driving mirrors and some vehicles move sideways down the road.

'Then to the driving test itself. You are taken on a short drive and then asked to reverse into an area marked out by four poles. You don't really have to pass as there is an unofficial fee that you can pay and you receive the licence regardless. Most applicants pay this fee, as it seems it doesn't matter if you have passed, you won't get the licence until it is paid.

'Now, all of the examples above may seem amusing and people who have lived in this region may say, "Well, that's Africa". But until the standards are raised for training and testing, the death tolls on the road will continue to rise and developing nations like Uganda will continue to spend millions of dollars a year to mop up the mess.'

And the expensive mess will now spread in England. Many Africans become driving instructors with the British School of Motoring.

YOU ARE WELCOME TO BRISTOL
One coconut and some Somalians

AMONG the likes of me, Bristol has long been known chiefly for its two football clubs, Rovers and City, and the rhyming slang associated with the latter. 'Bristols' (it is always used in the plural) means 'titties'. Other clubs with 'City' in their name have also been used to the same effect, with evidence that 'Manchester Cities' came first, but 'Bristols' is now used exclusively, almost certainly because of its alliterative similarity to 'breasts'. Peter Mayle used it in his *Hotel Pastis: A novel of Provence*: 'You're at the movies, right? By your side is a very tasty young lady you've had your eye on for weeks. Tonight's your big chance. You've got your arm round her, within striking distance of her Bristols. This. Could. Be. It.'

But now Bristol has become known for something far more sinister than a bit of harmless slang.

Bristol City Council's website states: 'Bristol has a changing population. New communities are settling in central parts of the city and beyond, bringing both advantages and new challenges around cohesion and integration.' In other words, the town is being swamped by settlers, creating insoluble problems.

Bristol has the highest proportion of Somalians of any city in the country and of any local authority outside London, and the third-highest Somali population in absolute terms behind London and Birmingham.

And it made headline news when two ethnic Bristol councillors went to court in the most ludicrous court case in British legal history.

On February 15th 2010 the case of Regina v Shirley Brown was heard by Bristol magistrates. Councillor Brown, a Liberal Democrat on the city council, stood accused of being a bit rude to a member of the Conservative Party. The official charge was causing racially aggravated harassment, alarm or distress, and I should mention at this point that the Conservative in question, Cllr Jay Jethwa, is South Asian via Uganda, and that Brown is black (so to speak).

A year before, the council was discussing the city's Legacy Commission, which was created to atone for Bristol's role in the slave trade. Atoning for slavery was an expensive business, for which the commission required £250,000 a year from the council. Cllr Jethwa said it was pointless posturing, a waste of money ill-afforded in a recession, while black Brown was of the opinion the commission was worth every penny. Black Brown said to Jethwa, 'In our culture we have a word for you... coconut.'

A human coconut, you see, is someone who is brown on the outside but white on the inside, who is an ethnic but promotes the interests of Whitey. It is a racial slur that goes back at least as far as 1988, when the influential political organisation Black Section expelled Janet Boateng, a former Lambeth Council firebrand, for being one. Millions of inhabitants of Britain consider it an insult. Another version is 'choc ice'.

The Chinese have their own variant - 'banana'.

Like so much else in the race relations industry, the insults all go one way. The opposite does not apply: there is no equivalent in the other direction. Jack Straw, champion of the rights of ethnics, has never been called a mushroom because some varieties of this fungus are white on the outside and brown on the inside.

Neither councillor came out of the ghetto. Brown had a comfortable upbringing in Bath, while Jethwa's rich family came to Britain after being thrown out of Uganda by dictator Idi Amin for being South Asian.

Brown's attack was received in silence but Jethwa subsequently said she was very hurt, had never been spoken to in that way before, it was an absolute disgrace, and so on. A couple of days later Brown apologised lavishly, albeit after complaining to reporters: 'How can I be racist? I'm black.' (So was Idi Amin, dearie, and he hated South Asians so much he expelled them from his country.)

And that should have been the end of it. Bristol Council could get on with running Bristol, atoning for the slave trade, that sort of thing.

So why did this playground name-calling case continue for so long?

Partly because the Conservatives reported Brown to the council's standards committee for 'causing embarrassment to the city'. She was found guilty of this and suspended from office. That verdict was overturned on appeal, but the case went back to court when she was charged under the Public Order Act with using 'threatening, abusive or insulting words, with intent to cause a person harassment, alarm or distress', a serious charge that comes with the threat of a criminal record.

As Brown had apologised, why was it necessary to turn this into a criminal prosecution? The Crown Prosecution Service stated that its approach was 'in the public interest... because it alleged an offence where the subject demonstrated hostility towards the victim based on discrimination against the victim's ethnic origin'.

The case was adjourned twice, until finally Brown was convicted, given a twelve-month conditional discharge and ordered to pay costs.

This farce is the legacy of the race relations industry: people can no longer tell the difference between racial hatred and vulgar abuse. If Jethwa was obese and Brown had called her a 'fat cow' that would of course have been a worse personal insult but not a criminal offence, or if the impulsive councillor had said, 'You have disregarded your cultural roots' she would likewise not have been taken to court.

The maximum penalty for this new offence, 'speech crime', is six months in prison or a £5,000 fine. Surely this is not enough for such a despicable crime. Maybe a second Legacy Commission could be set up to atone for the awful slur against Jethwa. Such suffering can hardly be compensated for. Would £150,000 a year be enough atoning?

At the same time, Bristol priest Richard Barrett was calling for the town to be made 'a city of sanctuary for asylum seekers'. In his column in the Bristol *Evening Post*, he wrote: 'Moves to make Bristol a "City of Sanctuary" are important. It's about taking a compassionate attitude to people who have had to flee for their lives, often after terrifying experiences and physical attacks, leaving their families and homeland, and arriving in a strange country with nothing.

'It's about actively welcoming them and affirming their contributions to our city life. It's not about increasing numbers. It will be a public declaration that we are a city proud to hold to the long-standing British tradition of offering sanctuary to the persecuted.

'Making the stranger welcome is at the heart of our faith. We should all sign up to the City of Sanctuary movement... '

And then, to add to the story of Bristol stupidity, Jon Kelly reported on the BBC that the town's Somalians, along with others in Britain, were 'keen to show their support' to Kent couple Paul and Rachel Chandler, kidnapped by pirates off the coast of Somalia.

'Sensitive to their homeland's reputation for civil war, piracy and lawlessness, Somalis across the UK have mobilized behind a campaign to release the pair,' Kelly wrote. 'TV and radio stations serving the [Somali] community are broadcasting regular appeals for the Chandlers' release, while demonstrations and public meetings demanding their freedom have been organized by Somali leaders across the country.

'They hope that the pressure will be felt back in their mother country - and that the strength of feeling among Somali Britons [*sic*] will be felt by the pirates themselves.'

Paul, 60, and wife Rachel, 56, were captured while sailing towards Tanzania. Their captors threatened to kill the couple if their demands for $7m (£4.4m) were not met. A recent video had shown Mrs Chandler saying that she was desperate and that she had been treated cruelly.

Kelly wrote, 'The couple's plight has prompted a series of displays of solidarity from the UK Somali community [*sic*], whose numbers were estimated at 101,000 in 2008 but which some observers believe could number as many as 250,000. Hundreds are expected to attend a public meeting in London on Sunday, called by community leaders in support of the couple. Somalis in Bristol have already launched their own campaign, when a large crowd gathered to witness the unfurling of a banner in support of the couple outside the Al Baseera mosque in the St Jude's area.

'Kayse Maxamed, editor of the Bristol *Somali Voice* newspaper, has spoken out about the plight of the Chandlers on the radio in the US and Africa. He believes Somalis in the UK owe a debt of gratitude to the country that has given so many of them shelter from war and violence. "The Somali community is very angry," he says. "We feel we have to do something. Britain welcomes Somalis. Many of us came as refugees, as asylum seekers, and now we live freely. Britain gives millions to the Somali people."'

(It was Britain's first Muslim minister, Shahid Malik, who, when Minister for International Development, generously gave all that money to Somalia, which, according to both Transparency International and the International Corruption Index, is the most corrupt country in the world. Virtually all of it was siphoned off long before it got anywhere near 'the Somali people'.)

Maxamed continued, 'We think the pirates really damage that relationship. They blacken our names. Because we are British now, we see our fellow citizens have been taken hostage.'

One organiser of the London meeting, a man named Omar Yusuf, said, 'We want people to use their influence back in Somalia. We want word to get back to the pirates that what they are doing is madness. We're emphasising the cultural aspect as well - it is un-Islamic, it is un-Somali, to take these people.'

Ah, what sweet Somalians! And we thought they were all jobless ponces! I stand corrected!

Who am I to comment, when I know almost nothing about Bristol? I have only one connection with the town, and that slight.

A couple I knew in Greenwich, Pete and Sheila Garrett, moved there a long time ago, soon after they were married. They now have a grown-up son who works abroad. We have kept in touch and they recently informed me they were leaving Bristol because of all the Somalians.

NOT FAIR
Scarlet and black

JACQUELINE Walker's memoir, *Pilgrim State*, tells the story of her mother Dorothy and herself from the time Dorothy was detained in a New York mental hospital in 1951. Deported from the United States,

Dorothy returns home to Jamaica, where she had left Jacqueline and Jacqueline's older brother Teddy with their grandmother. Dorothy, pregnant from an affair in New York, then fetches her children to England, where she hopes to start a new life. After a brief stay in Brixton they live in Deptford before being given a council flat in Greenwich. Dorothy has the baby, Roy, in the Miller Hospital. (She has another child, Pearl, who is somewhere in America. Dorothy has lost contact with her.) After she has Roy she contracts asthma and is unable to work. She dies after a fall at home. Jacqueline continues her own story up until 2004. The book was first published in 2008 by leading publisher Sceptre, received glowing reviews, and reissued in paperback the following year.

I found it especially interesting because much of the background is also my background.

Dorothy underwent electric shock therapy; so did my father. This controversial treatment is used for depression (which my father suffered from during his nervous breakdown) and schizophrenia (Dorothy's diagnosis). Some psychiatrists say it works for schizophrenia, others say they are not sure - they are in two minds about it. Ernest Hemingway committed suicide after undergoing it, saying it had destroyed his memory and therefore his ability to write. Certainly my father's memory was never the same afterwards.

And, like my family, hers lived in Deptford and Greenwich. Like Jacqueline Walker, I too have lived on Greenwich council estates. I do not want to get into a puerile, 'My council estate was worse than yours, nah.' But it was. I know the riverside Meridian estate, where her family was given a flat, and it is a prime location where properties are now worth a lot of money. I lived with my wife and infant son on a notorious estate that was on the site of the proposed Victorian Grand National Cemetery and has since been demolished as unfit for habitation. The cemetery was to have prevented 'the Danger and Inconvenience of burying the Dead within the Metropolis', with an inner area reserved for the very wealthy and 'great and distinguished persons whose wisdom, bravery, genius and talent have conspicuously contributed to the glory of the nation'. This plan being abandoned, there was built instead many years later, starting in 1970, a dumping ground of the living, persons at the other end of the social scale - 'one of the most deprived neighbourhoods in England', according to Greenwich Council. A mix of houses, maisonettes (in one of which we lived) and tower blocks, its structural and social deterioration became a casebook example of urban decay.

Everything in it except doors and windows was made of prefabricated light grey concrete slabs. All the outer doors for the public staircases to the overhead walkways had been glass: only the wooden frames remained, which you stepped through without opening. Draughts through the empty door frames blew about the litter - discarded wrappers of ice lollies and crisps, cigarette packets, fag ends. The stairwell was filthy, with graffiti and substances smeared on the walls. Adolescents thundered along the walkways on roller skates, stopping only to scribble a quick graffito or two on a urine-etched breezeblock. It was rumoured that the estate's architect later visited the site, and, after witnessing what had become of her vision, committed suicide; but this seems to have been said about the architects of all such estates.

Pilgrim State is a fine book, and I have no wish to denigrate it. Though it is in the settlers' suffering-and-hardship genre, it is only slightly mawkish in places. The tone is consistent and the few instances of racism encountered early on are not laboured. The instances of kindness received are given equal weight. I would like, however, to make three observations.

The first is how none of these settlers' tales, whether fictionalised or documentary or autobiography - *Notes from a Small Island* and all the rest - gives the slightest indication that the indigenous people might have entirely valid objections to diverse foreigners settling among them in vast numbers. None of these authors sees the bigger picture. Each is solely concerned with his or her own horde.

The second is how casually and in passing Jacqueline Walker mentions everything her family received from the state over many years.

Dorothy looks forward to the handouts while still in Jamaica: 'Ever since she'd left New York she had kept one dream going; the one that had her finding a place where she could make a good home for herself and her family, surely England must be it, the place where her children could go to proper schools, where there were free hospitals and government housing...' Then, when they are in Brixton: 'Dorothy could hardly believe they'd been in England for two whole weeks. Already she had got them a place to stay and soon, after the baby was born, she'd get off Social Security.' (She never did.)

And so it continues: 'Anyway, the children would be happy with jam on their bread and cocoa to drink - they got their dinner and milk free from school every day.'

'Soon after we got home we got a letter from the Housing Department saying there was a two-bedroom flat we could move to in Greenwich, on the Meridian Estate, by the river.'

'I can't get the [school] uniform yet, I have to wait till my mum gets the Clothing Grant from the Council.'

Also, the children were twice taken into care - more expense for Greenwich Council and the likes of my father. I do not want to appear curmudgeonly but how much did this one family, who contributed nothing, cost British taxpayers over the years?

It is no one else's fault that Dorothy had four children with different fathers and chose to try her luck abroad in a country still not fully recovered from a devastating war. For a long time after the war Londoners were still left with routine deprivation and indignities such as food queues, shortages and Spam fritters, and for many years the town was pock-marked by bomb craters (as Jacqueline Walker herself acknowledges). Its threadbare inhabitants had no reason to be in a generous mood. I would say that anyway, overall, in the circumstances, her family was treated with astonishing generosity.

My other observation is that Jacqueline Walker received funding from Arts Council England to enable her to write *Pilgrim State*. In spite of similarities in her story and mine, do you imagine the likes of me could ever receive Arts Council funding? The Arts Council on its website openly admits favouring ethnics. 'Championing diversity is one of our core ambitions,' it proclaims. 'We want to create an environment where the arts reflect the full range and diversity of contemporary English society.' Its 'race equality scheme' was 'implemented with a three-year action plan to ensure race equality was acted on internally and externally through our regularly funded organisations. We provided workshops, seminars and other support materials to our clients to help them devise their own race equality or diversity action plans. With the first race equality scheme action plan having been completed, work is now in progress to produce its successor for the period 2008-11. Our second race equality scheme will focus on taking strategic, leadership and development of Black and minority ethnic artists and organisations. It will be informed by the evaluation of our first race equality scheme and by consultation with Black and minority ethnic artists throughout the country.' Jacqueline Walker clearly benefited from this bias.

I too had problems with the colour of my skin. It used to keep going bright red.

I was cursed with blushing. I blushed at every little thing, at nothing at all and on behalf of other people if I felt they ought to be embarrassed. It is a crippling affliction, drastically limiting interaction with the world. It separated me from other people. Defenceless and denied retreat, I was at the mercy of everyone, no matter how hateful or stupid the person. I could not function socially and, because of it, avoiding confrontation became in me as strong as an instinct, a diffidence so extreme it amounted in itself to a personality disorder.

My connection with people and things was intermittent and unstable, my mind always seeming to be on something else, something that did not exist, as though I was forever unconsciously seeking an escape. Every now and then I feared with a sinking heart that I had never properly connected with anyone, that everyone else had a hidden capacity denied me. I felt that I lacked some essential human quality, that this resided in the folklore passed on by people who possessed a knowledge I was forced to supplement by reading books and observing others' behaviour and copying it. I studied appropriate reactions; they did not come naturally. I affected an ease of manner I did not feel, which took many years to perfect. If contradicted, I hurriedly corrected myself, changing my view utterly or so qualifying it that it amounted to an utter change of opinion, so that no one ever knew what I really thought. And I withheld innocuous but sometimes important information, not for any sinister reason but simply because I had never got into the habit of communicating. I grew accustomed to keeping to myself everything that I felt, to viewing the opinions, interest, help and even the very presence of others as a nuisance. I signalled to people from a distance, as though they were at the far side of a room in which most of the floor had collapsed. No one knew the secret of the difference between the parts I played and the detachment that ruled beneath them and which made all that behaviour an incessant dissimulation. In my social behaviour I gave a false account of myself. It was all an act. I regarded involvement in relationships as a wearisome game that I watched as an uninterested spectator, just as, later, as a sports reporter, I watched boring football matches as a chore.

Always, an irresistible indifference descended on me, which oppressed me cruelly. I took part in conversations only as an unwelcome obligation that I learnt to enliven with incessant, and sometimes inappropriate, levity, and humour, likewise occasionally misplaced, which made it less tedious and helped me conceal my real thoughts. This led to an absence of spontaneity. Timidity was an inner torment repressing feelings, freezing and distorting words. My efforts to socialise resulted in entanglements of misunderstandings, compromises, hesitations, failures to act; everything I said or did jarred, proved irresolute, clumsy, ineffective. For me the game was not worth the floodlights.

Because I was so ill-equipped to deal with people, I wondered to what extent I should try. Perhaps I should not bother at all. I felt that no matter what my status or achievements, I would never be respected. Flagrantly working-class, speaking in a strong gor-blimey Cockney accent, poorly educated, devoid of polish or grace, vulnerable, flinching from people, self-deprecating in speech and manner, I seemed designed to be over-looked. I often felt I had something important to say but no one ever took any notice. Throughout my life I have felt like Benny Hill's Japanese tourist saying plaintively to the customs officer who cannot understand him, 'Why you no rissen?' As soon as I retired, when keeping up the wearisome pretence of getting on with people was no longer necessary, I became a reclusive misanthrope.

I could write a book about it. I would, if the Arts Council paid me to do so as it did Jacqueline Walker. I wanted to devote myself to writing literature as a hobby in my retirement, not scribble these diatribes. But to apply I would have to answer impertinent questions about my racial category, which would not meet requirements.

When the Arts Council was set up after the war the sums it dispersed were minuscule - £2,000 for an orchestra. But an experimental grant of £235,000 (£9.4m in 2010 values) had by 2010 ballooned fifty-fold into a £450m annual settlement. And Arts Council England (thus shrunk in 1994) stands before the bar of Parliament as one of the least efficient public bodies and is regarded as a political police force. Following PM Tony Blair's Leninist mantra of education, education, education, arts ensembles now have to didactically teach as well as perform if they want to receive state subsidy. They carry a cartload of political correctness.

Arts audiences have to be measured to meet social inclusion targets. Theatres such as the Tricycle Theatre in Kilburn have to not only stage plays almost exclusively by and about ethnics but also employ statutory numbers of 'minorities'; and literature has to be ethnic literature.

My story would not be of any interest to the people at the Arts Council. I am the wrong colour. Going red all the time does not count. Jacqueline Walker was awarded funding because her skin was dark; not fair.

RICHARD EVERITT AND ST LAWRENCE
Nice work if you Khan get it

YOU will have heard of Stephen Lawrence, stabbed to death at a Greenwich bus stop in 1993 by a gang of white youths. The number of column inches dedicated to his case over the years is staggering. But have you heard of Richard Everitt, stabbed to death in Camden the following year by a gang of Bangladeshi youths?

Richard, aged fifteen, was a pupil in the main Camden secondary school, which was full of gangs united by their race. Known as a harmless, naïve boy devoid of aggression, he avoided the fighting between the other boys. His parents, Mandy and Norman, told the headmaster about their growing concern for Richard's safety as he was being bullied by Bangladeshi boys who had twice physically hurt him. On the second occasion one threatened him a knife.

Richard was murdered on the way to buy some chips near King's Cross station in the early evening of August 13th 1994.

A gang of Bangladeshi boys calling themselves the Drummond Street Posse felt they had been 'wronged' by a white boy and wanted revenge against all white boys and anyone would do. Tragically, they spotted Richard with two younger friends. Shouting, 'There's a white boy,' they isolated him, surrounded him and one of them stabbed him in the back.

He was targeted precisely because he was white, just as Stephen was targeted precisely because he was black.

One of Richard's younger friends, who had been headbutted, ran to get Richard's parents. The seven-inch knife wound had penetrated Richard's heart and lungs and he died cradled in his father's arms.

That night, the gang were hanging around Euston station and were picked up by the police for a separate incident. Although they were bailed that same night a policeman had noticed blood on the clothes of nineteen-year-old Badrul Miah and believed he was involved in Richard's murder. His clothes were taken for forensic examination and the blood was proven to be Richard's.

It took nine months for eleven arrests to be made, including that of Miah, by which time the actual killer had escaped to Bangladesh. The number then decreased to six and at a further committal hearing it dropped to three. Once at the Old Bailey it dropped again, to two. These two members of the gang, Miah and a boy named Showkat Akbar, were charged with 'joint enterprise', a well-established principle of law, and found guilty. The forensic evidence in connection with Miah was overwhelming and he received a life sentence (a tariff of twelve years). Akbar, also nineteen, was found guilty of violent disorder and sentenced to three years.

After the trial Mandy and Norman were the victims of threats and racial abuse. They had to leave their home and move out of London to Essex. The following year they received yet another blow with the discovery that the killers were appealing their sentences and that many of those backing the campaign for their release were educated, high-status professionals, including a Pakistani named Imran Khan, who was also solicitor for the family of Stephen. Imran Khan argued that there had been a 'miscarriage of justice' for the 'King's Cross Two' [sic]. The appeal failed but Akbar anyway served only eighteen months and Miah was moved to a less secure prison where he was allowed to go out on day trips and could be expected to be released within a couple of years.

Mandy and Norman never settled in Essex, feeling that it was still too close to London, and have now moved to Yorkshire, where they are trying to find some peace in their lives.

Few remember their son's case. Stephen Lawrence on the other hand has rarely been out of the news for many years, his juvenile murderers approaching middle age. The Lawrence case was given a public inquiry through manipulation by powerful pressure groups in the race relations industry. Sadiq Khan, son of Pakistani settlers, wrote the submission on behalf of civil liberties pressure group Liberty, of which he was chairman. This Khan was a 'leading human rights solicitor' who specialised in actions against the police.

Stephen's mother Doreen and Richard Stone, co-author of the notorious 1999 Macpherson report on the police handling of the murder, are now on the board of Liberty. The then home secretary Jack Straw said in 2012 that ordering the inquiry was 'the single most important decision I made as home secretary'.

Several decent, hard-working police officers had their career destroyed by the Lawrence case. One became a chiropodist.

The Khans meanwhile are doing very nicely for themselves. Sadiq is now a Labour MP and Shadow Secretary of State for Justice, succeeding Straw, who had changed jobs, while Imran continues to have a lucrative career representing ethnics, active in the Law Society and the Association of Muslim Lawyers. Also, one member of the Bangladeshi gang, who was also arrested but released without charge, has made a career in politics, standing as a candidate for the Labour Party in local elections.

Stephen Lawrence has been remembered incessantly by awards, prizes, an art gallery, a pavement plaque where he was killed, books, including one by his mother Doreen, a documentary play, a charitable trust, a bursary scheme open just to black people, and a training centre only for blacks. In 2012 his parents were given the freedom of the borough of Greenwich and the following year Doreen was elevated to the House of Lords as a Labour peer. Stephen is considered a martyr, a black St Lawrence. (The original martyred St Lawrence was killed in Rome during the persecution of Christians by Valerian in 258.)

But Richard Everitt has been forgotten by the Labour Party, the race relations industry, the media and the rest of the politically correct state apparatus. There are no memorials for Richard Everitt, no awards, no prizes, no art gallery, no plaque, no books, no documentary play, no charitable trust, no bursary scheme just for white people nor training centre in his name exclusively for whites. And not only have his parents not been given the freedom of the borough of Camden but they have been driven out of it.

There was no campaign by the Council for Race Relations, which denied the racist nature of the killing, nor recognition by Camden Council. When local Bangladeshis invaded Camden Town Hall, councillors cried publicly as they heard the descriptions of their 'traumatic overcrowding'. But there have been no tears for Richard Everitt.

The Labour-run council denied it was a racist murder in order not to upset Bangladeshi voters. (Ironically, because of this denial Labour has suffered at the polls in Camden.)

Meanwhile, the area where Richard was killed has worsened. The conflicts are now between rival Bangladeshi gangs, which initially claimed that they had been formed in self-defence to 'fight racism', and between these gangs and new Somali gangs in a racial turf war. Now they kill each other with knives and guns in Camden Market. The police, obsessed with diversity and, because of the Macpherson report, terrified of being labelled racist, are unable to confront the problem. Anti-racist groups are silent about the race war on the streets of Camden, just as they were silent after Richard Everitt was killed by a gang of Bangladeshis.

He was killed because he was white, and forgotten for the same reason.

Stephen's murderers were brought to justice after years of intense pressure by the race relations industry, which actually included changing an ancient law, enabling the killers to be brought to trial a second time. Meanwhile, no attempt was made to find Richard's killer in Bangladesh. And the killer's two friends, one of whom was splattered with Richard's blood, received such laughable punishment that justice for Richard's death cannot possibly be said to have been done.

Since his death, there have been thousands of white victims of racist crime, including another eighty murders.

Try Googling Kriss Donald, Gavin Hopley, Ross Parker and Charlene Downes as well as Richard Everitt. See how much media comment they have got compared to Stephen Lawrence. The contrast is truly shocking.

The establishment has never made a statement about any of these other murders. It is too committed to multi-culturalism, with Stephen Lawrence a cult figure, while the Khans make speeches about diversity to adoring crowds at human rights conferences.

HIDEOUSLY MUSLIM
Islam in the heart of England

FORMER black Labour minister David Lammy, current MP for Tottenham, once accused British museums of being 'too white', a bizarre accusation considering museums are by definition about history, and it is only in the last fifty years that Britain has become darkened by ethnics.

Likewise, a leading adviser to the government on 'community cohesion', Professor Ted Cantle, called Derbyshire 'unhealthily white'. (Prof Cantle's birthplace of Woolwich is now almost entirely Ethnic.) And, in 2004, Greg Dyke, then the BBC's director general, described the BBC's workforce as 'hideously white'.

'Hideous' is a strange, strong word to use. South Asians are now over-represented in medical colleges and law schools but no one would dare call medical colleges and law schools 'hideously South Asian'. Anyone who called the London borough of Tower Hamlets 'hideously Bangladeshi' would be labelled a fascist. Not only would any indigenous person who called Brixton or Lewisham 'hideously black' or Woolwich 'hideously ethnic' risk getting done for race hatred, but such places are invariably described by journalists and estate agents as 'vibrant'.

Birmingham, in the heart of England, is now largely made up of an assortment of Muslims from all over the world, including Afghanistan,

Yemen, Pakistan, Bangladesh, India, Sudan and Somalia - indeed, like other towns in the West Midlands, as well as other parts of England, Britain's second city can justly be called hideously Muslim - but beware of a tap on the shoulder from Politically Correct Plod if you do so.

An article in the January 2011 issue of the magazine *Standpoint* by a vicar's wife writing anonymously describes her four years in Birmingham.

She was glad to leave. 'I shan't miss some locals' assumptions that, being a white woman, if I was outside after dark, as I occasionally was, usually to walk the few metres between my house and the church, I must be a prostitute,' she wrote. 'I shan't miss the abuse my priest husband received: the daubing of "dirty white dogs" in red paint on the church door, the barrage of stones thrown at him by children shouting "Satan".'

She continued, 'Inner-city Birmingham has been a police no-go area for 20 years. Even during our time we saw the area change. When we arrived, the population was predominantly Pakistani. Now Somalis are there in equal number. Most of the run-down Irish pubs were turned into mosques.'

An increasing number of Muslims are arriving with EU passports. She asked one why he had come to Birmingham from Antwerp. He was surprised at the question: 'Everybody know. Birmingham best place in Europe to be pure Muslim.'

'I suspect there are few places in which they can have so little contact with the civic and legal structure of a Western state if they choose,' she wrote. 'It seems to be particularly easy to "disappear" if that is their intention. A parishioner once described a lorry pulling up outside his house, the side opening to reveal stacked mattresses full of sleepy, and presumably illegal, immigrants, who staggered out into broad Brummie daylight. We heard tales of how houses are exchanged for cash payments in our area. An untaxed car was once clamped by a frightened-looking official at 8am, but within hours the owner of the vehicle had organised the clamps to be sawn off, and he sped away.'

She noticed the Muslims' strong tendency towards denial. When her husband mentioned the 'dirty white dogs' graffito to a local Muslim, the response was, 'One of your people did it.' The police's response was no better. They chose not to believe it had happened, since all sign of it had been removed with buckets of anti-graffiti chemicals. They asked, pathetically: 'Are you sure it was racist?'

Meanwhile, one primary school in Birmingham is teaching more than half its pupils via computerised translators because they cannot speak English. Manor Park School uses Talking Tutor software. Teachers type instructions into the package, which translates the text and 'speaks' to the children. Headmaster Jason Smith said, 'This is a tool and definitely not a replacement for a real teacher. We have thirty different languages spoken in the school.' The software is in every classroom.

The situation in schools has always been an indication of the way things are going. Although political correctness in schools has been boosted over the last decade by the law, the most famous case remains that of a Bradford headmaster who, twenty-five years ago, was condemned as a racist, suspended and, at the age of fifty-one, forced into early retirement for warning that the policy of promoting multi-culturalism in schools was going to have a malign effect.

Ray Honeyford, the head of Drummond Middle School, said that the fear of offending Pakistanis and Bangladeshis was leading to the ghettoisation of education establishments, and that English was being relegated to a secondary language. As he later recalled: 'My philosophy at that time was a belief in integration, and a rejection of both racial prejudice and multi-culturalism, which I felt from experience was dangerously divisive and contained the seeds of future conflict.'

For making the innocuous and sensible point that English should be taught as a first language in English schools, and that promoting South Asian languages would lead to 'white flight', Honeyford was vilified and lost his job - even though the council's wish to pursue a multi-cultural educational agenda had not been requested by the local South Asians and was sometimes against the wishes of South Asian parents themselves.

A Bristol teacher who had vocally supported Honeyford was later asked not to return to his school after his colleagues told him that they 'no longer wished to work with him'.

But Honeyford's prediction of 'white flight' has come true. In parts of Bradford now, more than half the population comes from Pakistan. In February 2012 it was revealed that out of seven hundred pupils at one Bradford school, Byron Primary, just twenty-six speak English as their first language. About two thirds are Pakistani. And Drummond School is now totally Pakistani and been re-named Iqra School.

In September 2009 I read about another school and of another example of white flight, indirectly. *The Economist* published an article on a state school in Walsall, next to Birmingham at the heart of England, Palfrey Junior, where 98 per cent of the pupils were Muslims.

It was an interesting article, noting that the legal requirement for 'mainly Christian' worship was met with generic 'songs to God', that swimming was segregated by sex; at the request of the Muslim parents, there was no sex education and all food was *halal*. During Ramadan, pupils who fasted were kept indoors in case they became dehydrated. When the bell goes in mid-afternoon, most pupils head straight to a madrasa to learn the *Koran*. The article notes that these children spend a lot of time in a Muslim cocoon, with an experience of life that differs vastly from that of other young Britons, which complicates official efforts to boost social cohesion. And it noted that life in some British towns is steeped in Islam.

The renaming of a school in Bradford from Drummond to Iqra and *The Economist* article begged questions that struck me. What happened to the indigenous families whose children used to attend these schools? Where have they gone? Did they go in good grace or did they feel forced out by hordes of strangers? If the latter, are they to be branded racist, and, therefore, by extension, their views contemptible? The likes of London journalist Chris Blackhurst believe this to be the case. In one article he described attending a family wedding, at which, he wrote in indignation, 'I could not believe what I heard from distant relatives who explained that they lived in the countryside, to escape the Asians and black people taking over the suburbs'.

The Muslims believe they have a divine right to spread and multiply in England, because, like the Israelites, they are a superior people who do not have to consider the feelings of lesser mortals whose land they are taking. God said to Abraham, 'I will give to you and to your descendants after you, the land of your sojournings, all the land of Canaan, for an everlasting possession.' (Genesis 17:8). But Canaan was already populated. Many peoples had lived in that 'land of milk and honey' for centuries. The Israelites, as the self-proclaimed 'chosen people', disregarded this to such an extent that they massacred any Canaanites who resisted them, and, in the manner of all invaders throughout history, called the people they were invading enemies. King Solomon then used the survivors, those whom the Israelites had been unable to destroy utterly when they took possession of their land, as slaves to build his temple in Jerusalem. God said to the Israelites in Canaan, 'I gave you a land that you had never cultivated and cities that you had not built. Now you are living there and eating grapes from vines that you did not plant.' (Joshua 24:13). As Edward Gibbon wrote in *Decline and Fall of the Roman Empire*, 'The conquest of the land of Canaan, and the extirpation of the unsuspecting natives, cannot be reconciled with the common notions of humanity and justice.'

England is the latter-day Canaan. Betrayed and abandoned by our leaders, we too have foreign invaders among us, settlers who despise and hate us for not worshipping their deity and who, at the rate they are breeding and spreading, will eventually dominate our land, receiving our name without adopting our values.

WHAT A LOAD OF OL' SHIITE
Islam speaks

THE Islamic Republic of Iran was founded on the idea that Muslims await the reappearance of the 'twelfth *imam*', a messianic leader who was 'occulted' - hidden by God - in the ninth century. The concealment and the expected revealing of the True Imam or Mahdi is a core doctrine.

Iranian Shiite Muslims believe the martyrdom of the faithful in fighting the infidel and seeking justice for believers hastens the parousia, the second coming, of the absent *imam*. Until this miraculous event occurs, it is up to the clergy to run human affairs, under an arrangement known as the Guardianship of the Jurist.

The clergy aver that God has bestowed supreme authority on them and that most people are incapable of thinking for themselves and must blindly obey their religious and political leaders.

The president also claims to be the instrument of the hidden *imam*, carrying out his will and preparing the way for his reappearance, a claim that turns criticism of the president into criticism of the hidden *imam*, which is unthinkable.

With the numbing of the critical faculties of the population achieved, in April 2010 one of these Guardians, a senior Iranian cleric, blamed promiscuous women for earthquakes. Tens of thousands of people have died in Iran earthquakes in the last decade, including more than 25,000 when a powerful tremor hit the ancient town of Bam in 2003.

White-turbaned Hojatoleslam Kazem Sedighi told worshippers in Tehran that they had to stick to strict codes of modesty to protect themselves: 'Many women who do not dress modestly lead young men astray and spread adultery in society, which increases earthquakes. What can we do to avoid being buried under the rubble? There is no other solution but to take refuge in religion and to adapt our lives to Islam's moral codes. If an earthquake hits Tehran, no one will be able to confront such a calamity but God's power, only God's power. So let's not disappoint God.'

More than a billion Muslims all over the world are brought up to believe this sort of nonsense. And, as Voltaire said: 'Those who can make you believe absurdities can make you commit atrocities.' (Voltaire's play *Muhammed the Prophet*, an attack on hypocrisy and fanaticism written in 1741, can no longer be staged in France without police protection.)

The problem is, we are vastly outnumbered. The population of the Muslim world rose from 15 per cent of the world's population in 1970 to almost 20 per cent by 2000. It is expected to reach 23 per cent by 2025. The population of the Arab world alone has risen in the last fifty years from 80 million to 320 million. Half of that population is under twenty. Osama Bin Laden had no fewer than fifty-four siblings (twenty-five brothers and twenty-nine sisters) and he himself fathered twenty-five children (one of whom married a British woman in 2006).

Throughout history, civilisation has been challenged and often conquered by every variety of barbarianism. The relatively recent advance of secular liberal democracy is no different. Just as waves of nomadic Turks erased the lettered Byzantines, so we too will be overwhelmed.

These downfalls have usually been with the connivance of a ruling class softened by being too civilised. Roman historian Tacitus initiated his career with a monograph entitled *Germania* in which he eulogised the German tribes. Although they were known as barbarians, Tacitus wrote that they were unusually democratic, unsexist, maritally faithful and avoided vices such as pride and gluttony. *Germania* contained recurrent moral contrasts between the decadence of Rome and the crude vigour of the teeming, and potentially threatening, peoples beyond the Rhine. And indeed, eventually, many years later, these vigorous peoples played a major role in the eclipse of the Roman Empire in the West.

Praising your enemies has a long pedigree. Rulers do not seem to learn from history. The vast majority of the likes of me know by now that Islam poses a mortal threat to our civilisation. A survey by YouGov in 2009 suggested that 44 per cent of all respondents thought so. As presumably a big percentage of the other 56 per cent were Muslims, this means that most indigenous people agree with this statement. This has created a siege mentality that cannot be dismissed as paranoia - 'Islamophobia'. We feel threatened because we are.

The enlightenment that a few generations has achieved signals its own demise by the increased disinclination of the enlightened to bother multiplying. When highly cultivated people start to weigh up the advantages and disadvantages of having children, the great turning point has come. Their race is probably doomed anyway, under any circumstances, but when it is simultaneously menaced by millions of virile barbarians their demise is certain. Any civilisation that is neither reproducing nor defending its borders not only will not survive but does not deserve to survive.

If a people no longer has the strength or will to maintain itself in the political sphere, that is not the end of politics in the world, it is only the end of a weak people. As Hegel wrote in *Reason in History*: 'No power can destroy the spirit of a people, either from the outside, or from the inside, if it is not itself already lifeless, if it has not already perished.'

England is undergoing one of the most sudden and radical periods of transition in its history. All the guiding influences of truth and justice are being shaken and overturned.

Our civilisation is dying by its own act of self-destruction. No external enemy can destroy it the way the Spaniards once destroyed the civilisation of the Aztecs. Only inner enemies can threaten it. It can come to an end only if the ideas of liberalism are supplanted by an anti-liberal ideology hostile to social co-operation. And this is exactly what is happening.

Two periods have unfortunately combined, that of our ideological exhaustion and that of unprecedented demographic upheaval. It was only by coincidence that the policy of giving in to settlers' every whim and demand was adopted just before Muslims began to obey the Prophet's injunction to 'outnumber others'.

Now every week 20,000 Muslims fly from Manchester alone to Pakistan to visit relatives. Twenty thousand a week from Manchester alone! And they are all called British. In March 2012 the BBC headlined a package on its website, 'The most dangerous place in the world for Britons'. It turned out that the dangerous place was Pakistan and that the 'Britons' murdered there were Pakistanis visiting their homeland and getting caught up in violent family disputes. In the programme the BBC reporter, a man named Aleem Maqbool, interviewed two 'British' women in saris named Nasim Ather and Akila Naqqash.

AN ALLEGRA FOR OUR TIMES
Islam's useful idiots

DEVOUT parishioners in the isolated Pennine village of Dembury caused a stir in 2006 when they were discovered taking it in turns to dance on the village green ensuring someone was always dancing. It emerged this had been going on for ten months and they were doing it because their priest had told them to, saying God had instructed it and He had decreed that it was to continue for a year and a day.

This actually happened: but not in the Pennines and not in 2006. It is recorded as occurring in Saxony in the eleventh century. But transposing it conveys some idea of the idiocies you can expect in a society governed by religion. A religious debate initiated by a man from such a society did take place in Britain in the twenty-first century; and not only took place but was reported with great seriousness in British newspapers.

In March 2010 a Pakistani Islamic scholar issued a *fatwa* in London denouncing Muslim suicide bombers. In a document of six hundred pages, he claimed that these youths do not go to Paradise as they believe, but to Hell. All were agreed on what a fine upstanding bloke he was for denouncing mass murder; but no one raised the issue of an adult in the twenty-first century believing not only in Heaven and Hell but in angels and genies and other supernatural beings unknown to the likes of us.

The scholar, Dr Tahir ul-Qadri, who, according to Allegra Mostyn-Owen in the London *Evening Standard*, is regarded as a 'living saint' by his many followers, like all Muslims not only believes in genies, of the type that come out of the magic lamp when Aladdin rubs it, but also believes in beings called *nabis* and *rasuls*.

Muslim websites tend to be written in poor English but as far as I can make out from them, *nabis* are minor prophets living today who interpret and deliver Allah's decrees, while *rasuls* are higher prophets whose utterances, unlike those of relatively humble *nabis*, are to be regarded as so profound and ultimate that to disregard them warrants death for individuals and destruction for nations. Is that clear? You can snub a *nabi* but risk your life and face eternal damnation in the fiery pit if you disregard a *rasul*. All right? Be careful. If such a personage ever gets in touch with you, you had better swiftly ascertain whether he (or she - unlikely) is a *nabi* or a *rasul*. Your life depends on it.

Well, according to another badly-written Muslim website, admittedly penned by a mortal enemy of ul-Qadri, the eminent scholar once paused for a long time while delivering a speech, because, as he later explained, he was receiving a message, one assumes by extra-sensory perception, from a *nabi*, who was telling him that he, the *nabi*, could not attend a forthcoming event because he had no money for the fare and requesting that ul-Qadri please send him some dosh. The website was ridiculing not that such a thing could happen but that it could happen to ul-Qadri. It also says that ul-Qadri claims he is so holy that anyone who kisses him is guaranteed admission to Paradise. This website naturally predicts for this fellow devout Muslim not Paradise but the fiery pit.

Muslims discuss this sort of stuff solemnly and at great length. Many unbelievers in their ignorance treat them with respect. Then there are those who are not ignorant but write drivel for some other reason.

Allegra Mostyn-Owen's fawning profile of ul-Qadri was one of the yuckiest articles I have ever read. According to her, his revelation that killing people is wrong is an 'historic vision'. He gives his interview 'in a neat, terraced house in Barking where he emerges from his studies [of genies, *nabis* and *rasuls*, one assumes] resplendent in an elegant silk striped grey and white *juba* [*sic*] and a black woollen hat. She writes, 'I am honoured to be in his presence because he is considered a living saint by his followers... ' and so on, for two yucky pages. The accompanying photograph of her with her subject showing her wearing a headscarf and gazing at him like a sycophantic puppy, makes you cringe.

And to cap it all the gushing interview is accompanied by a panel in which Douglas Murray, director of the Centre for Social Cohesion, writes that what 'makes this 600-page ruling potentially important is that Dr ul-Qadri has a highly respected scholarly background'. Respected by whom? Others who believe in the existence of genies, *nabis* and *rasuls*?

If ul-Qadri had issued this *fatwa* in a Muslim country it would have been immediately judged the work of the devil by other 'esteemed Islamic scholars' with copious references to the *Koran*, citing different passages to the ones quoted by ul-Qadri, and he would be viewed as an 'apostate' and hence fair game to be murdered by any Muslim from a different sect or faction or who lives in a street or a village where they disagree with his views. The notoriously sensitive male youths of Islam would quickly be instructed to be offended.

Both Allegra Mostyn-Owen and Douglas Murray ignore the fact that ul-Qadri has many more Muslim enemies than followers; that he lives in Canada (why do none of these 'highly respected' Islamic scholars ever remain in their Islamic homeland?); and that the four hundred books attributed to him were in fact written by his students, a common practice among Muslims. Nor do they ask why it takes six hundred pages to make the obvious point that killing people is wrong. The Christian Book of Common Prayer needs only four words.

The likes of me are expected to go along with the wholesale introduction of alien words and concepts into our life and culture. Muslim readers of the *Evening Standard* will know what a *juba* is, but what about the rest of us? At the very least, this is poor journalism.

I suspect more sinister forces at work than inattentive sub editors.

Muslims make much of the Verse of the Sword in the *Koran*, one of the few verses that does not advocate killing unbelievers, because, they say, it 'cancels earlier verses', which do. This ignores two inconvenient facts. First, the *Koran* is saturated throughout, from start to finish, with exhortations to kill us infidels, and, secondly, it is not in chronological order of composition. Its chapters are arranged in order of length, the longest coming first. So the Verse of the Sword cannot take precedence over earlier verses because no one knows in what order they were written.

There are many other problems in deciphering the meaning of the *Koran*. The Arabic alphabet was invented two hundred years after the Prophet. As the kufic script in which the *Koran* was originally written contained no indication of vowels or diacritical points, 'variant readings are recognised by Muslims as of equal authority'. In other words, they can read into it whatever turns them on. Some chapters actually begin with cryptic words that no one has the least idea what they mean. They are literally meaningless. Islamic scholars are blind men in a dark room seeking a black object that is not there.

They claim that 3,000 years ago God, in His infinite wisdom and mercy, said to Himself through his white flowing beard, 'I shall intervene in human affairs' But humans had already existed for 100,000 years. What kept Him? (The priests of the other two monotheistic religions make the same claim but with less aggression.) Respecting them is like respecting children solely because they believe in Father Christmas, or respecting experts on the Harry Potter books.

Establishment Muslims naturally gushed over the *fatwa*, with the slimy Communities Minister Shahid Malik leading the way. Because one of the July 7th 2005 London bombers, Sidique Khan, lived in his Dewsbury constituency, Malik was considered qualified to pontificate.

'It is incumbent on Muslims to stand up for their faith,' he said. 'When 7/7 occurred those four evil young men killed themselves and over fifty innocent people because they followed a twisted and perverted interpretation of Islam which told them by doing so they would go to heaven. A clear and unequivocal message must go out that Islam teaches that these four are not martyrs going to heaven but sinners going somewhere very different indeed. Hence, I very much welcome the work of Dr Qadri in helping reinforce this most crucial message to Muslims and non-Muslims alike.'

This all seems well and good if you do not look into it too much. Close scrutiny of Malik however reveals an unscrupulous, hypocritical politician at work. Firstly, there are the usual suspicions of corruption that you see in the biographies of virtually all Muslim politicians. He lost his seat in 2010 after controversy over his expenses claims. Secondly, this MP in an enlightened secular country unashamedly confessed to believing sinners go to Hell.

Thirdly, his utterances to a different audience on different occasions reveal someone just as bent on the Islamification of Britain as suicide bombers but by different means - not bombs but the ballot box. The Islamic assault is the classic attack on all fronts.

Addressing a Muslim audience in an English town, this Lancastrian, one of six siblings born in Burnley to Pakistani parents, as the minister responsible for 'Race, Faith and Community Cohesion' opened his speech with a greeting in Arabic.

After conveying the good wishes of Jack Straw he proudly listed the amounts of taxpayers' money he had, as Minister for International Development, allocated as aid for Muslim countries, which in total came to more than £1 billion. This money was distributed through organisations such as Islamic Relief, Muslim Aid and Muslim Hands.

Malik called for a show of appreciation for these organisations, which the audience enthusiastically gave. (As all these Muslim countries are utterly corrupt very little of this money reaches the people it is intended for. See essay, 'You are Welcome to Bristol'.) He continued, 'Today, we're showing the true face of Islam. Our future in this country is very bright.' Reminding his audience that the first Muslim MP took office in 1997, he listed the growth in Muslim MPs since then; two in 2001, four in 2005, a projected eight in 2010 and sixteen by 2014.

'At this rate,' he said, 'the whole Parliament will be Muslim. We've got four Muslim MPs but there should be twenty Muslim MPs, and, *inshallah* [God willing], very shortly we'll see that. I'm confident that, *inshallah*, in the next thirty years or so we'll have a Prime Minister in this country who happens to share my faith.'

In all mass immigrations, there is a turning point when the offspring of settlers end up not just inhabiting but also shaping the country. They start to assert themselves, throwing their political weight around. The moment when natives discover they must share power with the aliens living among them is as fraught with tension as the time of the first settlers' arrival. In between, there is a period of calm. By the time it enters the minds of the indigenous people that the newcomers might eventually have claims to power, a point of no return has been reached.

Before the Muslims had gained even a foothold in any of Britain's democratic institutions, their eventual dominance of all of them was inevitable. When they are numerous enough to dominate British politics, which, as Malik rightly stated, will be soon, they will turn it into a weapon for the disempowerment and expropriation of the traditional British establishment. Later generations of British Muslims will remember the likes of me as the hostile reactionaries of the second stage of immigration, not as the generous hosts of the first.

Although Margaret Thatcher deliberately weakened Britain's ancient, elaborate and efficient system of local government for political reasons, it is still ample enough that a class of immigrant political leaders grows anywhere an immigrant population settles. Soon, as Malik predicted, there will be many Muslims in Parliament. Eighty Muslims stood for Parliament at the 2010 general election. (This at the same time as half of Muslim men and three-quarters of Muslim women are unemployed in Britain, according to the Equality and Human Rights Commission, which contradicts what Lord Ahmed said in June 2011: 'Ninety-eight per cent of Muslims in Britain make a fantastic contribution to the economy'.)

DEUTSCHLAND ÜBER ALLAH
Germinal

AN opinion poll showed that 55 per cent of Germans think their Turkish population is a burden on the economy. Germany has four million people of Turkish background, following a 1961 labour recruitment agreement between the town countries. Turks were invited - to work but not to stay. The agreement was tempered three years later when its 'rotation clause' was ended, partly because German companies did not want to constantly re-train new workers. But the impression remains that Turks are in Germany on sufferance, and multi-culturalism, which Germans disparagingly call 'multi-kulti' and which the German newspaper *Bild*, Europe's most popular newspaper, calls 'insanity', is now officially acknowledged to have failed - an acknowledgement due to just one book.

Thilo Sarrazin's *Deutschland schafft sich ab* ('Germany is abolishing itself') sold a million copies in a few weeks. Clearly his critique of multi-culturalism and the long-term impact of Islam found its mark.

On publication, he was forced to resign from his post on the board of the Bundesbank, the country's president said, 'Islam is part of Germany' and Chancellor Angela Merkel said Sarrazin's views were '*unerwünscht*', not merely mistaken but undesirable, even dangerous. She said Sarrazin's offerings were 'extremely injurious, defamatory and very polemical.' She also called them 'completely unhelpful' and said that 'a different tone is necessary.' But then Frau Merkel admitted in a speech to astounded young Christian Democrats that 'we lied to ourselves' about how successful the integration of Turkish Muslims into German society had actually been. To enthusiastic applause she admitted multi-culturalism had 'failed - utterly'.

Suddenly, Sarrazin's 'undesirable views' had, under pressure from public opinion, been adopted by the German government. This is how an open society is supposed to function. The German leaders had to recognise the difference between what Orwell called 'the freedom to say that two plus two equals four' and a diabolical world in which reason itself is denied.

Frau Merkel added, 'Not *sharia*, not the unity of state and religion, not the claims of the *umma* to infallibility, not the segregation of man and woman: none of these must be allowed to become part of Germany. That would be a betrayal of freedom.' Her speech was followed by a similar speech from French president Nicolas Sarkozy. After years of careful avoidance, Europe's leaders finally raised their voices to admit that multi-cultural society was not working.

But in Austria, a free speech activist was tried for drawing attention to the same problem. Elisabeth Sabaditsch-Wolff had been facing three years in prison, if convicted of inciting religious hatred, after she criticised Islam and *sharia* law. She was instead ordered to pay a fine of €480.

'I advise you not to burn the *Koran*, but to read it! Only by studying what Islam stands for, will we know how to face it down! Know your enemy!' she said at a demonstration. A left-wing Austrian magazine recorded and published a speech at one of her seminars, landing her in court on charges for 'a hate speech against Islam'.

'I have nothing against people who want to practise their faith, but I would like them to do this in the privacy of their own homes,' she said. Her ideas, she pointed out, are nothing new, and when Europe's political elite express them, they are not prosecuted for the same views. 'Multi-culturalism has failed and this is nothing new. My group and I have been saying it for years. And now all of a sudden Sarkozy, Merkel and others come out of hiding and agree with this. I do not know why.'

Multi-culturalism is now open to multi-criticism from some of Europe's most influential political leaders. It remains to be seen how their views might influence debate on the ground. But as far as the English are concerned at least, any debate now can only ever remain empty talk. It is too late. Our culture is in ruins, a flat wasteland of rubble. Around us is a colossal wreck. We sense this, and feel desperate without knowing the cause of the feeling and therefore cannot act. We scurry about here and there with a lot of fuss and clamour, for diversion as much as for a livelihood, but deep down are inert. The devastation has left each one of us horribly alone. A culture is like an active parent in that it provides security. You belong somewhere. Just as most delinquents are lost souls from a broken family, so we too are abandoned children whimpering for our parents, vulnerable to all sorts of evil, easy prey for sinister strangers. Hostile aliens are allowed to proliferate in our midst without the appropriate response. Our capacity for spontaneous and unselfconscious revulsion, a healthy instinct, has been rationalised out of existence. We are enjoined to love people we fear - the essence of sado-masochism.

When the Indians led by Mahatma Gandhi decided it was time to expel the unwanted British from their country, they did so. Can the British, on the same principle, now expel the Indians in their country? Of course not. That would be a breach of their human rights. I recently saw Africans loudly celebrating their country's independence at the seaside in Thanet, on the stretch of coast where Hengist and Horsa and Augustine landed. If Africans are so happy that the British were expelled from their countries why have they come to live among the British in such vast numbers?

Great failed social experiments normally do not survive. The Raj ended. The Soviet Union ended. The darkening of Albion has no end. The experiment of multi-culturalism, though now acknowledged at the highest levels to have failed, continues in perpetuity. A people can recover from an economic crisis or a war but not the replacement of its population. Without the English, England no longer exists. The ethnics are among us in their millions, solidly entrenched, breeding and spreading, never leaving, changing the complexion of the country for ever. Every year there is some new development. Things get worse and worse. A new wave of restrictions on the media is followed by journalists practising self-censorship, for a quiet life. The most common languages heard on Greenwich buses now are African languages. This is all very sudden. If, one summer, butterflies or flying ants descended on the borough on such a scale, clogging up everything, people would be asking why. Readers' letters about it would be published in newspapers, experts on butterflies or flying ants would explain the phenomenon. But when it comes to Africans, the subject is taboo.

There are very many ethnics. And their numbers increase all the time, as they breed and spread. A big proportion arrive with forged documents, and so are criminals from the beginning. They move easily in the murky dregs of London's life in this troubled time, bored and justifying their criminality with the fantasy of victimhood. Although life in the capital goes on with apparent normality - it has a police force and a civil service, newspapers, and television and radio channels devoted to it - its most important fact is ignored or denied.

This fact is that we Cockneys constantly squeeze ourselves into less and less space. Everywhere we go, an ethnic is in the way. Pavements, shops, public transport, all are crowded with ethnics, with new ones arriving daily, threatening and mysterious. We cannot understand why it is being allowed to happen, so obviously is it a strain on resources. Even if they all worked, this would still be the case; but many of them do not work, and so they wander around aimlessly during the working day, clogging up everything even more. In January 2012 the Greater London Authority's head of demography, himself an ethnic, spoke of how health-care and housing had been sufficiently planned until the 'crazy fertility numbers'. This is a polite way of saying that hundreds of thousands of Muslims and Africans are settling in the capital and breeding like rats. Every year the pressure mounts. London swells, expands, overflows.

Up until a year ago, when you took a train from Greenwich to the Kent coast once you reached Chatham after an hour's travelling you could reckon to be free of the sight and sound of ethnics. Now they teem at Chatham and neighbouring towns and in the coastal towns, few of them speaking English. A gigantic gaudy Sikh temple looms over the biggest town before Chatham, Gravesend. Given the rate the settlers are proliferating, in just a couple of years the old Saxon Shore will be the Ethnic Coast - and presumably the local people of Kent, like the local people of London, will be expected to pretend it is not happening.

IN BEDS WITH THE ENEMY
Devastating respect

IN 2010 an e-mail was widely circulated claiming that Bedfordshire police had to observe strict conditions when entering Muslims' homes in search of terrorists.

This is particularly relevant because a Bedfordshire town, Luton, is the Islamic stronghold of southern England. Stockholm bomber Taimur Abdulawhab al-Abdaly lived there, his fate (accidentally blowing himself up before he could murder hundreds of innocent Swedes) a reminder of the town's Islamification.

A settlement since pre-Roman times, the town, thirty miles north of London, now has more than 25,000 Muslims out of its population of 200,000, many of them Kashmiri. Most are on jobless benefits. Social housing and school places are scarce. Deprivation is due to overcrowding, which is due to them being there, and yet by twisted reasoning typical of Muslims they contrive to blame the infidel.

So their young males (who have no work to occupy them) become interested in terrorism.

The e-mail said the instructions to the police were:

❑Community leaders must be consulted before raids on Muslim houses.

❑Occupied bedrooms and bathrooms must not be searched before dawn.

❑The use of police dogs will be considered serious desecration of the premises.

❑Cameras and camcorders should not be used in case of capturing women in inappropriate dress.

❑If people are praying at home officers should stand aside and not disrupt the prayer. They should be allowed the opportunity to finish.

❑Officers should take their shoes off before raiding a Muslim house.

❑The reason for pre-dawn raids on Muslim houses needs to be clear and transparent.

One recipient of this e-mail wrote to Bedfordshire police asking if all this was true, and they posted this response on their website:

'The item you refer to is incorrect and is not "Bedfordshire Police's rules regarding terrorists and dangerous criminals" as is claimed.

'Bedfordshire Police does have guidance for entering households which was derived from National Home Office/Association of Chief Police Officers (ACPO) guidelines. While the information on the website is not the same, there are some similarities to our guidance for some basic considerations when entering Muslim households, especially for pre-planned operations, which is summarised below:

'Innocent occupants of a household such as women and children may be present and Police should never under-estimate the impact of any loss of their personal dignity. Muslim women may be more flexible in their choice of dress at home amongst family members than outside and police entry could contribute to a loss of dignity.

'Opportunity should be afforded for occupants to cover themselves sufficiently to comply with the etiquettes of "Hijab" if a non-family member is present - and that includes the head for women.

'The same level of etiquette and respect should be observed in Muslim households as in a Muslim place of worship, such as a Mosque.

'Female officers must be available wherever practicable to deal with females and there should not be any cross gender contact by the officers.

'Muslim prisoners should be allowed to take additional clothing to the station. All clothing needs to remain pure for prayer and the denial of appropriate clothing will be a very serious issue for the individual.

'If possible, officers should not take shoes into the houses, especially in areas that might be kept pure for prayer purposes - nor should they step on any prayer mats etc. This might be difficult in some cases but needs to be seriously considered - plastic overshoes may be an option in some cases if the cleanliness/purity of the overshoes can be maintained.

'Non-Muslims are not allowed to touch Holy Books, Qurans or religious artefacts without permission.

'In the current climate the justification for pre-dawn raids on Muslim houses needs to be clear and transparent. The aftercare of those not detained must be considered. Sufficient arrangements should be made to offer alternative accommodation to those who are removed from their homes whilst lengthy searches are carried out. If they are not removed from the house they should be allowed some flexibility and privacy. Deployment of family liaison officers should be considered to minimise the impact on the families and the local community.'

It may seem to some that all this is nearly as bad as the 'incorrect' claims.

Fear of offending Muslims permeates police forces throughout England, hindering their work. On January 5th 2011 *The Times* revealed that police and social services had adopted a culture of silence that facilitated the sexual exploitation of hundreds of white schoolgirls.

Agencies identified a pattern of grooming of under-age girls by gangs of Pakistani men in towns across the Midlands and northern England. But most forces publicly denied that ethnicity was a common factor. *The Times* found that of fifty-six men found guilty of grooming adolescent girls in seventeen court cases since 1997, fifty-three were Pakistani. A sharp drop in the price of drugs had led to the gangs losing considerable income, and selling girls was increasingly filling the gap. The girls were raped by gang members as a way of 'breaking them in' and then passed around various other men for sex.

Since then there have been several other cases, with the authorities desperately trying to play down the extent of these crimes and obscure the background of the criminals.

At one of the trials, in May 2012, when eight Pakistanis and an Afghan were convicted in Manchester, two Muslim councillors gave glowing character references for one of them. Rochdale councillor Aftab Hussain and former mayor Zulf Ali supported Abdul Qayyum, who was jailed for five years for conspiracy to engage in sexual activity with a child. Despite this, the following month Hussain was promoted to chair an important committee, enraging local indigenous people.

The pimps use takeaways and cab offices as their headquarters. Their methods are sophisticated and sinister. First, the girls are identified in locations such as parks, schools, leisure facilities and shopping malls, after which boys of their age are sent to befriend them. After a friendship is established, the boys introduce their contacts to young men who they often describe as cousins.

Then the grooming process gets really under way. The young man will take the girl out in his car, give her vodka, cigarette and cannabis, and take her to venues she would not normally experience until older.

Often giving the girl a mobile telephone as a 'gift', the pimp is then able to track her every move by calls and texting, which eventually will be used by him to send instructions as to details of arrangements with punters. The men sell the girls on to contacts for around £200 a time or as currency for a business deal. Another tactic of the pimp is getting the girl to despise and mistrust her own parents in order that he can achieve total control over her. The pimps routinely tell their victims that their parents are racist and that they disapprove of the relationships because the men are of Pakistani Muslim heritage, not because they are older.

The pimps know that the police do not want to be accused of racism. In 2004, Channel 4 withdrew a documentary that depicted parents trying to stop groups of young Pakistani Muslim males grooming white girls as young as eleven for sex after Colin Cramphorn, the then Chief Constable of West Yorkshire, joined groups such as Unite against Fascism in calling for it to be withdrawn. Channel 4 complied, saying that the issue was not censorship but timing because of the proximity with local and European elections.

One girl was only twelve when she was befriended by Pakistani boys about her own age who soon introduced her to relatives in their twenties and thirties. She had no idea she was being groomed and brainwashed until one day she was taken to wasteland and raped by the gang leader. The attack was watched by laughing gang members and recorded on mobile phones. The girl said, 'People ask me why I kept going back to Tarik, even after he raped me but he threatened to firebomb my home and rape my own mother if I tried to escape.'

The gangs want virgins and girls who are free of sexual diseases. Most of the men buying sex with the girls have Muslim wives and they do not want to risk infection. The younger the girl looks, the more saleable she is. Because male Muslims are pressured to marry virgins within their own extended family networks, they are more likely to view white girls as easily available and 'safer' than Pakistani girls.

Fear of being branded racist makes the police and social services reluctant to investigate the crimes as organised and connected.

One mother from Rotherham, whose fourteen-year-old daughter was groomed into prostitution and multiply raped for a year, said that almost every man convicted of these crimes in the north of England is Pakistani but that the authorities insist this is not relevant. One social services official said merely that it was 'interesting' to note that most of the men involved were 'Asian'. (See essay, 'Denis MacShane'.)

When another official in another case, in early 2012, this time as far south as Oxford, said, 'The experience of our members in the network is that both victims and offenders come from a wide range of cultural and social backgrounds,' we knew a cover-up was being attempted and, sure enough, when the men's names were published, they were all Pakistani names.

These gangs will be allowed to operate with impunity if their existence is denied in a twisted attempt to be anti-racist and culturally sensitive. Even calling the pimping gangs 'Asian' instead of Pakistani Muslim is to ignore the facts. Naturally, the Chief Crown Prosecutor for the North West, a man named Nazir Afzal, continues to call them 'Asian' (Japanese, maybe?) but many indigenous people, who should know better, also shamefully persist in doing do.

Grooming white girls for sex is endemic wherever Muslims have gained a foothold. Many of the victims are given alcohol or drugs before being forced to have sex in cars, rented houses or hotels.

Although the judge at one trial in 2010 said the race of the victims and their abusers was 'coincidental' even top useful idiot Jack Straw said there was a racial element to the grooming of vulnerable girls for sex, telling the BBC there was a 'specific problem' in some areas.

These young men, he said, were 'fizzing and popping with testosterone, they want some outlet for that, but Pakistani heritage girls are off-limits and they are expected to marry a Pakistani girl from Pakistan, typically. So they then seek other avenues and they see these young women, white girls who are vulnerable, some of them in care... who they think are easy meat.'

(Straw had remained resolutely silent about 'easy meat' - or any other controversial issues concerning his Muslim majority - until he had safely left office, and even on this he later made one of his grovelling apologies.)

Muslims naturally protested. The obnoxious Keith Vaz predictably called the comments 'pretty dangerous', saying Straw was wrong to 'stereotype a whole community', while Mohammed Shafiq, head of Muslim charity the Ramadhan Foundation, said, 'To suggest this is somehow ingrained in the community is deeply offensive.' (And it was in response to a later, similar, case that Lord Ahmed claimed 98 per cent of Muslims in Britain make a fantastic contribution to the economy.)

But, after the investigation by *The Times*, the facts could no longer be ignored. Detective chief inspector Alan Edwards of West Mercia Police called for an end to the 'damaging taboo' surrounding these crimes. 'Everyone's too scared to address the ethnicity factor,' he said. 'No one wants to stand up and say Pakistani men are recruiting young white girls and passing them around their relatives for sex.'

Other police sources said that those convicted represented only a small proportion of a 'tidal wave' of organised crime in some cities.

The Home Office said it had no plans to commission research into the ethnic and cultural background of sex criminals. But someone should, because, despite the indignation of the likes of Vaz and Shafiq, this is precisely a cultural issue. The convictions came on top of a new report from the Jill Dando Institute of Crime Science, which warned of the growing incidence of this kind of systematic abuse by Pakistani offenders.

Muslims regard white girls as sluts who deserve no better. One of the men in a failed attempt to blow up a London nightclub said in a tapped telephone conversation the girls who would be killed were 'just slags' and so, by inference, killing them was of no consequence. Combined with this contempt and the insistence on virginity is the sexual frustration caused by long-distance arranged marriages. A boy brought up in England has nothing in common with the illiterate village girl from Pakistan he is forced to marry. Longing for sex, he indeed sees English girls swanning around in mini-skirts and skimpy tops as 'easy meat'. Islam has taught these men that such girls are unworthy of respect. Under *sharia* law they would be severely punished.

The hypocrisy over such cases has nauseated commentators. Leo McKinstry wrote in the *Daily Express*, 'These noisy zealots constantly trumpet their commitment to women's rights, anti-racism and the protection of the vulnerable. Yet, suddenly, when confronted with the reality of vicious sexual exploitation of young white girls by Asian men, they drop their supposedly cherished principles. Instead they either deny the existence of the issue or, even worse, they collude with abusers by attacking those who tell the truth.

'In recent days these grotesque double standards have been fully on display in the wake of new evidence about the prevalence of Asian sex gangs in our society... In this twisted ideological world, it would seem that the hypersensitivities of an ethnic minority are more keenly protected than the rights of abused girls.

'The greatest crime is not the sexual brutality itself but daring to mention the ethnicity of the predators... To admit the truth would be to admit the failure of Britain's experiment in multiculturalism. Any difficulties in the creation of the new Britain are entirely the fault of racism among white people. In this narrative of social change, ethnic minorities always have to be cast in a positive light; they can never be seen as the oppressors, only as victims. That is why there has been such a long cover-up over Asian sex crimes. The illusion of multicultural success must be maintained even at the expense of the truth or childhood innocence.

'The same is true of reluctance to have an honest debate about forced marriages, or Islamic extremism, or knife crime or gang warfare.

'As one mother of an abused girl from Blackburn said: "People are scared it will start a race riot but it is this perception of racism that is putting up a barrier."

'But the sheer scale of the problem means that the establishment can no longer keep it a dirty secret. It is absurd to pretend that this has nothing to do with Islam. Only the politically blinkered refuse to see that Muslim culture promotes aggressive misogyny against women, who are often treated as little more than chattels.

'Muslim men's attitude towards women outside the faith can be even more contemptuous since they are regarded as infidels devoid of any morality. One white woman from Bradford who was repeatedly raped by a Muslim pimp recalled: "He told me I was making him do it because I was sinful, not a true believer, that he would not do it if I was a Muslim."

'It is a tragedy that the cultural values of Pakistan, one of the most hellish societies on earth, should have been imported wholesale into our nation.'

Melanie Phillips wrote in the *Daily Mail* that the issue was not race, as Straw suggested, but religion: 'Indeed, one of the many red herrings in this debate is that, if cultural characteristics are discussed at all, the gangs tend to be described as "Asian". But this is to besmirch Sikhs, Hindus, Chinese and other Asians. For these particular gang members are overwhelmingly Muslim men. And the common characteristic is not ethnicity, but religion. For these gang members select their victims from communities which they believe to be "unbelievers" - non-Muslims whom they view with disdain and hostility. You can see that this is not a racial but a religious animosity from the fact that, while the vast majority of the girls who are targeted are white, the victims include Sikhs and Hindus.'

One of the areas where this abhorrent crime is widespread is the West Midlands, where the police have been blurring Muslim issues for years. The explanation for this could be that West Midlands Police has had a Security and Cohesion department headed by a Muslim, one Anil Patani. The word 'cohesion' is always a giveaway. Police officers such as Patani, along with the useful idiots, have for a long time sought to promote 'cohesion' by obfuscating the activities of Muslim criminals, appeasing Islamic groups that are not quite as extreme as al-Qaeda and combating exposure of the bigotries of well-funded, Saudi-backed *imams*.

When in 2007 Channel 4 ran a documentary revealing such bigotries, Patani ganged up with Bethan David of the Crown Prosecution Service to accuse it of fraud. They referred Channel 4 to broadcasting watchdog Ofcom, an outlandish action for police and prosecutors to take, seeing that their job is to catch and charge criminals, not act as television critics.

Journalist Nick Cohen exposed their actions in an article in the *Observer*. He described how Channel 4 undercover reporters infiltrated radical mosques, where they recorded assorted *imams* calling for women to be subordinated to men, homosexuals to be murdered and for Muslims to reject the laws of a democracy in favour of *sharia* law.

Channel 4 took great care to ensure the accuracy of the programme, which was called *Undercover Mosque*. Its commissioning editors and lawyers swarmed over the script to make sure it complied with the law and Ofcom's regulatory guidelines. A fortnight before transmission they sent letters to every *imam* criticised in it explaining what Channel 4 had accused them of and offering them a chance to reply. The station aired its balanced and impeccably sourced documentary, and the forces of law and order cracked down - not on demagogic *imams* but on the broadcasters who exposed them.

Patani and Bethan David accused Channel 4 'of the splicing together of extracts from longer speeches'. They said the makers of the documentary seemed 'to have completely distorted what the speakers were saying'.

If the allegation of fraud was correct, it meant, for example, that Derby *imam* Ijaz Mian was a democrat whose words had been distorted by sly editing and trick camerawork. Among his words were, 'So you being a Muslim you have to fix a target, there will be no House of Commons.'

Similarly, when Abu Usamah of a Birmingham mosque roared on air, 'Take that homosexual man and throw him off the mountain!' Patani and Bethan David must have believed the image was an illusion created by scheming editors rather than a genuine murderous homophobic rant; and that they had put words in his mouth when he was shown saying, 'Allah has created the woman, even if she gets a PhD, deficient. Her intellect is incomplete', instead of him being in reality a raving misogynist.

Ofcom found no evidence that Channel 4 had misled the audience. The station offered Patani and the CPS the chance to apologise but they refused, so the station sued for libel, and the authorities, after wasting hundreds of thousands of pounds of taxpayers' money in a vain battle against the broadcaster, paid damages (more taxpayers' money) and issued a full, grovelling retraction. Patani and the CPS did not, however, condescend to explain their behaviour, and no one was disciplined.

Cohen concluded, 'Among the many casualties of their betrayal of liberal principles is serious investigative journalism, which they now treat as a species of racism. To their minds, journalists cannot reveal or argue against the doctrines of religious extremists, for to admit their existence would destroy multi-cultural illusions. They want us to live in a pretend country where no challenges to liberal values exist and those who claim that they do are bigots inciting racial or religious hatred.'

Far more vulnerable people than journalists are suffering from the betrayal. In 2008, researchers issued a report on honour killings and beatings. South Asian and Middle Eastern women's groups reported an increasingly widespread trend. Officials who should treat all women equally were deciding that religious and alien cultural practices took precedence over the law. A director of a women's refuge told the report's researchers, 'We don't visit the police station when certain Asian officers are on duty because some are perpetrators. One said he would not arrest someone who used force on his wife.' A worker in a women's group, too scared to give her name, said one Asian chief inspector had offered to help a family track down a girl who had fled them.

The report's authors noticed that women's groups seemed to have problems with one force in particular - Anil Patani's West Midlands Police.

NICE GUY
Ignorance no defence

BRITISH people of all types recoil from imagining the political evil of which Muslims are capable. It is a natural reaction and, in a strange way, even speaks well of us. But it makes us vulnerable, especially when we are ruled by traitors.

No one who is following these restrained and sardonic narratives of mine can fail to receive the impression of an ancient society helpless before a derisive enemy because of its politicians' treachery. My lifetime has been a time when our leaders could malignantly betray us without losing either office or public influence.

But at the grassroots level of politics, throughout the country well-meaning indigenous men and women betray us not rancorously but in all innocence. They are simply naïve. Their liberalism, a luxury of soft times, is not malevolent. Yet it is proving greatly destructive.

I recently read about the mayor of Newport, Gwent, walking in the vanguard of an annual intimidating 500-strong Muslim procession. Councillor John Guy led the march through the town by Muslims commemorating *Ashura*, the martyrdom of the Prophet Mohammed's grandson Hussein. In these processions, women walk at the back while the men chant and beat their hands against their chests.

Addressing the marchers, Cllr Guy said: 'The Muslim community send a wonderful example of hard work and community spirit. I wish you all success and all the best for this very important day.'

Every year throughout the world 'this very important day' is marked by bomb blasts and suicide bombers as Sunnis and Shiites kill and maim each other. In December 2011 alone, thirty pilgrims in processions were killed by a series of bomb blasts in Iraq, and a suicide attack killed sixty-three people at a shrine in Kabul where a crowd had gathered for the day of *Ashura* observation.

We do not know what was behind Cllr Guy's misplaced respect. As in many other towns, Labour in Newport needs the block postal votes of the Muslims to remain in power.

But I do not believe Cllr Guy was motivated by cynicism or political expediency. I think he is simply ignorant - and too nice.

A former policeman, he probably joined Labour with the best intentions, to represent the British working class, in the finest tradition of Labour politicians. As a councillor, he has probably always been well-meaning and meticulously honest - a thoroughly decent bloke, a nice Guy. Many of us know such Labour councillors. But their niceness is often now exploited by cunning settlers, especially Muslims.

During the term of office, elected mayors are non-political figureheads, not allowed to attend political rallies or become involved in any contentious issues.

But by leading this march and making that comment Cllr Guy unknowingly DID become involved in politics, for anything to do with Islam is automatically political.

This Muslim procession was just another date in his full diary, and, before dashing off to his next appointment, he spoke in politically-correct cliché. He probably knows nothing of the history or background of *Ashura*, or of anything else to do with Islam. He belongs to the great host of the blind.

The problem is political correctness. While our towns are being restocked by populations whose culture is alien to our own, undermining our sense of identity, we are forbidden to discuss the phenomenon meaningfully. Decades of deceitful lack of precision in language have had their inevitable outcome. To degrade language is finally to degrade civilisation. Political correctness has withered the reach of the English language - and numbed the critical faculties of the likes of nice Guy, predisposed to think well of their fellow human beings.

The deceit over the years has been profound. In the 1960s the official figure for immigrants was 'only 7,000 males every year' but the government did not announce that annually a further 50,000 dependants of established immigrants were also arriving.

Many of these were Muslims. And, breeding prodigiously and encouraging their offspring to reject our values, the Muslim hordes among us now plot to take over our country.

If they succeed, such a catastrophe would make the defeat at Hastings seem like a moderate misfortune. I cannot believe anybody still cherishes the smallest doubt that it is a real danger.

The fact that it remains shrouded in silence is uncanny enough. It is already uncanny when among the great host of the blind some few who can see are expected to not speak of it.

And it is not as though politicians such as nice Guy are being outwitted by a superior civilisation. The enemy is primitive.

Islamic civilisation made some contribution to scientific knowledge long ago before lapsing into an unscientific senility.

While scientists in Christian countries were making stunning discoveries over recent centuries, Islam has had no accomplishments in the fields of science, technology or welfare.

Not a single Muslim equals Copernicus, Galileo, Newton, Darwin, Pasteur or Einstein. For centuries, no Muslim has discovered or invented anything.

When forty-seven women in 1990 took their husband's cars and drove them round and round in the centre of Riyadh, the capital of Saudi Arabia, in protest at the ban on women driving, they were arrested and denounced by the chief religious authority at the time, blind sheikh Abdul Baz, as 'Communist whores'. Baz also believed the world was flat.

But still the Archbishop of Canterbury, Rowan Williams, called for *sharia* law to be widely applied in Britain. As the *Koran* says repeatedly of the infidel: 'Has he not eyes to see?' Is Williams as blind as a Baz?

His utterances remind me of a *Not the Nine O'Clock News* satirical sketch, a solemn mini-documentary entitled 'The Devil: Is He All Bad?', in which a trendy vicar played by Mel Smith earnestly argues that the Devil needs understanding and should not be condemned outright, and a nice suburban couple give careful accounts of the mitigating features of their practice of sacrificing virgins. The vicar predicts approvingly that the Devil will soon be accepted into the Church.

It is a wonderful parody of fair-mindedness. The Christian clergy has long preached the doctrine of pusillanimity.

Not so the Muslims. They are constantly being reminded they need not obey British law. The Muslim Parliament of Great Britain says in its Founding Charter, 'For a Muslim, the observance of his host country's laws is optional. A Muslim must obey the Sharia and the Sharia alone.'

Demography is used as a political weapon. The mosques, of which there are now more than four hundred in London alone, are conducting an organised replacement of our population. In every mosque in Britain Friday prayers are accompanied by the *imam*'s exhortation: 'Bear at least five children each couple.'

Five children each couple is nowadays rather a lot. But the situation is even worse than that. Muslims, remember, are bigamists. So a male Muslim with two wives will produce at least ten babies; if he has three wives, fifteen babies. And do not remind me that in Britain bigamy is illegal. Indeed, British bigamists are jailed. But if the bigamist is Pakistani, Bangladeshi or Somali or some such, it is called polygamy and no one touches him. And not only that. Even though bigamy is indeed illegal in Britain, the rules on receiving benefits have been changed to allow for it. In February 2008 the Department for Work and Pensions issued guidelines giving recognition, and some benefits, to additional spouses (meaning Muslim wives). 'Where there is a valid polygamous marriage [*sic*] the claimant and one spouse [wife] will be paid the couple rate,' the guidelines ran. 'The amount payable for each additional spouse [wife] is presently £33.65.'

And the likes of nice Guy still believe insidious Islam is not a threat. Why are they so naïve? Have they not eyes to see? Once power is attained Muslims will abandon the lie that Islam has moderate elements. Through their many pressure groups they will have continued their creeping advance, worming their way ever deeper into society. Things that once seemed outrageous will become the norm, and, with the foundations of traditional society rotting, its active virtues undermined, the indigenous people will be utterly confused, paralysed by incomprehension.

Islamic religious instruction among Muslims has been carried out by immigrant *imams* who have a clear agenda aimed at inculcating their British-born wards with disdain and even hatred for the surroundings.

Maintaining the loyalty of the Muslim diaspora, the *umma*, is a top priority. Despite this obvious clash of loyalties, the Home Office has allowed into the country many Muslim clerics from Pakistan and the Middle East who speak no English; who, while living on benefits at the expense of the likes of me, simultaneously call on young Muslims, many likewise also on benefits, to take up arms against the 'enemies of Islam', meaning us, denouncing Britain as 'the spearhead of blasphemy that seeks to overthrow Muslims and the Islamic caliphate'. These young Muslims, restless and angry, funded by Saudi sheikhs as well as by us, creep backwards and forwards between Britain and Muslim lands, full of mischief, capable of ill-judged mayhem.

Throughout world history invaders have invariably called the people they were invading enemies, with no consideration that if they, the invaders, had stayed at home, there would be no cause for enmity. With malice always goes the fear that credits others with harbouring malice too.

Because Muslims' religion compels them to be politically ambitious, they cynically become local councillors, stand for Parliament, form alliances with other types of settlers, often in one of the numerous Black and Minority Ethnic organisations that now cover most fields of human activity, and which they quickly dominate. Some profess moderation in order to be awarded a peerage. Muslims' success at the ballot box is seen as a 'manifest victory' (*fath mubin*) of their religion. And all Muslim politicians, as well as parading their commitment to Islam, because of their culture of dishonesty invariably sooner or later are suspected of financial corruption.

Nice Guy, blinded by political correctness, cannot see any of this. He is not hostile to our civilisation, far from it, but obviously democracy is endangered when corruption, politics and a totalitarian religion are so intertwined, and such councillors have to be held to account for their unwitting contribution to the crisis. As in law, ignorance is no defence.

Refined, happy but vulnerable ancient Egypt at the height of its power erected precautionary bulwarks against depredations from the east, manned by warriors with orders not to allow in desert riff-raff. When we think of the primitive chanting that fills the streets of Newport and other British towns on *Ashura* marches, actually encouraged and supported by local leaders, we can only wonder what is occurring in our land.

ATILLA, ALAN AND...
Ab-who?

ALTHOUGH there are more Turkish Cypriots in England than in Cyprus, I have only ever known two (though I am the friend of a friend of artist Tracey Emin) and by coincidence they were both murderous criminals. By a further coincidence, they were both sentenced to seven years in jail.

One was a Muslim terrorist. I knew him before he hatched his cunning plan to earn Brownie points for admission to Paradise by the means of mass murder. He achieved ignominy under the name of Abu Abdullah, though his real name was Atilla Ahmet. ('Atilla' is not the usual spelling of this name. Many displaced foreigners cannot spell their own name properly.)

As a bodyguard of the notorious cleric Abu Hamza he was described as Hamza's right-hand man, a vital job considering Hamza lacked a right hand of his own. Hamza had lost both his hands and the use of his left eye, supposedly as a result of wounds sustained in helping to clear land-mines in Afghanistan. When not using Ahmet as his right hand he used a distinctive hook. Hamza was formerly the *imam* of North London Central mosque in Finsbury Park, where he ran the Supporters of Sharia group dedicated to the establishment of Islamic law in Britain.

Ahmet was convicted in March 2008 after pleading guilty to three charges of soliciting to murder. The judge accepted that he had acted partly because of his 'love of the limelight' at public meetings. 'You always found an excuse not to go on any training camp if it involved loss of comfort,' the judge said. In spite of such a love of home comforts, Ahmet used to call himself 'the number one al-Qaeda in Europe'.

On January 7th 2005 he was taped pontificating to co-religionists, when he said, 'How can we go home and sleep at night knowing there are millions of Muslims screaming for our help? Do we not have a conscience? Brothers and sisters, the time has come for us to stand up and be counted. Behave like Muslims. You will find reward in *Yaum al-qiyameh* [Paradise]. Otherwise, the fire is beckoning.'

And on the weekend following the July 7th 2005 London suicide bombings in which fifty-two people died, he was taped teaching children a sick song praising terrorists. At an Islam private school called Jameah Islameah near Crowborough, East Sussex, he crooned the words, 'Come, mister Taliban, come bomb England, before the daylight come you wanna see 10 Downing Street done' to the tune of Harry Belafonte's innocuous *Banana Boat Song*.

Brought up in Lewisham, in his youth he was known to friends as Alan. Before he embarked on *jihad* he was a manager in a big south-east London youth football league, managing at different times youth teams of clubs Sydenham Boys, Athenlay and Fisher Athletic.

As a football reporter on a local paper, I met Ahmet when he was managing the under-16 team of Fisher. His team had reached the League Cup finals, an annual springtime festival of football held at private playing fields where the finalists in all age groups competed for that age group's cup.

Because of his unacceptable conduct at previous matches, Ahmet had been banned by the league from attending. One league official, informing me of this, said to me, 'He's a nutter, very volatile and takes it far too seriously. Once, when his team was playing, I had to referee the managers, not the game.'

Ahmet's Fisher won 2-1 and so won the 1998 under-16 League Cup. I had been told to take a photo of every winning squad with their trophy, including the managers. When I lined up the Fisher boys in their black-and-white striped shirts for their team picture, suddenly behind them, to be photographed with them, in a bobble hat and ostentatious bushy beard, up popped Ahmet. He had been skulking in the bushes to watch the match and could not resist dashing out to share in his team's glory.

This put me in a quandary. He was banned from the ground. He should not have been there. But there he was, proudly standing behind his goalkeeper, Jason Brown, who went on to have a long career as a keeper for several professional clubs. I took the picture, and it appeared in the paper.

This was Ahmet's football swansong. To judge by the beard he was already a Muslim, and by the time the following season started in the autumn the married father-of-four had abandoned the game to devote himself fully to mass murder.

Fisher Athletic was a big club led by Dogan Arif, the other Turkish Cypriot I have known.

Fisher's first team were semi-professionals in the Conference, the league just below the Football League. In English football's pyramid system of promotion and relegation, the team that came top in the Conference automatically entered the Football League. Naturally this was the ambition of all Conference clubs, and Fisher had a better chance than most because they could attract the best players with the highest wages, despite drawing crowds of only two hundred, as Dogan Arif was a leading gangster who had amassed a fortune from armed robbery, drug trafficking, contract killing and other racketeering-related activities in London's underworld. As well as paying his players handsomely, he also ploughed large amounts of money into improving the club's infrastructure, which police later realised was money laundering.

For a while Fisher's ambition seemed realisable, as every season they finished near the top of the table and twice reached advanced stages of the FA Cup, by coincidence each time losing 1-0 to a Bristol club, first Bristol Rovers and then, the following season, Bristol City. He had already made enquiries about the club taking over the site of the Millennium Dome to use as a stadium.

I used to attend Fisher's post-match press conferences, where Dogan would jovially supply me and my fellow hacks with drinks and quotes in a relaxed, informal interview. He could well have had a gun on him but what was that to me? It was interesting, because I had never met a gangster before. I had met some dodgy dealers, crooks calling themselves businessmen, but a gangster was something completely different. One Saturday after a match he failed to appear. He had been arrested. He got his seven years for conspiring to supply £8m worth of cannabis. He was said to control the family fortune from jail. The family maintained ties with relatives in Turkey who oversaw shipments arriving in mainland Europe. In September 2000, now released from jail, Dogan was ranked seventh in the *Sunday Times'* 'Criminal Rich List'.

Following the downfall of the Kray brothers, the Arifs were one of several criminal organisations who took control of the London underworld including Clerkenwell crime syndicate the Dailey gang and the Brindle family with whom the Arifs were engaged in a highly publicised gangland war throughout the 1990s, which ended in eight murders.

The Arif family had settled in the Old Kent Road area in the 1950s. They built up a business around property, pubs and clubs. By 1980, led by brothers Dennis, Mehmet and Dogan, they had become one of the most feared gangs in south London, and soon the Arifs were considered the leading crime family in the whole of London. In 2004 the *Irish Daily Mirror* called the Arifs 'Britain's No 1 crime family'. The London *Evening Standard* reported that the godfather of the family was Dogan, 'said to favour attracting someone's attention by sticking a gun down his mouth'.

Another brother, Bekir, one of seven brothers in the family, had convictions dating back to 1977, when he was imprisoned for his role in an armed robbery that resulted in the death of a security guard. In May 1999 Bekir, known as 'The Duke', was convicted of conspiracy to supply 100kg of heroin worth £12.5m and jailed for twenty-three years.

He told the jury during his trial that he was nothing more than a 'Del Boy' businessman, referring to the wheeler-dealer main character in the television comedy series *Only Fools and Horses*. He claimed he had no idea he had become involved in a drugs deal. But police cameras and listening devices had recorded hundreds of hours of conversations between Bekir, his associates and a drugs supplier. The conversations were recorded in October 1997 during a year-long police surveillance operation.

Passing sentence at the Old Bailey, the judge told Bekir: 'Your role was plainly that of principal and your conduct was as cynical and dishonest as has been your defence. In my view there is no mitigation.'

Bekir was the third of the seven brothers to receive a major prison sentence. Dennis and Mehmet are currently serving twenty-two and eighteen years respectively for an armed robbery in which an accomplice was killed. Wearing Ronald Reagan masks and wielding shotguns, they were arrested in Reigate, Surrey, as they attempted to rob a Securicor van. Mehmet, who was driving a pick-up used in the robbery, was shot by police but survived. His passenger, Kenneth Baker, was armed with a sawn-off shotgun, and shot dead as he attempted to open fire on officers.

Dogan, having served his term, went to live a life of luxury in the Turkish republic in north Cyprus, which had no extradition treaties with the outside world. He has a secluded £2m villa near the coastal town of Lapta, with minders who are constantly armed.

Without Dogan's financial support Fisher swiftly declined. The first team was relegated two seasons in a row, making promotion to the Football League impossible. But the club continued to run a thriving youth section, which Ahmet proudly joined - and then left, as he lost all interest in football, concentrating on *jihad*.

Now calling himself Abu Abdullah, Ahmet was at the centre of arguments with the trustees at the Finsbury Park mosque. After Hamza's arrest in 2004, he became more outspoken.

He was accused of being an al-Qaeda official after he gave a controversial interview to the American news channel CNN in February 2006. In a second interview with CNN in August, he said the attack on the World Trade Centre was 'a deserved punch on the nose' for America and described Prime Minister Tony Blair as 'fair game' for a terrorist attack. He relished the news that insurgents had killed coalition soldiers in Iraq and Afghanistan. His hatred of non-Muslims was matched only by his contempt for *munafiqs*, the Arabic word for hypocrite, which he used to describe any Muslim who did not support *jihad*.

Ahmet boasted he would happily go to prison for fifty years if he got the chance to publicise his hate-filled views in the media but after only a few hours of questioning at Paddington Green police station he started having claustrophobia-induced panic attacks.

In the bleak high-security Belmarsh prison in Woolwich where he was sent to serve part of his term, fellow defendants spoke of him 'cracking up'. Said to have become paranoid, he accused them of being MI5 spies, and sacked his legal team. He now pleaded guilty, which they maintained was a desperate attempt to be released early. They said he was ridiculed and friendless.

There Ahmet had to endure much more vilification of his religion than outside, for in prison strangely was a freedom not to be found in the free air, since infidel prisoners could curse Islam without fear of arrest as they were already arrested. Despite his earlier infidelophobia, only in prison did he learn just how much Islam was hated.

Another problem was not realising that non-believing South Asian criminals call themselves Muslims in order to get preferential treatment and to frighten other criminals, who feel, with some justification, that Muslims are capable of anything. A report by Nick Francis in the *Sun* revealed that South Asian drug dealers reason that if Muslims were going to be considered extremists they may as well use that fear. One said, 'The reality is that Asian gangs don't care about religion but with Islam comes fear, and with fear comes power… Young Muslim gangs aren't worried about what Allah makes of their criminal ways - they don't believe in it to that extent. Through religion we can even use mosques as a safe place away from the police or other gangs.' Francis claimed that most of Britain's prisons are dominated by Asian gangs calling themselves Muslim. They are allowed prayer meetings every Friday, which is free time away from the guards, so they can plan new crimes and make new contacts. Muslims also get better food. They have money sent in for their kitchens from Muslims outside and receive special *halal* dishes.

And, according to an anonymous inmate of high-security prison Long Lartin, 'If we attempt to cook pork in the communal kitchen it is deemed dangerous, even a threat to your life.' In a letter to prisoners' magazine *Inside Time*, he wrote, 'The kitchen is usually occupied by 90% Muslims and we have been told if we cook pork we will be stabbed.'

In Belmarsh, Ahmet himself had to be isolated in a hospital wing for his own safety after telling Muslims the *Koran* does not justify violence (a bizarre stance considering he was inside for plotting to blow up people). He also upset them by stepping in to protect a warden they were attacking.

He remained a devout Muslim, praying five times a day in Belmarsh, where the nastiest men in the country are cooped up not knowing what to do with themselves to relieve their boredom and frustration.

Their day starts at 8am when they are let out of their cells (which warders are now supposed to call 'rooms'). This is a particularly dangerous time for the warders. The prisoners have been locked up for thirteen hours and are tense. The warders never know if they are going to get a kettle full of boiling water thrown at them. Prisoners add sugar so the hot water sticks to the skin. After exercise, meals (warders are not allowed to use the word 'feed' because that is what animals eat) and recreation, the prisoners are returned to their 'rooms' for the night at the uncomfortably early hour of 7pm, still bursting with virile energy. Naturally they hate this. They yell, bang tin cans against the bars and kick their doors.

Ahmet, in the prime of life, while his compatriot-in-crime Dogan sunned himself in the beautiful land of their fathers, was an incarcerated figure of ridicule, who, after rolling out his prayer mat and saying his prayers, laid on his bunk for the entire evening. To his chagrin, he was not even called any more by his adopted Muslim name.

A Muslim convert sentenced with him, a young Jamaican named Kibley da Costa, who changed his name to Abdul Khaliq, had the same problem. He told the court his family would not use the name. 'Mummy has not adapted to Abdul Khaliq,' he said.

BANGLADOSH
Currying favour in the East End

ACROSS the Thames from Greenwich, the East End has been taken over by rogues from Bangladesh, leaders of a horde so big and influential that one East End district has been officially renamed Banglatown. So many Muslims now live in the East End that every Friday thousands kneel on sheets of blue tarpaulin laid in the road for prayers because the mosques are packed out.

(No other group would be allowed to regularly block the road like this. Maybe a new red-bordered triangular warning sign will be devised, which, instead of showing silhouettes of running children or an elderly couple walking with a stick, will show a silhouette of a crouching Muslim.)

Bangladeshis began arriving in the East End in the 1970s, at the same time as the Greater London Council changed the policy for the allocating of council housing, switching from one based on a waiting list, in which local couples with young children lived in overcrowded conditions with parents, sometimes waiting patiently for many years, to one based on need. This new criterion naturally favoured the many newcomers from Bangladesh, for they were indisputably homeless - they had voluntarily left their Bangladeshi home. It is recorded that even at this early stage of mass immigration, any locals who voiced concern in the Housing Department at what they regarded, justifiably, as foreigners jumping the queue, were threatened with having the police called to deal with their crime of racism.

Bangladeshis exploited the new rules with aggressive campaigning and an organised squatting movement. Some Bangladeshi men started taking over empty properties in 1973, in preparation for the arrival of their families.

The first mass Bangladeshi squat was organised by one Abbas Uddin, who later, significantly, became the first Bangladeshi councillor in the borough of Tower Hamlets.

The Bengali Housing Action Group, BHAG, was formed in 1974 to unite the various squatting groups that had sprung up. Its acronym was clever, neatly expressing its predatory nature - *bhag* in Bengali means 'tiger'. The force and concentration of the *bhag*, the tiger, were used as the settlers made the area their territory, helped by having Cllr Abbas Uddin in a position of authority and power.

The mayor of Tower Hamlets is now a vile Bangladeshi named Lutfur Rahman, who had been sacked by Labour as its candidate over his close ties with the extremist Islamic Forum of Europe and concerns over vote-rigging. He was deselected after Labour's Helal Abbas submitted a dossier to the National Executive Committee claiming Rahman had been 'brainwashed by extremists'. Abbas, who was backed by an MP named Rushanara Ali, was installed in his place - and lost.

Labour was thrown into chaos by Ken Livingstone campaigning for Rahman, who ran as an Independent but was backed by a number of busi-nessmen including a millionaire 'curry king' named Shiraj Haque, and the campaign was marred by dirty tricks, including the distribution of 90,000 copies of a freesheet in Bengali carrying smears against Abbas, calling him the 'wife-beating candidate' and a racist.

Abbas had been installed as Rahman's Labour replacement rather than John Biggs, second in the Labour selection, despite Biggs being eminently well qualified, having spent his life representing the area. The party thought one thing disqualified him: he was not Bangladeshi.

Rahman slickly said in his victory speech, 'The people of Tower Hamlets spoke today. All I want to do is serve the people. Please work with me. What this campaign shows is that the will of the people will always prevail.' Afterwards Rahman, now running an Olympic borough with a billion-pound budget, refused to answer questions about dirty tricks, saying, 'This is about my victory, nothing else.' On the steps of the town hall about three hundred Bangladeshis chanted his name. The London *Evening Standard* carried an ominous photograph of the scene - a London town hall over-run by jubilant swarthy foreigners.

The same noisy mob have brought a menacing atmosphere to the council chamber. The council's Tory group leader, Peter Golds, who is Jewish and gay, reports he has suffered racist and homophobic abuse from the gallery, and in May 2012 a councillor named Kosru Uddin was arrested for allegedly threatening to kill a fellow councillor named Rania Khan in a Town Hall argument. During an extraordinary confrontation there was chaos and screaming that was described as a 'violent fracas' by onlookers, begun when Khan referred to Uddin as a *chamcha*, a Bengali word that translates as spoon but is used to mean lackey or lickspittle. He is then said to have had an angry confrontation in the council chamber with Khan's mother, also a councillor, named Lufta Begum. Khan, the cabinet member for culture on the council, is a Rahman supporter. Golds said, 'The meeting was extremely acrimonious and unpleasant.' Police had already been called to the Tower Hamlets council chamber several times after Bangladeshis had taken it over.

And political and financial corruption had also immediately become endemic. Livingstone was rewarded with electoral fraud throughout Tower Hamlets in an attempt to help him regain the position of mayor of London. (In spite of Livingstone's scandalous history of tax avoidance, cronyism and treacherous support of Argentina during the Falklands War and for Islam, Labour was backing him again in his mayoral bid.) Rahman was hopeful his close contacts with Livingstone's circle would ease his way back into the Labour Party before too long. Livingstone had achieved this; why not Rahman?

Other Rahman supporters, even the millionaires among them, were rewarded with council flats or heavily subsidised housing association houses meant for people who could not afford to buy property in the area, in which there is an acute housing shortage.

Haque, the 'curry king' who supported Rahman, is now the tenant of a housing association house in Bethnal Green despite owning at least eight properties, a chain of restaurants and a supermarket.

Similarly, a councillor named Shahed Ali in 2011 registered a new company, giving his home address as a flat which is a council property, though he owns at least four properties - an Essex curry restaurant, the neighbouring property and two flats. The council flat came on to the public record soon after Ali announced his support for Rahman.

Ali later that year liquidated his restaurant business owing £25,000 to the Inland Revenue, though the restaurant continues to be owned by him, and still serves its curry dishes as it always has done. In December he bought himself a Porsche worth £87,000. As Rahman's cabinet member for the environment, he is responsible for spending about £70m of taxpayers' money. He says however he will not be paying the money his company owes in tax.

Another corrupt East End councillor was Shelina Akhtar, an Independent (who had previously stood for Labour) for the Spitalfields and Banglatown ward in Tower Hamlets, sacked after being jailed for sixteen weeks for dishonestly claiming tax benefits for a property in Blackwall Way, Poplar.

This was the second time an offence of this nature was committed by the thirty-three-year-old. During the time of the offences - which ran for two periods between November 2009 and September 2010 - Akhtar was actually living somewhere else and sub-letting the first property.

She failed to turn up in court at the start of the case, sending a doctor's letter saying she was ill and therefore unfit to stand trial. The judge dismissed her claim and issued a warrant for her arrest. The warrant was later withdrawn when Akhtar surrendered herself.

The housing benefit that she falsely claimed totalled £1,085. Prosecutor Michelle Fawcett said: 'She is a local councillor and the case, therefore, was more serious. This defendant has previous convictions for identical matters.'

In July 2010 at Thames Magistrates' Court, Akhtar had been handed one hundred hours of unpaid work and ordered to pay £250 costs after being found guilty of dishonestly claiming jobseeker's allowance, housing benefit and council tax benefit.

She won her seat in the May 2010 elections, where she originally stood as a Labour candidate but later defected to become an Independent to work alongside Rahman. She was one of eight Tower Hamlets councillors who were expelled from the Labour Party after deciding to support Rahman when he was dropped as Labour's candidate for mayor.

Even after her first conviction and her arrest on the second set of charges, she claimed in her official council engagement log to have attended thirty-four hours of 'group meetings' with Rahman supporters and thirty-eight hours of 'mayoral engagements' with Rahman himself.

Electoral Commission rules state that a councillor will be automatically barred from office if sentenced to three months in jail or more, so Tower Hamlets Council had no choice but to sack Akhtar.

But the most outrageous case of Bangladeshi corruption in the East End is that of Baroness Uddin.

Like her compatriots Shiraj Haque and Shahed Ali she too lives in a subsidised dwelling despite being rich and owning properties - in her case, including a family mansion. Baroness Uddin lives with her husband and their five children in a rented, heavily-subsidised housing association house in Tower Hamlets meant for a needy family. It is a pleasant 1990s-built three-bedroom gaff in a quiet street.

Her corruption is so great it requires a separate essay, which follows.

BARONESS UDDIN
Muslim faith and acting in bad faith

BARONESS Uddin was born in a Bangladeshi village. She moved with her parents to London in 1973, when she was thirteen, and grew up in the East End, where her family were given a council house.

She began her ascent to power and riches as a pushy, precocious adolescent speaking poor English who had been in the country just five years. She formed and led 'community working groups'.

Then, aged twenty, she somehow got a job as a Youth and Community worker with the Young Women's Christian Association. Why a Christian organisation should employ a Muslim is unknown.

Then she became a liaison officer for Tower Hamlets Social Services; and then manager of Tower Hamlets Women's Health Project. She then worked for Newham social services. In 1990 she became the second Uddin to be elected a Labour councillor in Tower Hamlets, following Abbas Uddin, and the first Bangladeshi woman to hold such an office of a local authority in Britain. She then became the deputy leader of Tower Hamlets council. Having long campaigned for increasing the skills of South Asian women, she created the first purpose-built education and training centre for them in Britain, the Jagonari Centre, in the East End.

This is the sort of career that usually can, at most, as one approaches retirement age, be rewarded with an MBE. But for some reason she was raised to the peerage, aged only thirty-eight. She swore in by saying '*Allahu akbar*' while holding a copy of the *Koran* as she took her seat in the House of Lords.

(The first Muslim life peer, Baron Ahmed of Rotherham, also took his oath on the *Koran*, as did our most senior Muslim politician, Baroness Warsi - see next essay.)

Baroness Uddin was the youngest woman on the benches and the only Bangladeshi woman to be appointed to the Lords, to which she was invited 'for her contribution to the advancement of women and of disability rights'.

Her fraudulent activities quickly followed. Not only did she claim more than £100,000 between 2005 and 2010 by stating her main residence was a small flat in Maidstone, Kent, when in fact it was her Tower

Hamlets heavily-subsidised housing association house, she also claimed mileage to Kent even though neighbours said the flat had never been occupied and remained unfurnished.

This also allowed her to claim the second-home allowance on her London house, a scheme that ostensibly exists to compensate politicians living outside London for the cost of accommodation close to Parliament.

Her London home is owned by Spitalfields Housing Association, which gets more than £37.8m a year from the taxpayer. The average rent for its properties is £124 a week, a sixth of the market rate.

With stunning hypocrisy, Baroness Uddin has had the gall to make a speech in the House of Lords about the plight of 25,000 families on the waiting list for social housing in East London.

Her husband even denied having a property in Kent when questioned on the issue, and she has appeared on the electoral roll at her London address from 1996 to date. Additionally her Facebook page states how she has lived in the East End of London for more than 30 years.

Baroness Uddin claimed £29,675 for accommodation in 2007/8, when the maximum daily accommodation claim was £165 a day. Her bill represents a claim at the maximum possible rate for 179 days, more days than the Lords actually sat that year.

Scottish National Party MP Angus Robertson called for an investigation by House of Lords authorities and the police. Based on Land Registry records, it shows Baroness Uddin bought the flat in central Maidstone for £155,000 in 2005.

She has in fact claimed her main home has been outside London since 2001, earning an extra £83,000 as a result. Despite repeated questioning she refused to state the location and details of her main home for which expenses were also claimed. Baroness Uddin also has one of the highest claims for overnight subsistence of any member of the Lords.

Legally, a housing association tenant must live in social housing as their 'only or principal home', so she could have breached her agreement. But because the tenancy is joint with her husband, the housing association says it cannot (or will not) evict her.

Peter Golds, the Tory group leader on Tower Hamlets Council, wrote to Housing Minister Grant Shapps demanding her eviction.

'It's scandalous that a state-funded housing association has not kicked her out,' he said. 'Lady Uddin is depriving a low-income family of a home which was built for the needy at public expense.'

The House of Lords authorities passed her case to the police for possible prosecution for fraud. The *Daily Telegraph* reported that she was refusing to co-operate with the police investigation, declining to answer any questions. The Crown Prosecution Service announced that she would not face any charges on the grounds that a senior parliamentary official ruled that a peers' 'main house' might be a place they visit only once a month. There were no indications that the expenses would be paid back.

Further expenses claims by Baroness Uddin were later discovered when the *Sunday Times* revealed that her family owns a mansion in Bangladesh. The mansion was described as made of Italian marble with tiles and mosaics. It was built after she became a peer.

The *Sunday Times* wrote: 'A Labour baroness who lives in low-cost social housing has a palatial family holiday mansion overseas. Baroness Uddin lives in a three-bedroom house in Wapping, East London, which is heavily subsidised because it is intended for people who cannot afford to buy property in the area.

'However, for almost a decade her husband Komar has also owned the mansion in Bangladesh, which is decorated with Italian marble and bears a crest similar to that of the House of Lords on its gates.'

The Uddins' mansion overlooks a river in a market town where Komar comes from. One friend of the family there said Komar proudly filmed the entire construction process and used to boast about every detail of the costs, from the specially carved doors to the marble brought in from Italy. Another friend who had visited the property said, 'It is a very beautiful house. There were tiles and mosaics and a very beautiful balcony.'

The *Sunday Times* continued, 'At the same time, the Uddin family has continued to live in the Wapping house. The area has some of the most desperate housing needs in the country.

'The Uddins are likely to pay about £6,000 in rent a year for their house, based on average prices for properties owned by the housing association. This is a third of the cost of normal commercial rents for a property of that size.

'There are still unanswered questions about claims by Uddin for the period between 2001 and 2005. She got £83,000 in overnight allowances for staying in London - even though she bought the Maidstone flat only in September 2005.

'One of Uddin's friends said she had not owned a property in the UK before her brother bought the Maidstone flat on her behalf. Uddin said her main home in 2001-5 was a property outside the capital but has failed to provide any evidence for this, despite repeated questions.

'From September 2005 she designated the Maidstone flat as her main home. This enabled her to claim about £100,000, even though her closest neighbours said they had never seen her there.'

A plumber who went into the flat said it looked like someone had left it ages ago. It was very dusty. There was an old mattress on the floor of one bedroom, where the bed was not made. In the other bedroom was a fold-up clothes dryer. He confirmed the flat did not look lived in.

However, Uddin claimed she travelled by car to and from the Maidstone flat at least every week the Lords was sitting. This allowed her to also claim £2,000 in mileage.

On October 18th 2010 the House of Lords Privileges and Conduct Committee ruled that Baroness Uddin had 'acted in bad faith' and recommended that she should be asked to repay £125,349 as well as being suspended from Parliament until Easter 2012.

But in November 2011 it was revealed that no formal mechanism existed to prevent Baroness Uddin's return to the House of Lords, even if she refused to repay the expenses that were fraudulently claimed, leading many members of her own party to call for her to resign rather than bring the House of Lords into further disrepute.

Still, in December 2011 the House Committee in the Lords recommended that Uddin not be allowed back to the Lords until the outstanding expenses had been repaid. The amount of money quoted in her case, £125,349, is probably the largest amount in any of the House of Commons or House of Lords expenses scandals.

But, like so many of her kind, she thumbs her nose at the authorities. She has kept her title, remains living in the Tower Hamlets house paying rent heavily subsidised by taxpayers, has not faced criminal charges nor repaid a penny.

Uddin, who has held highly-paid directorships in companies such as Carlton Television, claims she cannot afford to repay the £125,349.

Discounting the fictitious programme *EastEnders*, the East End of London is known mainly for bearing the brunt of Nazi bombing. What a tragic irony that it is now home to a horde of invasive foreigners whose leaders, as well as becoming increasingly active and powerful in British politics with a plot to conquer the country, are also shamelessly, utterly corrupt.

BARONESS WARSI
A Gurkha or a Buryat, maybe?

A FEW weeks after that Clash of the Pygmies, the 2010 general election, Conservative Party co-chairman Sayeeda Warsi blamed electoral fraud for depriving her party of an outright majority in Parliament.

Speaking in an interview with the *New Statesman*, Warsi, also a baroness and Britain's first female Muslim cabinet minister, said there were 'at least three seats where we lost, where we didn't gain the seat, based on electoral fraud'.

She refused to say exactly which seats they were, but then conceded that they were 'predominately within the Asian community'.

Asia begins at the Urals in Russia and the Bosphorus at Turkey and ends at the Pacific. This vast area of the world, containing towering mountains, wide lakes, endless forests, the sand of scorching deserts and the ice of the frozen *tundra*, is home to many peoples. So which of them is she talking about? Gurkhas from Nepal? Buryats from Siberia? No, of course not. What she actually meant, and was too coy to say, was Muslims from Pakistan.

Later that day she pulled out of an appearance on the BBC's *Question Time*.

According to reports, police had launched fifty criminal inquiries into claims of voter fraud during the election. In the same week that the interview was published five Muslim Conservative Party members in Bradford, including two former councillors, were jailed for their part in a postal vote scam aimed at getting a Tory candidate elected. Former Bradford city councillors Jamshed Khan and Reis Khan were jailed along with Mohammed Sultan, Mohammed Rafiq and Alyas Khan for attempting to pull off a vote fraud that involved making up more than 3,000 fraudulent votes. And in May of that year, a Conservative councillor in Walsall, Mohammed Munit, appeared in court charged with voter fraud relating to his victory in the May 2008 elections. There were also many cases of electoral fraud by Muslims in the Liberal Democrat party. And all this in a country that had never experienced voter fraud before.

But it is not surprising, for Pakistan, one of the most corrupt countries in the world, has no record of successful participatory democracy and politics is used solely for personal gain and enrichment.

Voter fraud has been imported by settlers from a part of the world that has no tradition of democracy or probity. They have brought their culture with them. Culture is not like a coat that can be taken off at the arrival desk of an airport. A deeply dishonest people remain deeply dishonest wherever they are; and, as E M Forster showed in his 1924 novel *A Passage to India*, justice, legality and honesty mean nothing on that sub-continent, where court cases are decided not on what is true or false but on what is the less untrue. Before independence, two years were spent on drawing up a constitution, only for India to slip back into its customary manner of conducting politics, through routine nepotism and bribery backed up by the occasional assassination. In England, Muslim politicians at all levels, from local councillors to government ministers, are inordinately involved in corruption scandals, both electoral and financial. They instantly claim innocence and many of the cases remain unproven but the sheer number of these suspicious cases is itself compelling.

The *New Statesman* interview was conducted at the Conservative Campaign Headquarters, the interviewer being a fellow ethnic named Mehdi Hasan, who reported that at her first cabinet meeting she wore a pink-and-gold '*shalwar kameez*', with no explanation, as though the likes of me could be expected to know what a *shalwar kameez* is. This sort of stuff is becoming increasingly common in articles about Muslims. It illustrates Muslims' sinister cultural encroachment.

And during the interview, Hasan glances over his shoulder at the open-plan office behind him, where dozens of young men and women are hunched over computers - 'yet,' he writes, 'Warsi and I seem to be the only non-white faces on the entire floor'.

Now he knows how the likes of me feel on any bus in London.

Warsi also once said on television that fellow Muslims who had just pelted her with eggs in a Luton street were 'idiots who do not represent the majority of British Muslims'. Apparently Muslims who plant bombs or throw eggs do not count. She accused them of not being proper Muslims. They said the same of her. They shouted abuse at her in Arabic and Urdu even though she was born in Dewsbury and they too were born in England, apart from one who came from Jamaica, who converted to the religion of peace while in jail for grievous bodily harm.

When Labour was still in power she also said she did not want to see more Muslim members of parliament. Speaking at a dinner in Yorkshire in honour of the president of Kashmir on May 4th 2010, she said, 'One of the lessons we have learnt in the last five years in politics is that

Muslims that go to parliament don't have any morals or principles.' She contradicts this thought in the *New Statesman* interview. Now, when she is herself in a position of power, she sets herself up as a champion of all ethnics: 'We will play our role and then we will have a new generation of BME [Black and Minority Ethnic] politicians.' This new generation of 'BME' politicians will naturally include many Muslims.

In May 2012 Warsi was continuously in the news for a string of murky dealings, both financial and political. First it was divulged that she had knowingly concealed rental income from a property she owned; then that she claimed reimbursement for rent she had never paid; then that she failed to register with the House of Lords authorities a controlling stake in a company, in breach of regulations that instruct peers to declare their commercial interests, especially if they are the principal shareholders in a company; then that her business partner, a relative named Abid Hussain, went along with her on a governmental trip to Pakistan, where he met leading politicians; and then that Hussain had been a prominent member of Hizb ut-Tahrir, the radical Islamic group the Conservative Party had promised to ban while in opposition. (Warsi described Hussain as a 'community activist'.)

This is not a paltry record of intertwined financial and political skulduggery, even for our most senior Muslim politician.

Warsi had been on seventeen trips abroad while in office, when her role as party chairman was simply to adopt relations with ethnics in Britain.

She claimed a payment for accommodation while actually being at the home of party donor Wafik Moustafa, who said he did not charge rent. She said she made an 'appropriate payment' to tenant Naweed Khan for the times she stayed at the property.

Khan is a party official who is her special aide.

Warsi's business transactions, revealed in company documents, led to calls for a detailed investigation into whether she had broken parliamentary rules. Statements for her company, spice-maker Rupert's Recipes, said she owned a 60 per cent stake, and the Lords code of conduct states peers must register share holdings in companies in which they hold a governing interest or if they are valued at more than £50,000.

The code requires 'unremunerated directorships' to be registered, as 'certain non-financial interests may reasonably be thought to affect the way members of the House of Lords discharge their public duties'.

Particulars also emerged of the extent and funding of Warsi's travels abroad. Of her seventeen trips, eight were paid for by the government, one by an Azerbaijani expatriate group - and, in a sinister revelation, two were funded by Saudi Arabia. Six had taken place since January and funding details had yet to be made public.

All this, remember, is after she cunningly said Muslims should not be trusted in politics as they are invariably corrupt. You will never get to the bottom of Muslim duplicity. Speaking of an honest Muslim politician is like speaking of a tabby panther or a striped leopard.

You will see from the names of all those she has dealings with that, though born in Yorkshire, Warsi has lived her entire life in a Pakistani environment. She took her oath in the House of Lords on the *Koran*; got married in an Islamic ceremony; all her friends and business associates are Pakistani...

Is it any wonder she has conducted her political and financial affairs according to Pakistani customs? How could it be otherwise?

In January 2011 she made a speech in which she attacked 'bigotry' against Muslims. Prejudice against Muslims has become widespread and socially acceptable in Britain, she claimed, blaming 'the patronising, superficial way faith is discussed in certain quarters, including the media'. She described how prejudice against Muslims has grown along with their numbers, partly because of the way they are often portrayed. She called this portrayal 'taking a pop at Muslims'. This is like saying conservationists are taking a pop at Japanese knotweed.

Islam was not discussed in our land before its vast hordes came here. We never had any problems with its customs and beliefs, any more than we did with those of cannibals or head-hunters. Now we are expected to take seriously Islamic customs and beliefs just because Muslims are among us in their millions demanding that we do so. Now there is indeed a growing disquiet at the increasing influence of the Islamic world-view. Perhaps this is due, not to a lack of understanding, but greater under-standing, of what the *Koran* and Muslim traditions teach.

Warsi also revealed that she raised the issue of Islamophobia with the Pope on his visit to Britain, urging him to 'create a better understanding between Europe and its Muslim citizens'. This, while Christians were being driven out of Iraq, churches were being bombed in Egypt, non-Muslims are permanently banned from entering Mecca, and in her parents' homeland of Pakistan Christians suffer not only from prejudice and intolerance but also from legal discrimination, enshrined in law based on *sharia*. In March 2012 the Grand Mufti of Saudi Arabia said that all churches in the Arabian Peninsula must be destroyed. Grand Mufti Sheikh Abdul Aziz Bin Abdullah, the highest official of religious law in

Saudi Arabia, as well as the head of the Supreme Council of Islamic Scholars, cited the Prophet Mohammed, who said the Arabian Peninsula is to exist under only one religion.

The useful idiots who call for tolerance and a 'dialogue between civilisations' are easily refuted by the authority of the *Koran*, which has many verses rousing believers to wage *jihad* against unbelievers. Anti-Jewish sentiments are frequently found in Islamic religious texts, and apostates are to be executed, according to *sharia*.

Further, the attitude of pious Muslims to non-Muslims can be seen in the Arabic word *kafir*, which goes far beyond the neutral English word unbeliever. A *kafir* is to be shunned. Muslims are not to befriend such people (The *Koran*, 3:28). Schoolchildren in Saudi Arabia are taught to not even shake hands with a *kafir*.

Can it be that *kafirs* such as me understand Islam better than the likes of Baroness Warsi?

Medieval thinking was steeped in superstition, a phantasmagoria of devils and sorcerers, of saints and relics, of the threat of a ghastly hell inhabited by demonic hybrids, part-human and part-monster. As late as the eighteenth century someone as educated as Samuel Johnson could still be terrified at the prospect of hell. No sane person would choose to live in such a world. And yet this is the world Muslim politicians will take us back to.

It was above all ignorant; and the prophets occupied a special place in that realm of ignorance. Baroness Warsi has urged us to respect Muslims because they unquestioningly accept that the *Koran* is the infallible word of their deity. Why should we? Not only is it not true but their wrong, mistaken, silly belief threatens our civilisation.

KEITH VAZ
Burglar with the keys

LIKE all mafias, the race relations version has several branches. This makes it hard to describe in an episodic book. Trundling on about one of the many devious ethnics operating in this country, I would come across a new name and do some research with a view to mentioning him or her in passing, and discover a whole new biography of deceit, greed and corruption.

Thus I came across the Right Honourable Keith Vaz MP. While I was writing about the Millennium Dome, he was mentioned as having been fêted by the dodgy Hinduja brothers for becoming the first Asian MP since 1929. Seeking to add just a couple of sentences, I look him up, and find he is himself involved in so much scandal that linking him to other ethnic duckers and divers in different essays requires daunting organisational skill. All these ethnics are connected to each other. Sayeeda Warsi, a Tory, is a close chum of Labour peer Lord Ahmed of Rotherham (whose biography also contains many scandals, mostly over him inappropriately supporting Islam but including as well a term in jail for killing someone while simultaneously driving and texting). And Vaz, as well as being a pal of the Hindujas, is also a mate of Ali Dizaei, the hero of another of my essays. I could not embark on a long digression on Vaz while writing mainly about the Hindujas in one essay, nor in the one devoted to Dizaei.

Reluctantly, for I have a straightforward Anglo-Saxon mind and cannot easily follow the tangled threads of Muslim deceit, I realised that Vaz had to have an essay of his own, even though this would inevitably entail some overlapping with other essays. So here it is.

Keith Vaz was born in 1956 in Aden, Yemen, to Indian parents. They fetched him to England with them when he was nine. In 1987 he became MP for Leicester East, elected by 16,000 Muslim voters. From then until 1992 he was a member of the powerful Commons home affairs select committee, which has an important voice in issues of law and which he now heads.

He says he is a Christian but this is clearly part of his immeasurable cunning, for throughout his career he has supported Islam, and been supported by Muslims. He is a Muslim in all but name.

In 1989 he led a protest in Leicester against author Salman Rushdie when Rushdie published his fantasy novel *The Satanic Verses*. Addressing 3,000 Muslim demonstrators, Vaz said, 'Today we celebrate one of the great days in the history of Islam and Great Britain.' This great day for Great Britain included the act of book-burning. He predictably accused Rushdie of Islamophobia.

After the alpha males of Islam told their hordes a passage in the book was blasphemous, *The Satanic Verses* was banned in India and was the subject of a violent riot in Pakistan. A *fatwa* issued in Iran called on all good Muslims to kill or help kill Rushdie and his publishers, after which he was put under police protection. Thirty-eight people were killed in violence against those connected with the book, including a translator in Japan. Among the supporters of the murderous Muslims was Prince

Charles. He said, 'I'm sorry but when someone insults the profound beliefs of a people...'

(The heir to the throne has a scandalous record of supporting Muslim murderers. He is matey with Chowdhury Mueen-Uddin, one of England's most important Muslim leaders who is being charged with eighteen murders by a war crimes tribunal in his native Bangladesh. Mueen-Uddin, who has a senior role in the NHS, is accused of abducting, torturing and killing eighteen journalists, academics and doctors in Bangladesh's 1971 bloody war of independence with Pakistan. His tortures included gouging out the eyes of an eye doctor, cutting out the heart of a cardiologist and cutting off the breasts of a woman journalist. He is now director of Muslim Spiritual Care Provision in the NHS and is also chairman of the Multi-Faith Group for Healthcare Chaplaincy. And Charles also aided the building of the Finsbury Park mosque that became a centre of al-Qaeda.)

Vaz wrote in the *Guardian* urging Rushdie not to publish *The Satanic Verses* in paperback, maintaining, like Lady Uddin and all the other Muslims who have reached positions of power in our liberal, open society, that 'there is no such thing as absolute freedom of speech'.

In that same month, Vaz caused outrage when he suggested that an IRA bomb detonated at Leicester Army Recruitment Office might have been planted by the British army.

And in May 2012, after eight Pakistanis and an Afghan were jailed for sex-grooming under-age English girls in Rochdale, the latest in a long string of such cases, all concerning gangs of Muslims (see essay, 'In Beds with the Enemy') he said fatuously, 'I don't think it is a particular group of people.' Many of the girls were repeatedly raped on a bare mattress above a kebab shop.

This immigrant from a hellish country once said he was 'glad that Britain had been transformed'. Britain now more closely resembles the hellish countries the transformers left. Mass immigration is like mass tourism in that it destroys the original attraction.

The serial corruption charges against him began when parliamentary standards watchdog Elizabeth Filkin opened an investigation after allegations that he had accepted several thousand pounds from a solicitor named Sarosh Zaiwalla that he had failed to declare. Both men of course denied the allegations. Additional allegations were made that Vaz had accepted money from other businessmen (all ethnic and all rich).

Mrs Filkin also wrote to Vaz asking how many properties he owned, and he replied three. But BBC Radio 4's *Today* programme revealed that he owned four. It was also discovered that he had transferred the ownership of a fifth property to his mother eight days after Mrs Filkin had requested details of all his properties. Vaz said the timing was a coincidence. The property was put on the market by Mummy Vaz six months after the transfer. Land Registry documents showed that Baby Vaz had become the owner of the property on August 5th 1988, and the Electoral Register showed that it had been his address in 1988 and 1990. Between 1992 and 1996 the property was the address of another ethnic, called Reza Shahbandeh, an Iranian by the sound of his name, who Vaz denied all knowledge of when asked.

The Filkin report cleared Vaz of nine of the twenty-eight allegations of various financial wrongdoings but Elizabeth Filkin accused him of blocking her investigation into eighteen of the allegations. He was censured for a single allegation, that he had failed to register two payments worth £4,500 in total from Zaiwalla - whom he later recommended for a peerage. Mrs Filkin announced in the same month a new inquiry that would focus on whether or not a company connected to Vaz received a donation from a charitable foundation run by the Hinduja brothers.

Two months before, immigration minister Barbara Roche had revealed in a written Commons reply that Vaz, along with Peter Mandelson and other MPs, had contacted the Home Office about these brothers. She said that Vaz had made inquiries about when a decision on their application for British citizenship could be expected.

Vaz had become the focus of Opposition questions about the Hinduja affair and many parliamentary questions were tabled, demanding that he fully disclose his role. Vaz said through a Foreign Office spokesman that he would be 'fully prepared' to answer questions put to him by Sir Anthony Hammond QC, who had been asked by the Prime Minister to carry out an inquiry into the affair.

Vaz had known the Hinduja brothers for some time. He had been present when the charitable Hinduja Foundation was set up in 1993, and also delivered a speech in 1998 when the brothers invited Tony and Cherie Blair to a *diwali* celebration (see the O_{no} essay).

On January 26th 2001 PM Tony Blair was accused of prejudicing the independent inquiry into the Hinduja passport affair, after he said that the Foreign Office minister Keith Vaz had not done 'anything wrong'.

In March Vaz was ordered to fully co-operate with a new inquiry launched into his financial affairs by Mrs Filkin. Foreign Secretary Robin Cook urged Vaz to fully answer allegations about his links with the Hinduja brothers. Vaz met Mrs Filkin on March 20th to discuss a complaint that the Hinduja Foundation had given £1,200 to a company run by his wife, in return for helping to organise a Hinduja-sponsored reception at the House of Commons. Hubby Vaz had previously denied receiving money from the Hindujas, but insisted that he made no personal gain from the transaction in question.

In June he said he had made representations during the Hinduja brothers' applications for British citizenship while a backbench MP. Tony Blair also admitted that Vaz had 'made representations' on behalf of other ethnics (all of them filthy rich).

On 11th June Vaz was officially dismissed from his post as Europe Minister. The Prime Minister's office said that Vaz had written to Tony Blair stating his wish to stand down for health reasons.

In December Mrs Filkin cleared Vaz of failing to register payments to his wife's law firm Fernandes Vaz by the Hinduja brothers but said he had colluded with his wife, who works under her maiden name of Maria Fernandes, to conceal the payments. Mrs Filkin's report said that the payments had been given to his wife for legal advice on immigration issues. (Mrs Vaz specialises exclusively in immigration and nationality law.) It concluded that Hubby Vaz had gained no direct personal benefit, and that Commons rules did not require him to disclose payments made to his wife. But Mrs Filkin did criticise him for his secrecy, saying, 'It is clear to me there has been deliberate collusion over many months between Mr Vaz and his wife and to prevent me from obtaining accurate information about his possible financial relationship with the Hinduja family'.

And now on to the next Vaz scandal.

In 2002 he was suspended from the House of Commons for a month after a standards and privileges committee inquiry found he had made false allegations about a former policewoman, Eileen Eggington. The committee said that Vaz 'recklessly made a damaging allegation against Miss Eggington to the Commissioner, which was not true, and which could have intimidated Miss Eggington or undermine her credibility'.

Eileen Eggington, a retired police officer who had served thirty-four years in the Metropolitan Police, including a period as deputy head of Special Branch, wanted to help a friend, Mary Grestny, who had worked as personal assistant to Vaz's wife. After leaving the job, Mary Grestny dictated a seven-page statement about Mrs Vaz to Miss Eggington in March 2001, who sent it to Mrs Filkin. The statement included allegations that Mr and Mrs Vaz had employed an illegal immigrant as their nanny and that they had been receiving gifts from rich ethnic business-men such as the Hinduja brothers. The allegations were denied by Vaz and the committee found no evidence to support them.

Later that year Vaz complained to the police that his mother had been upset by a telephone call from 'a woman named Mrs Egginton', who claimed to be a police officer. The accusations led to Miss Eggington being questioned by police. Vaz also wrote a letter of complaint to Mrs Filkin, but when she tried to make inquiries he accused her of interfering with a police inquiry and threatened to report her to the Speaker of the House of Commons. Miss Eggington denied that she had ever telephoned Vaz's mother and offered her home and mobile telephone records as proof. The Commons committee decided she was telling the truth.

A letter to Mrs Filkin from Detective Superintendent Nick Gargan made it plain that the police did not believe that Vaz's mother ever received the phone call and the person who came closest to being prosecuted was not Miss Eggington but Vaz. Gargan said that the police had considered a range of possible offences, including wasteful employment of the police and an attempt to pervert the course of justice. The police eventually decided not to prosecute: 'We cannot rule out a tactical motivation for Mr Vaz's contact with Leicestershire Constabulary but the evidence does not support further investigation of any attempt to pervert the course of justice.'

The complaints the committee upheld against Vaz were that he had given misleading information to the standards and privileges committee and Elizabeth Filkin about his financial relationship to the Hinduja brothers, that he had failed to register his paid employment at the Leicester Law Centre when he first entered Parliament in 1987 and that he had failed to register a donation from the Caparo group in 1993.

It was concluded that he had 'committed serious breaches of the Code of Conduct and showed contempt for the House' and it was recommended that he be suspended from the House of Commons for one month.

So - on we go to the next scandal vis-à-vis a Vaz.

In 2001 it was revealed that he had assisted Anglo-Iraqi billionaire Nadhmi Auchi in his attempts to avoid extradition to France. Opposition MPs called for an investigation. Auchi was wanted for questioning by French police for his role in the notorious Elf Aquitaine fraud scandal that led to the arrest of a former French Foreign Minister. The warrant issued by French authorities in July 2000 accused Auchi of 'complicity in the misuse of company assets and receiving embezzled company assets'. It also covered Auchi's associate Nasir Abid and stated that if found guilty both men could be jailed for life.

Vaz was a director of the British arm of Auchi's corporation, General Mediterranean Holdings, whose previous directors had included Lords

Steel and Lamont. Vaz used his political influence on GMH's behalf; this included a party in the Park Lane Hilton to celebrate the twentieth anniversary of GMH on 23rd April 1999, where Lord Sainsbury presented Auchi with a painting of the House of Commons signed by Tony Blair, Opposition leaders and more than a hundred other leading British politicians. Lord Sainsbury later told the *Observer* that he did this 'as a favour for Keith Vaz'. In May 1999 Vaz resigned his post as a director after he was appointed a minister. In a statement to the *Observer*, a GMH spokesman said that Vaz had been invited to become a GMH director in January 1999, yet company accounts showed Vaz as a director for the financial year ending December 1998.

Labour confirmed in May 2001 that Auchi had called Vaz at home about the arrest warrant to ask him for advice. A spokesman said that Vaz 'made some factual inquiries to the Home Office about the [extradition] procedure'.

Vaz helped many other rich ethnics as well as the Hinduja brothers to get a British passport. It was becoming clear that he was for sale and that he had only two stipulations - those he helped had to be rich and had to be brown.

Despite this, not only did Vaz remain an MP - he was even promoted after his lying and corruption had been exposed.

He had extended his Labour power when the party's national executive committee voted to resurrect the defunct Black Socialist Society (BSS) in 2006. As part of this, the party set up an Ethnic Minority Taskforce. (Thus following the hateful new trend of ethnics ganging up when the only thing they have in common is not being white.) Tony Blair appointed Vaz to chair this taskforce. When membership of the BSS exceeded 2,500 in early 2007 the society qualified for its own seat on the NEC. Vaz was elected to this post in March 2007.

More power came in July, when he was elected chairman of the home affairs select committee, in unusual circumstances. Select committee members are usually proposed by the quasi-independent committee of selection, but Vaz was nominated by Commons leader Harriet Harman.

As the select committee has a crucial role in law-and-order issues, appointing the ducker and diver Vaz its head was like entrusting your spare set of house keys with a known burglar.

Suspicions were inevitably soon roused. In September 2008 Vaz faced pressure to explain why he failed to declare an interest when he intervened in a court case on behalf of a 'very, very dear friend'. Race lawyer Shahrokh Mireskandari was a convicted Iranian fraudster, a Labour Party donor who played a role in several racial discrimination cases against the Met Police, including representing Britain's top ethnic policeman, Assistant Commissioner Tarique Ghaffur, in his £1.2m claim against Met chief Sir Ian Blair. Mireskandari paralysed Scotland Yard with his campaign of multi-million-pound litigation, even boasting he would 'destroy Sir Ian and his golden circle' of white officers.

His accomplice in many of the cases was a fellow Iranian, Met Commander Ali Dizaei, head of the National Black Police Association, who had just been suspended after the *Daily Mail* revealed disturbing links between the pair and who would shortly be jailed for corruption (see next essay).

The Solicitors Regulation Authority began an investigation into Mireskandari's legal firm, Dean and Dean, in January 2008 after a number of complaints about its conduct. Vaz wrote a joint letter with fellow ethnic Labour MP Virendra Sharma to a High Court judge, brazenly on official House of Commons stationery, trying to halt proceedings against the firm, which had lavished hospitality on him and his family, including the best seats at Wembley Stadium football matches and pop concerts. He cited a complaint he had received from Mireskandari and alleged 'discriminatory conduct' in the authority's investigation into Dean and Dean. The authority was forced to set up an independent working party to look into whether it had disproportionately targeted ethnic lawyers for investigation.

At the time that Vaz wrote to the judge, Mireskandari's firm was involved in a long-running and costly legal dispute with an airline over a £500,000 legal bill that threatened the solicitor with bankruptcy. In the letter to the High Court, Vaz wrote, 'We are deeply concerned about the apparent way in which this ethnic-minority firm of solicitors has been dealt with.'

Mireskandari had convictions in the United States and bogus legal qualifications, and was suspended from practising law in Britain.

Also in September 2008, Vaz came under pressure when it was revealed that he had sought the private views of Prime Minister Gordon Brown in connection with the select committee's independent report into government plans to extend the detention of terror suspects. The *Guardian* reported that e-mails suggested that Vaz had secretly contacted Brown about the committee's draft report and proposed a meeting as 'we need to get his [Brown's] suggestions'. An e-mail was sent in November 2007 to Ian Austin, Brown's parliamentary private secretary, and copied to Fiona Gordon, Brown's political adviser. Another leaked e-mail showed that Vaz had also sent extracts of the committee's draft report to a former Lord Chancellor for his comments, when, according to Parliament's standing orders, the chairman of the select committee cannot take evidence from a witness without at least two other committee members being present. This was compared to a judge deciding a case privately contacting one of the parties to seek their suggestions.

Naturally, Vaz was in on the Great Parliamentary Expenses Scandal. As reported by the *Daily Telegraph*, he claimed £75,000 in expenses for a second home just twelve miles from his main home. His main home is declared to be in a north-west London suburb. Bought with his wife for £1.15m in 2005, it is forty minutes from Westminster by Tube, raising questions as to whether billing for a second home (a £545,000 Westminster flat) was essential for his work as an MP.

He also flipped property: claiming for the Westminster flat's service charge and council tax (£2,073 and £1,022), then renting this flat out, switching his second home to a house in his Leicester East constituency, fitting it with around £16,000 of furniture and soft furnishings, as well as £600 a month of un-receipted cleaning, service and repair bills, then flipping back to the Westminster flat again, allowing mortgage interest to be claimed on the flat once more.

Vaz is clearly odious. And his biography teems with fellow repellent ethnics.

How could all those lords and leading Labour politicians be fooled? Were they blinded by political correctness or greed or, what seems to be increasingly common, a convenient mixture of both? I was at a meeting on a local issue once with Tory MP Jonathan Aitken shortly before he was jailed in 1999 for perjury and perverting the course of justice, by which time he had enjoyed many years in the top echelons of British politics. I saw immediately that he should not be trusted or believed. Can a gor-blimey Cockney like me be more perceptive than our lords and masters? Types like Aitken and Vaz should not fool mature, experienced people.

Vaz apparently has one of the most affected voices in politics. *Daily Mail* parliamentary observer Quentin Letts has written that Vaz blatantly uses the home affairs select committee as a publicity vehicle for his own self-grandeur. 'Most committee chairmen,' Letts wrote, 'will talk of witnesses being at the "table". Mr Vaz talks of it as a "dais".' Vaz revels in events such as Diversity Night at Labour Party conferences.

Vaz was caught out so many times acting dodgy you wonder how he survived all those years. His nickname in the Commons is 'Vazeline', as nothing sticks. But he not only survived - he prospered. After many charges over many years, Labour still appointed him to chair one of the most powerful select committees in Parliament - where he soon faced yet more accusations of corruption. Detectives went to court to obtain production orders requiring several high street banks to provide full details of his financial affairs. They apparently showed huge sums of money for an MP earning less than £100,000 a year being moved in and out of his bank accounts. The police alleged that the funds were 'of a suspicious nature'. Vaz said that he was 'not worried' and that the sums had come from a house sale and 'a drawdown of equity'.

At his prayers, Vaz must daily praise whatever deity it is he genuinely worships - Allah, God or Mammon -for removing him from Yemen and placing him among the gullible of the Earth.

As my father would have scornfully said: 'Gertcha, you cow-son.'

ALI DIZAEI
Not One of Us, indeed

E-MAILS from the Metropolitan Police these days have a long disclaimer at the bottom, stating that the message must not contain 'racist, homophobic, transphobic, sexist, defamatory, offensive, illegal or otherwise inappropriate material'. The fact that a police force has 'illegal' at the end of the list and 'racist' at the top shows us the way we live now.

In this environment, Muslims have managed to reach top positions in the police not because of their ability but because they are members of the race relations industry, which now resembles a powerful mafia. Nothing moves in Britain without its consent, without being checked first against dodgy quotas on 'diversity', 'equality' and 'fairness' - in effect, seeing what is in it for them, which is their only interest, just like mobsters.

The sentencing in February 2010 of Met Police commander Ali Dizaei to four years imprisonment, convicted of perverting the course of justice and of misconduct in a public office, revealed how much this mafia has contaminated the fight against crime.

This corrupt Iranian thug made the highest ranks solely because he ran the National Black Police Association, when the only thing black about him was his hair dye.

Olive-skinned, contemptuously swaggering around London with his third wife, the implausibly named Shy, who looked more like a gangster's moll than Mrs Dixon of Dock Green, he resembled an archetypical

Mafioso more than a policeman.

As a cunning manipulator of racial politics, he naturally fooled staff at the BBC, who had made his dishonest memoir, *Not One of Us*, its Radio 4 Book of the Week. Interviewees are required by the BBC to state their ethnic origin beforehand. Checking any further than that is obviously not deemed necessary.

Dizaei comes from a family of *baseej*, a police force notoriously thuggish in a part of the world where the only law is the arbitrary *fatwas* of Islamic rulers, who regard issues such as allowing men to wear a tie or to shave their beard as 'complicated religious questions' best left to them to resolve otherwise it 'weakens the government', and the idea of justice is *sharia* laced with the revenge of clan feuds. You would have thought that this alone would have made even the BBC wary.

Then, once in Britain, he had the gall to write a PhD thesis on racial discrimination in the British police force and, bursting with insincere indignation, to become a regular media commentator on ethnicity and religion.

All this sort of thing, and there is a lot of it, is done with a degree of cynicism incomprehensible to indigenous Britons. It is this incomprehension, this inability to understand such evil, which allows the settlers to get away with it.

In 2006 a secret, high-level Met Police report concluded that Muslim officers were more likely to be corrupt than indigenous officers because of their cultural and family backgrounds. Of course, the report, which was actually written by an Asian detective chief inspector, was howled down as 'racist' - exactly the same defence that Dizaei hid his dirty deeds behind. Dizaei's career shows that the racial politics of modern policing has deliberately divided the public it serves into the 'white community' and the 'black community'.

It is a form of racism, cynically and lucratively propagated by the likes of Dizaei.

Even before his conviction for corruption, he had faced allegations of taking drugs, spying for Iran, accepting bribes, using prostitutes, fiddling his expenses, abusing his police credit cards and fabricating evidence.

The investigation into the allegations, code-named Operation Helios, cost £4m and involved more than fifty officers. It was the most expensive operation against a single officer in the history of Scotland Yard.

He was suspended in January 2001, charged with perverting the course of justice, misconduct in public office and submitting false mileage expense claims, but welcomed back in September 2003 by Commissioner

Sir John Stevens after being cleared of the charges, and promoted.

The National Black Police Association, of which Dizaei was president, demanded a full independent inquiry into the investigation. This demand was naturally met, and the inquiry, headed by Lord Morris, concluded that the investigation was disproportionate and that Dizaei's race and ethnicity played a part in the manner in which the investigation was conducted. Not only was Dizaei acquitted; after he was reinstated he then brought his own claim for racial discrimination in the conduct of the investigation and was awarded £60,000.

All these suave knights and lords, with their plummy accents, being taken in and exploited by a slimy thug from Tehran!

Dizaei then made even more money from the case by publishing his version of his career to date and of the Operation Helios investigation. *The Times* and BBC Radio 4 serialised it, and the *Guardian* gushed.

In June 2007 another knight, Sir Ian Blair, the Met Police chief commissioner, apologised for Operation Helios. In March 2008, at the third attempt, Dizaei was promoted to the rank of Commander. Six months later he was the subject of a complaint alleging he had improperly provided advice to a solicitor named Shahrokh Mireskandari, a fellow Iranian, close friend and convicted fraudster who was defending a woman accused over a fatal hit-and-run accident. (See next essay.)

The Metropolitan Police Authority was still investigating this alleged misconduct, which he naturally denied, when he was suspended again just six days later, accused of yet another offence, this time the one for which he was finally nabbed. Outside a London restaurant called Persian Yas owned by his uncle, Sohrab Eshragi, in which Dizaei had just eaten a meal with his wife after attending a ceremony at New Scotland Yard for new recruits, the officer assaulted and falsely arrested a young man who said in court he came from Iraq and was named al-Baghdadi, in a dispute over £600. At the trial a police doctor told the court injuries Dizaei claimed had been caused by al-Baghdadi were probably self-inflicted. When officers arrived, Dizaei had handed them the metal mouthpiece of a *shisha* pipe, held on al-Baghdadi's key ring, and claimed he had been stabbed with it, but the doctor concluded that two red marks on his torso did not match the pipe.

The jury also heard that Dizaei rarely paid for his meals and while at the restaurant habitually left his unmarked car on a double yellow line.

Eshragi told the jury Baghdadi was 'a crook, basically', adding, 'His history... everybody knows he's not a good gentleman. I was worried about this man. He was in a fight before and disappeared before the police arrived.' Confirming the perception that Dizaei resembled a Mafioso, Baghdadi told the jury he saw Dizaei as a gangster 'like Tony Montana', the Cuban mob boss played by Al Pacino in the film *Scarface*.

But in December it was revealed that al-Baghdadi had used a false name and nationality when he appeared in court. Documents seen by BBC News suggested al-Baghdadi's real name was Maleki and that he too was Iranian. This contradicts statements he gave to the Independent Police Complaints Commission and evidence he gave under oath in court.

These people ALL seem dodgy. Uncle Eshragi's history probably does not bear too much scrutiny either. We are constantly expected to forget that the mindset of these interlopers is different to ours.

Maybe their descendants will assimilate (though Dizaei's son goes on about what a fine, noble chap his father is, which does not augur well, and this again raises the question of who will assimilate whom) but even if they do, my generation meanwhile has to co-exist with this generation, share our land with swarthy duckers and divers, dusky spivs, brown adventurers up to every trick going and inventing more. I feel surrounded by alien predators. And they are encouraged in their criminal activities by Britain's farcically lenient sentences.

In one month alone a woman living near me in Greenwich named Olajumoke Ajadi was sentenced to do a bit of unpaid work as punishment for a series of thefts from purses, bags and desks while working as a cleaner in a school, and a single mother named Moriam Ologunro living in the Greenwich area of Thamesmead, the 'fraud capital of Europe', was jailed for only eighteen months for fraudulently obtaining benefits worth £100,000 over ten years, first using a false birth certificate and false passport to get an NHS job and then claiming income support, housing and Council Tax benefit under a false name.

In Iran, the charge of 'corrupt on Earth' carries the death penalty. Where Dizaei comes from, he would have been topped. Olajumoke Ajadi too, wherever it is she comes from, would certainly have been imprisoned, while Moriam Ologunro would have been put away for far longer than a laughable eighteen months.

Apparently, at his trial Dizaei glared at the jury throughout, unable to desist from his habitual attempted intimidation. But the jury refused to be bullied; as did inmates at Edmunds Hill prison in Suffolk, where, just days after being sent there, he had excrement poured over his head and was knocked unconscious in a violent attack. This was good news. It showed that at least the lower orders understood the nature of the likes of Dizaei even if the knights and lords were fooled.

The combination of Britain's libel laws and the power of the race relations industry has made investigative journalism an expensive luxury. Newspapers that reveal anything dodgy about any ethnic risk losing a lot of money.

In late 2009 Dizaei received huge sums in damages from no fewer than three newspapers. In September he won a High Court action against the *Daily Mail* and the London *Evening Standard* over what they had written about him. They were forced to issue an apology and pay substantial damages. On receipt of the apology he issued further proceedings against the *Daily Mail* for an allegedly defamatory article. Then, only three months later, in December, he accepted a substantial payout and an apology from the *News of the World* for false allegations in an article. The paper backed down and apologised in the face of legal action from Dizaei, after it claimed the officer 'employed an illegal immigrant as his right-hand man and took him to the heart of the British establishment.' The paper also paid the said immigrant, one Ace Bakhtyari, who was later jailed for having a fake passport and deported. One can fairly assume not only that Bakhtyari kept his payout but that he immediately obtained a new false passport and came straight back. The problem is, Britain's libel laws act in the reverse manner to the rest of British law, which is the widely acclaimed principle of being innocent until proven guilty. When it comes to libel, the opposite applies. What with this twisted legal bias and the risk of newspapers being branded racist, ethnics, especially Muslims, make merry. Dizaei, already earning a considerable salary as a leading policeman, supplemented his earnings with vast sums from litigation. In 2009, it amounted to a lucrative career in its own right.

Dizei was released after serving a year of his sentence when the Court of Appeal quashed the conviction. But then guilty verdicts for a second time, at a retrial, meant there was now no way back for him, although his new three-year sentence would be reduced by the fifteen months he had already spent behind bars. He had won his job back with the Met before the retrial and would remain a senior police officer until the bureaucratic formal process of throwing him out of the force could be completed. He would then be sacked for gross misconduct and could face losing all or part of his pension under further measures aimed at punishing corrupt officers.

What a performance, all caused by rampant political correctness!

An article in the *Daily Mail* on February 16th 2012 by a former colleague of Dizaei showed how political correctness was ruining Britain's police. Former detective chief superintendent Kevin Hurley wrote that the Met has been paralysed by fears of being branded racist.

'The Metropolitan Police continues to stumble from one self-inflicted crisis to another, weakening its ability to fight genuine crime,' he wrote. 'It is a force that for too long has been gripped by a dangerous cocktail of poor leadership, politically correct dogma, warped priorities and tactical incompetence.

'Those flaws have been graphically illustrated by the appalling case of Ali Dizaei, the notoriously corrupt Iranian-born officer who was this week sent back to jail for a second time after his conviction for perverting the course of justice.

'Only an organisation obsessed with the creed of diversity and lacking in moral integrity would have allowed a swaggering, criminal bully like Dizaei to rise up its hierarchy and gain a senior position.

'He should have been drummed out long ago, not constantly rewarded with promotion.

'But Dizaei is a symbol of the rot within the top ranks of the Met. Too many senior officers seem to have forgotten that their central duty is to protect the law-abiding British public. Instead of taking tough decisions - like challenging Dizaei - they indulge in politicised manoeuvres designed to protect their own backs and further their own careers. The high command of the Met inhabits a culture where cowardice is dressed up as pragmatism, where a talent for spouting jargon trumps determination to take on the criminals. The biggest losers from this approach are not just ordinary decent British citizens, but also the constables out on the streets, often doing a heroic, selfless job only to be undermined by their selfish, careerist superiors. It is no exaggeration to say that the Met frontline are lions led by vacillating donkeys.

'As a former detective chief superintendent at the Met myself, I have been appalled by the Dizaei saga. I was actually the borough commander in West London at the time when he tried to frame al-Baghdadi. The incident ultimately led to two criminal trials and Dizaei's conviction this week. But from the moment Dizaei hauled al-Baghdadi into Hammersmith police station on charges of assault, I had the severest doubts about his tale. This was not just because of the unconvincing nature of his story that al-Baghdadi had attacked him, which turned out to be a pack of lies, but also because of Dizaei's appalling record of dishonesty, corruption and abuse of office.

'Like almost everyone else in the Met, I had always known that he was a wrong 'un.

'On a superficial level, he could be charming and personable, but his easy manner barely disguised his dark side. He was a figure of epic venality, ambition and ruthlessness, his entire career geared towards furthering his own interests, regardless of the legality or probity of his methods. When he joined the Met as a superintendent in 1999, former colleagues in the Thames Valley Police, where he was an officer for more than a decade, warned us to beware, telling us of his enthusiasm for playing the race card to achieve his ends.

'But in a climate of hysteria over accusations of "institutionalised racism", the Met's top brass were desperate to recruit more ethnic minority senior officers.'

The warnings from Thames Valley Police were grimly fulfilled. Dizaei was a master at using fears about racism to thwart any challenge to his increasingly aggressive, self-serving conduct. The National Black Police Association was his chosen instrument with which to bully and intimidate the Met's hierarchy.

'He became a law unto himself. The Met's terror of taking any action against him made him feel even more invincible.

'Even the Independent Police Complaints Commission, normally all too keen on enforcing the politically correct code, urged the Met to discipline Dizaei - but top commanders were too pusillanimous to do so. Most had prospered by avoiding tough decisions.

'They were not going to risk all by taking on a formidable adversary who loved to smear his critics as racists.

'Thanks to their lack of courage, he got away with behaviour that would have led to the sacking of any other Met employee.

'So he gained a PhD with a thesis attacking the Met on racism, while in 2007 he wrote an autobiographical book called *Not One of Us*, which contained severe criticism of the Met. Yet instead of being sacked for gross disloyalty, he was promoted.

'Can you imagine any successful company that would behave in such a pathetic manner towards a senior member of staff making money out of trashing the firm's reputation?

'Fuelled by his invulnerability, Dizaei's ego was legendary among the rank-and-file. On one occasion he alleged that two constables had damaged his private car. On investigation, it turned out that the damage was inflicted by one of his many mistresses.

'Any other officer behaving in that way would have been disciplined or sacked, especially because he had shown such a contemptible lack of respect towards the two constables.

'But nothing happened to Dizaei, protected as he was by the shield of spurious anti-racism. On another occasion, he drove into the station and parked so carelessly that he blocked the exit of the emergency response vehicles. Almost immediately, the emergency vehicle was needed. "Can you move your car?" called out the officers, needing to rush to the scene of the incident. "You move it," replied Dizaei, throwing them the keys and marching brazenly inside. That was the arrogance of the man. He had no sense of public service, not a shred of decency.

'He was a brute in uniform, who once threatened to kill the mother of one of his mistresses "like a dog". But he was clever enough to exploit the political pressures on the Met for more than a decade.

'And, of course, political correctness was to blame for the pusillani-mous way the rampaging gangs of looters and vandals - many from ethnic minorities - were dealt with during the riots last summer. Paralysed by political correctness and accusations of racism, terrified of being account-able for controversial decisions over public order, the Met's senior officers allowed the mob to control the streets for five days before launching a crackdown. This is not the police force that the public deserves.'

The Met has its own group for black officers, the Metropolitan Black Police Association. Having these groups is of course racist, as a Tory peer admitted on April 5th 2013. Lord Waddington said there was 'nothing more institutionally racist' than the existence of the Metropolitan Black Police Association.

His comment came after the group said on the 20th anniversary of the death of Stephen Lawrence that discrimination at Scotland Yard was still institutional.

(This anniversary was marked by a renewed tsunami of publicity rarely seen for anyone outside royalty or religion, a nauseating, sinister tidal wave engulfing the country.)

The group also said it 'works hard to attract officers from black and ethnic communities'. Following the trend in these numerous Black and Minority Ethnic organisations that have appeared all over the country covering most aspects of human life, it is dominated not by blacks but by Muslims.

Throughout the Muslim world men join the police for the money they can make from intimidation, bribery and their own crimes, often violent, which go far beyond the old occasional British 'bent copper', and, natu-rally, quite a few do this here also. In 2010 a corrupt London policeman named Mesut Karakas was jailed for fourteen years for leading an ethnic gang in a plot to kidnap a bank manager and steal £100,000.

Karakas was sentenced for planning to snatch the Lloyds TSB manager and his wife in London. The five-man plot involved staging fake roadworks outside the bank manager's home as a distraction. But the gang was under surveillance by Scotland Yard detectives who bugged Karakas's car and arrested them. Transcripts of the gang detailing the plan reveal Karakas referring to his fellow-ethnic gang members as 'bruv' and 'blood' and to his Met colleagues, childishly, as though acting in an American crime film, as 'feds'. The 'feds' found four sets of false number plates, industrial gaffer tape, dust masks, a balaclava, handcuffs, industrial ear protectors and the van intended for the snatch.

Other law enforcement agencies, as well as the police, are also vulnerable to Muslim corruption. The Crown Prosecution Service (CPS), which reviews evidence gathered by police and then decides if cases should go to court, has irresistible opportunities for bribery for a case to be dropped.

In July 2010 a Muslim senior crown prosecutor who accepted a £20,000 bribe to drop a case was jailed for four-and-a-half years. Sarfraz Ibrahim, who worked for Gwent CPS, was caught in a police sting. He was jailed at Swansea Crown Court for corruption, perverting the course of justice and misconduct in a public office.

He and an associate were put under surveillance and an 'integrity test' devised to see whether he and the associate were prepared to act corruptly. The associate was eventually identified as a man called Saifur Rahman Khan, who lived near Ibrahim. Over four months, until their arrest, both men were gradually tested to see whether they were honest. A fictional scenario was created which presented them with a chance for Ibrahim to use his position to intervene in a case in exchange for money. It centred on an assault case which Ibrahim was able to 'manoeuvre' in such a way that he was eventually able to mark it 'no further action'. Unknown to either man, the case was bogus, created to test their honesty.

In the West the comprehension of the true principles of criminal jurisprudence has grown over the last two hundred years with the growth of science - with the triumph, in mental habits, of ordered reason and experience and the understanding of the nature of evidence. In Muslim countries justice remains the plaything of superstition, fear, folly and greed. Naturally, law is ignored - or exploited. Muslims in our land retain or adopt this attitude - including many who enter the legal profession.

The judge told Ibrahim his actions had had a 'potentially corrosive effect beyond this case'. Indeed. With the likes of Dizaei and Ibrahim operating at high levels, Muslim corruption has the potential to corrode law enforcement in this country. Gertcha, you cow-sons.

THE THIEF-TAKER'S LAWYER
and friends

'ALI Dizaei recommends Shahrokh Mireskandari to Tarique Ghaffur'. This could have been a headline in some South Asian or Middle Eastern newspaper in 2008. Ghaffur and Dizaei were both top policemen, Mireskandari a leading lawyer. All are Muslims.

But all three were operating not in Dhaka or Mecca but in London; and, well I never, would you believe it, two of them have criminal convictions! All three belonged to the race relations mafia.

Ghaffur's parents were Punjabis who fled to Uganda to escape the massacres of Muslims by Hindus. When South Asians were expelled from Uganda by black racist dictator Idi Amin, he came with them to Britain, where he became a top bobby, in fact Britain's highest-ranking Asian Muslim police officer. He often used his position to comment on issues of alleged racism in the police service, and on alleged discrimination against Muslims as a factor in creating terrorists.

Like so many Muslims in Britain, Ghaffur was devout when it suited him and ignored Islamic law when it did not. His first marriage ended after he committed adultery, which, as even us infidels know, is a crime under Islamic law for which the punishment is death by stoning. The stones thrown during the execution 'should not be so large that the offender dies after a few strikes, nor so small as to fail to cause serious injury.' In Iran adultery is an offence 'against divine law' and is the only crime punishable by stoning. Men are buried up to the waist while women are buried up to the chest. In Afghanistan under the Taliban it once happened that a woman still alive after lengthy stoning had to receive the *coup de grâce* of a rock dropped on her head. Ghaffur, following his Islamic capital offence, lived on to marry again, benefiting from living in a civilised country at the same time as plotting to undermine its institutions.

In June 2008 he accused the Metropolitan Police of racism, claiming, among other things, that he was not properly consulted over the proposed law involving forty-two-day detentions for terror suspects, and on August 28th took the issue further by accusing Met Police Commissioner Sir Ian Blair of racial discrimination against him personally and confirmed speculation that he would take proceedings against Sir Ian and the Metropolitan Police Service at an employment tribunal, claiming £1.2m.

In the following days, Ghaffur claimed he had received death threats that he said he believed came, in part, from within the Metropolitan Police Service. He said he considered a leave of absence as a consequence and hired a firm of personal bodyguards. Although he made these claims to the press he did not report the death threats to the police, saying he had lost faith in the ability and willingness of the police to protect him.

On November 25th the Metropolitan Police Authority announced that Ghaffur had agreed an out-of-court settlement for £280,000 in his racial discrimination claim against Scotland Yard. Both sides agreed to a confidentiality clause and two days later Ghaffur resigned from the police.

Obviously, accepting only a fraction of his claim and losing his job and credibility was a defeat for Ghaffur. He had made one big mistake.

He had been persuaded by his close friend Dizaei, who was himself mired in litigation and whose own criminal activities were at last soon to be proved, to appoint as his lawyer a convicted Iranian fraudster - Mireskandari.

Shahrokh Mireskandari, as well as being one of the many dodgy ethnic donors to the Labour Party, had already played a role in several racial discrimination cases against the Met Police. While working on behalf of Ghaffur he was suspended from operating as a solicitor following exposure by the *Daily Mail* as a convicted conman with dubious legal qualifications. This was a huge embarrassment for Ghaffur.

After stepping down, Ghaffur described himself as 'an old-fashioned thief taker'. This could be construed as some kind of Freudian slip, for the original thief-takers were the most successful gangs of thieves of the eighteenth century, all the while appearing to be the nation's leading policemen. The most famous of them, Jonathan Wild, in 1718 called himself 'Thief Taker General of Great Britain and Ireland'.

Leading a gang of thieves, Wild would arrange the return of property stolen by his own underlings. To keep up the belief that he was working legitimately he would even hand over some members of his own gang, who would be publicly hanged. He himself was hanged in 1725. Wild's hanging was a great event, and gallows tickets were sold in advance for the best vantage points, at the bottom saying, 'Pray bring this Ticket with you'.

By his testimony, he sent more than sixty thieves to the gallows. His 'finding' of lost merchandise was private but his efforts at finding thieves were public. Wild's office in the Old Bailey was a busy spot. Victims of crime would come even before announcing their losses, and discover that

Wild's agents had 'found' the missing items. After his villainy was exposed he became a symbol of corruption and hypocrisy.

Ghaffur, our modern thief-taker, should have been more careful than to hire a bent lawyer. A former colleague of his said: 'It's a great shame Tarique didn't sniff out his lawyer as being a crook.'

It was also a blow to Dizaei. Already deep in scandal, he was now suspended from duty over allegations he had an improper relationship with his close friend Mireskandari.

The Solicitors Regulation Authority, the legal profession's watchdog, scrutinised Mireskandari's qualifications, conduct and the running of his West End law firm, Dean and Dean, investigating him over alleged dishonesty, accounting malpractice and other serious misconduct.

The *Daily Mail* had revealed that Mireskandari, who insisted on being addressed as 'Dr' and claimed to hold a BSc (Hons), MA (Hons) and JD (Hons), gained his law degree from a discredited 'mail drop' university in Hawaii that was shut down by the authorities. He failed to provide evidence of his qualifications. He told clients he had twenty years' legal experience in the US before coming to Britain but US authorities had no record of him practising as an attorney.

The *Daily Mail* also disclosed that he was a convicted conman who in 1991 was given three years' probation over a tele-marketing scam in California. Following the revelations, the High Court in London heard that he had produced a forged letter of reference from a former employer to gain entry to the law profession in Britain.

There were also allegations of other serious 'dishonesty' as well as a 'whole list of concerns' raised about Mireskandari's conduct by all levels of the British judiciary, the hearing was told. Investigators removed dozens of boxes of files from the offices of his law firm.

Mireskandari would charge his clients as much as £750 an hour, among the highest fee rates in London. Such fees paid for his £2m flat overlooking Lord's cricket ground, decorated with pictures of himself.

'Masterminding' was how many described his powerful influence. Mireskandari, a liar, crook and friend of billionaires and royalty, boasted while working for Ghaffur that he was 'tearing the Met apart' and that his team was 'running rings' around the force.

These comments backfired spectacularly when Ghaffur was suspended for the 'media campaign' run by his advisers. Most of Ghaffur's pay-off consisted of legal costs and his salary up until the following April, when his contract was due to expire.

Meanwhile Mireskandari was pursuing his own £10m action against the Solicitors Regulation Authority, which he accused of having racially harassed and defamed him. Both the Met and the SRA are mighty institutions. But Mireskandari also had powerful associates, many in the race relations industry.

As well as being the legal representative to his best chum, the fellow crooked Iranian Ali Dizaei (see previous essay) who was the president of the National Black Police Association, for which Dean and Dean provided official legal advice and which was backing Ghaffur, Mireskandari was also a confidant of the Labour chairman of the home affairs select committee, the Rt Hon Keith Vaz MP (see essay before that) who had called Mireskandari the best lawyer in Britain and one of the best in the world; who, at the Palace of Westminster, presented his pal with the 'Asian Solicitor of the Year' award; and who was a frequent VIP guest of the bent solicitor. Mireskandari represented royal families, billionaire tycoons such as the dodgy Hindujas (see essay, 'O$_{no}$') and powerful politicians, many of whom were invited to his annual Christmas party at a Park Lane hotel, which was recorded on a 'souvenir' DVD.

At social functions this crooked lawyer rubbed shoulders with the likes of Leader of the Commons and Labour Party deputy leader Harriet Harman. And then Ghaffur, number three at Scotland Yard, goes and puts his legal affairs into the hands of this fraudster with doubtful qualifications who had left a trail of appalling litigation and blighted lives. As with the Hindujas, Mireskandari was like Trollope's Melmotte, the deceitful financier with a murky past in *The Way We Live Now*. All were simply buying their way into society. As Melmotte says in the novel, 'All I have to do is throw a few dinners and the thing is done.'

Mireskandari was born in Iran in 1961 and came to Britain aged six. At thirteen he was sent with his older brother to a Dorset boarding school. Having failed all his O-levels, he moved to London, where he failed the exams again. He returned to Iran just before the Islamic Revolution, upon which he fled to Turkey. He says he rode five hundred miles on a pony across the mountains but you cannot believe anything these types say and he probably just caught a scheduled flight at the airport. From Turkey he went to the eastern United States, where he claimed political asylum and lived with his father.

By the late 1980s he had moved to California, where he worked as a chauffeur, driving the gold Rolls-Royce of a Beverly Hills businesswoman. But he wanted riches himself, and to this end he set up a tele-marketing business, cold-calling victims to say they had been 'randomly selected' for discount international air fares and hotel accommodation.

Part of the deal was to buy a camera.

Of course, the air fares were not bargains, the camera's price was grossly inflated and when travellers turned up at the hotels with their certificate from Mireskandari's firm 'no one knew anything about it', said the district attorney's office.

When he had gone through all the phone books in the area he moved to the town of Ventura, where he opened an office in an employee's name and bought a Jaguar with a mobile phone using her social security number to get the account. With a friend, he charged up to $1,000 at a time to her credit card and never paid her back. Because he would not pay for anything she eventually had to file for bankruptcy. He even bought a piano on her credit. He then moved on to a Los Angeles law firm, his job being to find clients among the town's wealthy Iranian expatriates. When he was charged with the tele-marketing offences the firm stood by him, representing him in court.

As the *Daily Mail* reported: 'The DA's office wanted a prison sentence, his attorney remembers. However, when he faced the judge on "misdemeanour" charges (which carry a maximum jail sentence of twelve months) it became evident that a plea bargain could save him from the Ventura County Jail. According to the attorney involved in the case, which was reported in the *LA Times*, Mireskandari was sentenced to three months on the "criminal justice work release programme".

'This meant that instead of being jailed around the clock he would be allowed to attend his place of work during the day, returning to prison in the evenings. The weekends would be spent behind bars. Because Ventura was a ninety-minute drive from his new place of work, said the attorney, he was allowed to attend a government-run halfway house fifteen minutes from his office. "He was living with persons about to be released from the prison system." On top of this Mireskandari had to serve three years' probation and pay back $6,814 to his known victims.

'In time, according to his ex-attorney, California state law allowed Mireskandari to have his guilty plea bargain struck out and his criminal record expunged. The conviction became spent.

'Unless, of course he applied for something like an attorney's licence.

'Senior attorneys at the LA law firm which employed him were persuaded to give him another chance following his conviction. "There was a time when he seemed sincere,' one told the *Mail*. "We tried to help him.

'"His main academic credential was a bachelor's degree from the University of Pennsylvania (the university has no record of it).

'"He had documentation which seemed to support this, although having seen his written work, I am sceptical he could have graduated from any college, anywhere at any time. Nevertheless, on the strength of this degree and our letter of recommendation, he started a law course at a minor local university. Unfortunately he failed his exams miserably at the end of his first semester. He failed his retakes and that was that. I want to make it clear that he never worked for us as a lawyer."

'The attorney said that Mireskandari worked for the LA law firm until the mid-1990s, when the relationship was "terminated and not amicably".

'What would he do next? He would return to the UK and become one of London's most expensive lawyers.

'So how did he manage to accumulate so many letters after his name: BSc, MA and JD, all with honours?

'A profile of him in the *Law Gazette* states that he gained "a business degree in the United States followed by a doctorate in law and a masters in international law".

'This summer the Solicitors Regulation Authority sent investigators to the US to examine the veracity of Mireskandari's qualifications.

'One man they spoke to was Jeffrey Brunton, head lawyer for Hawaii's Office of Consumer Protection. He said the SRA had interviewed him about a law degree which it said had been awarded to Mireskandari by the American University of Hawaii.

'Mr Brunton said the "university" was founded in the early 1990s by a couple from Arizona. They based it in Hawaii because of the "lax laws" at the time. It was then sold to an American-based Anglo-Iranian named Hassan. "He ran the American University of Hawaii until our courts shut it down," said Mr Brunton.'

Of course it is possible Mireskandari has a legitimate law degree from a credible university somewhere. But when the *Mail* asked him repeatedly to specify where he gained his qualifications he refused to answer.

'For the record the State Bars in California and Virginia both said that they had no listing of any licensed lawyer by the name of Mireskandari.

'By 1999, with the discredited Hawaiian doctorate to his name, Mireskandari was back in London and founding Tehrani and Co, Solicitors. His US qualifications were convincing enough for him to be accepted on the Law Society's rigorous Legal Practice Course, a conversion course for overseas-qualified lawyers.

'Surprisingly, perhaps, he passed, qualifying as a solicitor in 2000.

'Did he disclose his conviction?

'A spokesman for the SRA said: "We run a criminal record check as standard practice. All applicants have to divulge all criminal convictions from the past. A conviction would not necessarily bar someone and we use our judgment. But if it had something to do with financial dishonesty that would be a very serious matter indeed."

'By 2003 the firm's name was changed to Dean and Dean, with Mireskandari its figurehead. An LA attorney who knew him says: "I remember him saying there were thousands of personal injury cases in the UK. It was like shooting fish in a barrel."

'Instead, Mireskandari was to specialise in race relations and the wealthy Middle Eastern, Asian and Russian expatriate communities. He plans to open offices in Moscow and Mecca. His "expertise" doesn't come cheap. One former client was charged £10,000 for a day's work.

'An American attorney who has given a statement to the SRA said he had been told it had received numerous complaints "from people who have been cheated out of their life savings and paid for services they never got". One of his clients was Iranian-born academic Dr Sheida Oraki. She employed Mireskandari, then a trainee solicitor, for an agreed fixed fee of £1,000. Yet when it was presented his bill had risen to £19,000. She refused to pay and made a complaint to the Law Society. After litigation she offered to pay, but Mireskandari forced her into bankruptcy as she would not withdraw her complaint. He is still pursuing her for more than £150,000 in costs.'

Another cause célèbre was Mireskandari's even more expensive battle with former client Angel Airlines, which refused to pay a grossly inflated bill of £500,000. A specialist costs judge estimated that a reasonable bill would have been one fifth of that figure. Mr Justice Coulson pointed out that Mireskandari's pursuit of the full fee had occupied fifty days of court time and the participation of twenty-four judges. One fellow judge had described Dean and Dean's case as 'an appalling piece of litigation'.

Mr Justice Coulson agreed. He said, 'The multiplicity of proceedings, appeals and applications is the product of what I consider to be an abuse of process by the proposed applicants, Dean and Dean.'

Mireskandari was finally booted out of the legal profession on June 21st 2012 and ordered to pay £1.4m in costs. He was struck off after it was proved he had faked his legal qualifications and hid his criminal convictions. The conman was found guilty of an incredible hundred and four breaches of the rules governing solicitors' conduct by a central London disciplinary tribunal, which ruled he racked up debts, overcharged clients, conducted improper litigation, failed to keep proper records and used clients' cash to pay staff salaries.

The decision to kick him out of the legal profession followed a six-week misconduct hearing dogged with attempts by him to halt the proceedings. After getting the hearing adjourned for fourteen months, he failed to return from Los Angeles to give evidence, instead bombarding the tribunal with applications to adjourn on medical grounds. He was represented by seventeen barristers but the panel ruled that allegations of dishonesty had been proved, adding that it was 'not credible' that he could have achieved top marks in his doctorate at the discredited American University of Hawaii, while at the same time working full-time and being thrown out of three law schools for poor performance.

It also ruled that 'without a shadow of doubt' he acted dishonestly when he hid his criminal convictions for fifteen counts of tele-marketing fraud in America from the Law Society and the SRA when he returned to England. The tribunal found he racked up huge debts at Dean and Dean and then 'dishonestly and recklessly' used clients' cash to prop up his business. One client's mortgage account fund was pilfered by him to pay off debts. Another client's £200,000 bail bond was withdrawn without permission from the court. When a judge ordered it be repaid, Mireskandari was forced to borrow £250,000 from a client to cover the shortfall. He was also found guilty of reproducing images of a client's injuries, using a make-up artist, before passing them off as police photographs to the home secretary. On being slung out of the profession, Mireskandari claimed he was the victim of a racially motivated vendetta.

With this record of deceit and criminality, could Mireskandari really have represented Britain's top ethnic policeman? Could the Rt Hon Keith Vaz MP, chairman of a committee with a crucial role in law-and-order issues, really had described Mireskandari as the best lawyer in Britain and one of the best in the world? What is occurring?

The likes of Mireskandari and his friends seem to believe they can get away with anything. They play for high stakes, brazen and confident, believing that the game is not one of chance but of skill, and feeling unbeatable with the race card up their sleeves. You cow-sons. Gertcha.

JACK STRAW
'The English as a race are not worth saving'

SETTLERS could not have come to our country in such vast numbers without the connivance of traitors among us. The biggest of these, the one who has wielded the most power, is Jack Straw, home secretary in the last Labour government.

The Labour Party's election manifesto of 1997 said, 'Every country must have firm control over immigration, and Britain is no exception.' On being elected the new leaders secretly adopted a different strategy, that of initiating unrestricted immigration with the deliberate aim of transforming it racially; partly, it seems, according to a gabby former Labour adviser who in 2009 revealed the deceit, to spite the Tories.

The edicts encouraging hordes of settlers were concocted with great subterfuge by Straw, who knew that the indigenous people would strongly object if they were made aware of the full details and implications of such a policy.

The former adviser revealed in the *Daily Telegraph* that Labour ministers secretly threw open Britain's borders to mass immigration to help socially engineer a 'truly multi-cultural' country, and exposed their reluctance to discuss such a move publicly for fear it would alienate its core working-class vote.

Sir Andrew Green, chairman of the Migrationwatch think tank, said: 'Now at least the truth is out, and it's dynamite. Many have long suspected that mass immigration under Labour was not just a cock-up but also a conspiracy. They were right.'

Labour wanted mass immigration to dissolve English national identity and advance the cause of international socialism.

Another possible motive, suspected by many, was that settlers would be likely to vote for Labour in elections.

In the publicity that followed the revelation, it emerged that 20 per cent of Labour seats, INCLUDING STRAW'S, depended on Muslim votes. His constituency of Blackburn has the highest proportion of Muslims in Britain outside London. Twelve per cent of the population of Blackburn was not born in Europe, and no fewer than 25 per cent of its residents are Muslim.

Surely Straw did not care so much about remaining member of parliament for Blackburn that he would jeopardise his civilisation? Was it misplaced altruism or political cynicism, or a mixture of both, that led him to pass his calamitous act? Such mixtures can easily happen and are in fact quite common. Exactly opposite qualities may on occasions be blended in someone's nature.

Straw in fact even admits in his autobiography that he owes his political survival to the votes of settlers, and praises influential Muslim settler Baron Patel of Blackburn for his help in securing these votes.

Patel in turn praises Straw for his work to solve the race problem, saying, 'Jack is making more progress on the race issue than anyone ever before.'

So the main culprit in creating a problem is praised for his efforts in solving it!

Straw and Patel are such close chums that Straw spent his honeymoon at Patel's house in Gujarat. Like all close chums, they are forever doing each other favours.

Straw helped pal Patel secure a £1.5m donation from the Emir of Qatar to build a mosque in Blackburn. A Muslim Lib Dem councillor said that the Blackburn Labour Party used Straw's involvement in the mosque donation to garner votes from local Muslims.

The £1.5m Qatari gift was half the £3m that pal Patel needed to build the five-storey mosque, which is one of thirty-five mosques in the town. He disclosed that Straw gave him 'a reference letter' that helped him solicit the donation during an appeal for funds to several Middle Eastern governments.

Inevitably, Straw suffers from the misguided guilt, revels in the pleasurable masochism, now prevalent among our leaders.

His performance on the famous *Question Time* programme of October 2009 where he appeared with the leader of the British National Party, Nick Griffin, was illuminating. When a mature negress in the audience told him she 'cringed' every time she heard him say, 'Afro-Caribbean.' - 'It should be AfriCAN-Caribbean' - instead of telling her to grow up, he raised his hand in APOLOGY!

The ancestors she identifies with cringed under the slaver's lash. She cringes because a word is not pronounced to her satisfaction.

Clearly neither of them had read the August 12th-25th issue of *The Trumpet* (slogan 'Africans now have a voice...'). On page 2 was a half-page advertisement for the 'Miss Afro-Caribbean Beauty Contest'. ('This event,' it said, 'is in aid of promoting togetherness and share one purpose between this two continent that have so much in common.' [*sic*].)

In 2002, when foreign secretary, he blamed British imperialism for most of the problems in the Islamic world.

And, displaying the astonishing ignorance also widespread among our leaders, in 2005 he told the UN that Muslims invented mathematics (more than a 1,000 years after Pythagoras!) and the 'digital age'.

Throughout his career, Straw has championed foreigners as a basic policy.

Before 1997 immigration was unplanned - bureaucratic drift, lack of concentration. No one wanted it and the Tories tried to limit it, for example with a rule that restricted large numbers of male settlers' wives and extended families entering Britain by a marriage deliberately arranged beforehand to enable them to follow the male to Britain.

As soon as Straw became home secretary, he first abolished this rule and then, the following year, with dubious, protean arguments, passed the Human Rights Act, a piece of political posturing that was to have devastating consequences. When it was ratified, he said the act 'makes it clear that it is the duty of states to promote and protect all human rights. Human rights are for everyone to enjoy everywhere'.

'Human rights' entered the vocabulary of political discourse as a throwaway line in an Allied declaration in 1942, which included among war aims the defence of 'life, liberty, independence and religious freedom' and the preservation of 'human rights and justice in their own lands as well as in other lands'. It was mere sloganeering. But, meant simply to bolster the war effort, two decades after the end of the war universal human rights slowly began to dominate international law.

The European Convention on Human Rights was formed in 1959; by the mid-1970s its court in Strasbourg had only judged seventeen cases; now it has 120,000 undecided cases.

Clearly the process no longer properly functions. The court's impressive increasing volume of business, far beyond what it can cope with, is due to the fact that it has treated the convention not just as a safeguard against despotism, the specific original aim of human rights legislation, but as a template for most aspects of human life.

Enthusiasts keep discovering more and more rights, so that there seems to be no end to them. A woman from Oldham who claimed her baby daughter was wrongly taken into council care took her case to the European court. Over the years, its language seeped into the language of British courts until, following pressure from the likes of top judge Lord Bingham, it was enshrined in an Act of Parliament.

Making British law subject to the European Convention on Human Rights confused the whole issue of mass immigration, enabling its apologists to mix together economic, moral, philosophical and political justifications, to adopt new arguments in its favour as earlier ones were too strongly disputed and disproved.

Straw deliberately went too far, because he was convinced it was the right thing to do, with the bonus of gaining the approbation of a decisive number of the Blackburn electorate. He passed his law and then sat back and let it all happen, little by little... lost control, admitted it but was happy to go along with it.

When home secretary, he every now and then vowed to be tough on bogus asylum seekers. These statements resemble the nonsensical comic song 'I've got a little list' (of society's offenders who never would be missed) sung by the Lord High Executioner Ko-Ko in *The Mikado* - just a bit of fun not meant to be taken seriously, which can be, and often is, adapted to the times, as in an amateur production in May 2011, just a few days after the killing of Osama Bin Laden:

And that bearded terrorist,
I had him on the list!

Possibly on one such farcical little list presented to the House was the Colombian drugs baron fleeing from the revenge of a rival gang whose members he had murdered, and the deposed African dictator responsible for the execution of political opponents. They both got in anyway.

A Bolivian illegal immigrant was allowed to stay after being found out because he had a 'settled home life' with a legal UK resident, the proof being that they had a cat. It was decided deportation would breach his human rights.

One of the few Straw actually did refuse asylum to was a man fleeing Saddam Hussein's regime, because, said Straw, 'We have faith in the integrity of the Iraqi judicial process and that you should have no concerns if you haven't done anything wrong.' Six years later Hussein was hanged for crimes against humanity. Whether the unfortunate man Straw so unwisely returned was still around is unknown.

By then Straw was the foreign secretary who had approved the invasion of Iraq, presumably having changed his mind about the nature of the regime. He recently said, 'I could have stopped the war... I could have stopped Britain's involvement.'

All politicians make mistakes, but to be responsible for TWO mistaken devastating invasions, that of Iraq and the ethnic invasion of Britain, is a record that would have made any honourable Roman senator contemplate suicide. I do not know how Straw lives with himself, the main policies of his career so clearly turning out catastrophic.

Everything Straw did has miscarried. All he touched he blighted.

He was the key figure for thirteen years in a government that tore apart the fabric of Britain. Through his ideological enthusiasm for mass immigration, parts of our towns now resemble Islamabad, complete with *sharia* law, political corruption, paedophile grooming gangs, *burkas*, oppression of women and female genital mutilation. Twenty-five thousand immigrant girls suffer this abuse every year in Britain, with not a single arrest for this criminal offence.

How many types of foreigners can a people reasonably be expected to put up with? How many alien practices? How much difference? Respecting the diversity of dozens of cultures is not only beyond the mental capacity of the most well-meaning of indigenous citizens but such race-mixing is one theory for the cause of the fall of Rome.

Britain is now a society loosened to its very foundations by a copious admixture of foreigners, an imperfect fusion of races, its people disunited by successive immigrations and threatened by a totalitarian religious ideology. The contemporary sound of our island is the noise of the Tower of Babel.

And all this was deliberate policy, epic treachery on a scale with that of classic traitors such as Coriolanus, who waged war on his native Rome, and Judas, the greatest sinner in Dante's *Divine Comedy*, in which traitors suffer the worst torments in the deepest part of Hell.

(The Prophet Mohammed is also consigned to this part of Hell by Dante, as a 'sower of discord', described split down the middle with his entrails spilling out.)

At the age of thirteen, Straw wrote to each of the main parties asking what they intended to do for their country if they won the forthcoming 1959 general election. Four decades later he said, 'The English as a race are not worth saving.'

Who could have thought that such idealism in adolescence would have become so dangerously perverted in adulthood?

Human rights are only the creation of governments, and can be manipulated by any government as appropriate. Like any other 'right' they can be applied selectively without limit, making them the perfect rhetorical excuse for arrogant politicians to tear apart the traditional local culture. Those following this policy are either oblivious to the damage they are inflicting on the social fabric or know it but do not care.

Straw, playing God, imagined he was creating a new race upon the Earth, an island rainbow nation. And all he has done is destroy.

KEN LIVINGSTONE
A nightmayor

IN March 2012 Ken Livingstone, the Labour candidate for mayor of London, seeking to regain the post he once held, declared in a London mosque that if elected he would make London 'a beacon of Islam'.

This promise came in a speech in the notorious North London Central mosque, also known as Finsbury Park mosque, formerly controlled by the terrorist recruiter Abu Hamza.

Livingstone pledged to 'educate the mass of Londoners' in Islam, saying: 'That will help to cement our city as a beacon that demonstrates the meaning of the words of the Prophet.'

He described Mohammed's words as 'an agenda for all humanity'. Praising one sermon, he said: 'I want to spend the next four years making sure that every non-Muslim in London knows and understands its words and message.'

He said this from the same pulpit at which Hamza had repeatedly preached war!

On this very platform Hamza had said, 'No drop of liquid is loved by Allah more than the liquid of blood' and that direct action was necessary: 'Those who do not take part in direct action, as defined by Islamic practice, constitute lesser Muslims. He is too coward, he is inexperienced, he doesn't want to take the challenge. This is wrong.'

In the *Koran*, passages urging war are far more frequent than those speaking peace. Very few verses of tolerance abrogate or even balance out the many that call for infidels to be fought and subdued until they either accept humiliation, convert to Islam or be killed.

The remarkable stress on violence in the *Koran* has contaminated world history with suffering and sorrow. Typical is this letter Mohammed sent to two kings, neither of whom were threatening Muslims: 'Embrace Islam... If you two accept Islam, you will remain in command of your country; but if your refuse my Call, you have to remember that all your possessions are perishable. My horsemen will appropriate your land, and my Prophethood will assume preponderance over your kingship.'

And, although the *Koran*'s chapters are arranged generally in order of length, the longest coming first, sometimes the period of the recitation can be gleaned from the context, and from these instances it emerges that Mohammed spoke peace until he was strong enough to wage war. And it is these hypocritical early recitations that are now quoted by our cunning Muslims when it suits them, not the later quotes, by when Mohammed had a large army and was allowing his men to rape traumatised women on the very day the men had slain their families in the name of Islam.

No one can read the *Koran* and not see a link between Islam and Muslim violence. This must mean that Livingstone has not read it.

At the time of his speech the mosque was controlled by the Muslim Association of Britain, which is tied to the banned terror group Hamas and which encourages its members to vote certain ways in elections. In other words, it gets involved in politics.

Since Muslims make up more than ten per cent of the local population in forty political seats, the Muslim Association of Britain believes Muslim voters can influence the results in forty seats.

A man who has acted as spokesman for the current mosque leadership, Azzam Tamimi, told the BBC's *HARDtalk* programme of his readiness to become a suicide bomber.

And one of the mosque's current directors, Mohammed Sawalha, was described by the BBC as a former senior figure in Hamas who 'is said to have masterminded much of Hamas's political and military strategy' from his post in London. In 2009 Sawalha also signed the Istanbul Declaration, which calls for attacks against the allies of Israel, which include the UK. The British government interpreted it as calling for attacks on British troops.

In 2010, Labour MP Khalid Mahmood resigned from the mosque's board of trustees and reported it to the Charity Commission, accusing the mosque of forging his signature on key legal documents.

In that same year, Livingstone campaigned in the London borough of Tower Hamlets to support the corrupt Bangladeshi settler Lutfur Rahman in his bid to become mayor of Tower Hamlets after Rahman had been sacked by Labour for his links to a Muslim extremist group, the Islamic Forum of Europe (IFE).

During Livingstone's former mayoralty, 2000-2008, his London Development Agency channelled hundreds of thousands of pounds to the East London mosque in Tower Hamlets, which is controlled by the IFE, even though senior agency managers strongly opposed the grant.

In return, IFE activists campaigned strongly for him at the 2008 mayoral elections, boasting that they 'got out the vote' for Livingstone and achieving dramatic swings to him in their East London heartland. Their support almost won him back the mayoralty. He lost by fewer than 150,000 votes.

Livingstone also gave thousands of pounds of public money to the Muslim Welfare House, a charity closely associated with the Finsbury Park mosque, which signed an open letter backing his re-election campaign in 2008.

The Islamic Forum of Europe is dedicated to changing the 'very infrastructure of society, its institutions, its culture, its political order and its creed, from ignorance to Islam'.

It is especially active in Tower Hamlets. The 'Islamic Republic of Tower Hamlets', as it is known, teems with Muslim clerics called the Tower Hamlets' Taliban, who seek to impose *sharia* law on the capital.

The Tower Hamlets' Taliban regularly issue death threats to women who refuse to wear Islamic veils. Streets have been plastered with bright yellow posters declaring, 'You are entering a Sharia controlled zone: Islamic rules enforced.' Street advertising deemed offensive to Muslims is regularly vandalised or blacked out with spray paint. Leaflets are pushed through letterboxes saying, 'Verily, it is time to rejoice in the coming state of Islam. There will be no negotiation with Islam. It is only a short time before the flag of Islam flies over Downing Street.'

Rahman, known to be linked to jihadists, has dedicated much of his time as mayor to diverting public money to the IFE, and to stocking public libraries in Tower Hamlets with books and DVDs containing the speeches of banned Muslim clerics.

He is a close ally of a fanatic named Anjem Choudary, a *sharia* court judge based in London who believes in the primacy of Islam over all other religions, and who campaigns for Islamic law to be implemented throughout Britain. In 2011 Choudary burned poppies on Remembrance Day as a two-minute silence was observed nearby by service personnel and their families. He also chanted slogans such as 'British soldiers burn in hell'. He led a group based in Tower Hamlets called Muslims Against Crusades that launched a campaign to turn twelve British cities into independent Islamic states.

The 'Islamic Emirates' would function as autonomous enclaves ruled by *sharia* law and operate entirely outside British jurisprudence. He said, 'With several Islamic emirates already well-established across Asia, Africa and the Middle East, including Iraq and Afghanistan, we see this as a radical, but very realistic step in the heart of Western Europe, that will, *inshallah*, pave the way for the worldwide domination of Islam.'

Muslims Against Crusades has since been banned but it was the eighth name for an organisation that simply changes its name every time it is banned.

In June 2013 Choudary said soldier Lee Rigby, who had recently been hacked to death in Woolwich by two Muslims, would 'burn in hellfire'.

Choudary, who receives state welfare payments of up to £25,000 a year, said he could not feel sorry for Rigby and that the young soldier would be tortured in hell for not being a Muslim.

He added, according to the *Sun* newspaper, 'Allah said very clearly in the *Koran*, "Don't feel sorry for the non-Muslims." So as an adult non-Muslim, whether he is a part of the Army or not part of the Army, if he dies in a state of disbelief then he is going to go to the hellfire. That's what I believe so I'm not going to feel sorry for non-Muslims.'

Choudary was also reported by the *Sun* as saying, 'We invite non-Muslims to embrace the message of Islam. If they don't, then obviously if they die like that they're going to the hellfire.'

He said he thought Rigby's murderers were doing what they believed to be Islamically correct. 'Only Allah can judge them in the hereafter for what they did in their life,' he said. 'In their eyes they are martyrs and what I say is, Allah may accept them into paradise. I believe all Muslims will eventually go to paradise.'

And it is not true that only fanatics like Choudary support murder in the name of Islam. Many Muslims gleefully blow their horns when driving past the spot where Rigby was killed.

Livingstone allied himself to sworn enemies of our civilisation.

And, as Muslim fraud at elections is the norm, he is automatically implicated in political corruption. In April 2012 police probed voting fraud in Tower Hamlets. An editorial in the London *Evening Standard* read: 'The British electoral system is remarkable for its integrity and freedom from corruption. That makes it all the more important that we take seriously threats to that integrity.'

Never in any of these moralising editorials in British newspapers is there the slightest hint that these threats come solely from settlers, who, inevitably, have fetched with them the practices, standards and values of their home country; that swarthy men from the back alleys of Dhaka, Sylhet and Chittagong and innumerable villages in the Ganges Delta, having moved in like cuckoos pushing out the rightful inhabitants, are now feathering their stolen nest.

In Britain, voting registration forms are sent to every address in the country and the head of the household fills in the people who live there. There is no check on the accuracy of this information. Everything is done on trust. The system worked well in tight-knit, homogeneous communities fifty years ago, when there was also a high level of honesty, but it is now abused on a massive scale by settlers. There are now an estimated two million 'ghost voters' in the UK as a result of this weakness in the system. Small flats are found to have up to fifteen voters registered at them. Once, seventy postal voters were found to be registered in one two-bedroom terraced house.

Though Livingstone was not personally involved with abuses, the prevalence of them - multiple occupancy was also alleged in previous elections in Tower Hamlets - indicated a condoning of them consistent with his record of hypocrisy.

He pulled out of a BBC mayoral debate because the BNP candidate was taking part, saying, 'The far right want to destroy our democracy and stand for the elimination of our basic rights. They cannot be treated as a legitimate part of politics. I will not share a platform with the BNP and it is a point of principle to me that I never will do.'

This personification of hypocrisy had the gall to use the word principle in regard to himself!

In reality the only threat to democracy in this country comes from Islam.

Livingstone became a professional politician aged only twenty-seven and never did anything outside politics afterwards. An early campaign to give settlers more of Lambeth's better housing stock was followed by forty years of hypocrisy.

In 2012 it was revealed he channelled his income through a small firm to minimise his tax, after he had repeatedly attacked 'rich bastards' for similar tax avoidance.

His appeal to Islam could have regained him the mayor's office. He only lost, again narrowly, because the Muslim vote for him, including all the fraudulent ones, was outweighed by indigenous Londoners voting Tory who would have voted for a different Labour candidate.

I do not know why Livingstone espoused the cause of hostile strangers, whether it was ignorance, stupidity or a personality disorder.

He has always over-estimated the sufferings of those he sympathised with, a trait they have ruthlessly exploited. His type are easily fooled by Muslims seeking a justification for their existence by identifying themselves with historical and current events in the Middle East, no matter where they come from. People born in Lancashire to Pakistani parents say, 'It's all your fault, you invaded us,' meaning by 'us' some country in the Middle East. After the bombs exploded in London on July 7th 2005, killing fifty-two people, Livingstone explained it would not have happened if the Arab countries had been left alone and not exploited for their oil, even though three of the four bombers' parents came from Pakistan, and the fourth bomber was Jamaican.

When London mayor, Livingstone vowed that the British would never follow the French example and ban headscarves in schools, saying, 'It marks a move towards religious intolerance that we in Europe swore never to repeat, having witnessed the devastating effects of the Holocaust.' His hero, who he once brazenly embraced in public, is the notorious Yusuf al-Qaradawi, a top Muslim supremacist with a special loathing for Jews.

In Livingstone's very long autobiography, which, typically, is longer than most biographies of great world statesmen, he writes that George Orwell's *1984* influenced his political beliefs more than any other book. He cannot see that if Islam is allowed to prevail the sort of totalitarian society depicted in the novel will be what England will have in just a few decades.

DENIS MACSHANE
Rotten in Rotherham

FORMER Labour MP for Rotherham Denis MacShane, as well as being a traitor, is a liar and a thief.

He began his twin careers of deceit and treachery while an official at the National Union of Journalists in the 1970s, when he was responsible for drawing up the NUJ's *Guidelines on Race Reporting*, an influential document in the suppression of free speech in this country.

It stridently champions diversity and multi-culturalism, banning NUJ members from even the slightest criticism of ethnic settlers. In tone it resembles a Communist Party directive in the Soviet Union, rigid instructions more than guidelines.

For decades journalists have used their influence to manipulate public opinion and the main reason for that are these strict guidelines, which all journalists must respect and which dictate what can or cannot be written or broadcast. These guidelines imposed by the NUJ have had a baneful effect on British democracy by establishing systematic censorship.

Three weeks after two Muslims hacked to death soldier Lee Rigby in

Woolwich, and tried to decapitate him, just down the road in Thames-mead a man named Daha Mohammed slit the throat of a disabled man in a wheelchair named Colin Greenway. Journalists could not cope with this murder. It came too soon after the Rigby killing, was too nearby and had a similar element of Muslim butchery. And so there was a news blackout.

The guidelines state clearly that parties opposed to mass immigration must be reported only in negative terms, that journalists must promote immigration and diversity and whenever settlers commit a crime their ethnicity should ideally not be revealed.

And these guidelines were created by one of the most despicable of all British politicians, a man who, prior to becoming a politician, was even sacked by the BBC for gross dishonesty.

MacShane was fired after using a fake name to call a radio phone-in programme he worked on at the time. During the call, he accused leading Conservative politician Reginald Maudling of being a crook, with Maudling threatening to sue as a result.

MacShane remained an NUJ official after his sacking despite having been discredited as a journalist, even becoming its president for a year, his salary paid out of members' contributions. Some members who were aware of this naturally objected. Renowned *Times*' columnist Bernard Levin wrote:

'I do not much care to be told how to do my job as a journalist by a journalist who was sacked for professional misconduct, has been unable to find regular employment ever since, and at present lives on a payment which comes out of the union subscriptions paid by me and my fellow members of the NUJ.'

The BBC enthusiastically adheres to the guidelines drawn up by MacShane. So the organisation that sacked him now obeys his rules!

MacShane then entered politics, in which, as the Labour MP for Rotherham, he stole thousands of pounds of taxpayers' money by filing fraudulent expenses claims.

Over four years he submitted fake invoices for air fares, meals and hotel bills. He claimed for eight laptop computers in three years.

He funnelled money through a bogus front organisation he called the European Policy Institute (EPI), which had no formal structure, offices or staff - although it did have its own letterhead on stationery that he had specially printed. This allowed him to claim for 'consulting and translating services' at up to £950 a time. The bills were all signed by a fictional 'general manager'. Names given for directors were all old friends of MacShane. He controlled the bank account and wrote cheques to himself, drawn on the British taxpayer. In November 2012, MacShane resigned as an MP after the Commons Standards and Privileges Committee suspended him for a year for the 'gravest' abuse of expenses they had seen. The Standards Commissioner said he 'plainly intended to deceive' Parliament's expenses authorities.

MacShane had already been suspended from the Labour Party when his deception first came to light. He was re-admitted only after police announced they were not pursuing fraud charges against him, on the advice of the Crown Prosecution Service.

At the time, neither the police nor the CPS had access to all the evidence that was eventually put before the committee. Scotland Yard later came under pressure to reopen the case after MacShane made a 'number of frank admissions' about his expenses in letters to the Standards Commissioner in which he admitted he faked nineteen invoices totalling £12,900.

He obviously deserved to be jailed but remained free because he insisted the damning evidence against him was protected by parliamentary privilege and could not be used in court, which Commons officials conceded was true.

It was a contemptible affront to justice. MPs should not be able to use parliamentary privilege to escape prosecution for outrageous criminal behaviour. Parliamentary privilege is designed to allow MPs to name individuals they believe to be involved in illegal activity without fear of being sued for libel. It is not meant to be used by thieves like MacShane, and the courts had already rejected a defence of parliamentary privilege in the case of other expenses cheats.

The Commons had the chance to clarify the position on privilege three years earlier at the height of the expenses scandal but MPs voted against changes that would have made evidence such as MacShane's letters automatically available to the police. Absurdly, they pretended that any such changes would have a 'chilling effect' on freedom of speech.

It was not the first time MacShane was caught cheating. He had already pocketed £125,000 over seven years in expenses by claiming his shabby garage was his constituency office. He was forced to repay only a pittance. This time he was bang to rights, by his own admission. He should not have been allowed to hide behind parliamentary privilege. He should have been arrested and charged with fraud.

MacShane also charged taxpayers more than £8,000 for 'translation services' that turned out to be payments to his brother. He submitted more than a dozen invoices to the Commons bearing the heading of his EPI, with each bill justified by just one line - 'research and translation' - followed by a demand for fees ranging between £550 and £950.

The names and signatures on the bills, sent between August 2005 and January 2008 and totalling £8,050, were blacked out by the Commons censors, but it was established the EPI was run by his brother, Edmund Matyjaszek. The link between the brothers was not apparent from the documents submitted by MacShane because Matyjaszek, a poet and playwright, kept the surname of their father, Jan Matyjaszek, while his brother took the maiden name of their mother, Isobel MacShane, at the request of the BBC when he joined it in 1969.

Such fraud linked to nepotism is typical behaviour of Muslims, which raises the interesting question of whether MacShane became contaminated through long close contact with many Muslims or he was attracted to their culture in the first place because of something in his own character.

Maybe it was his pathological dishonesty that drew him to Muslims? Maybe he felt more comfortable in their environment of deceit than among his own kind?

In any event, he wholeheartedly joined in their deceit. In November 2001 an article was published in the *Observer* under the name of Muslim MP Khalid Mahmood. A few days later it was revealed that the article had not been written by Mahmood but by MacShane. Mahmood simply agreed to put his name to it.

This deceit would be reprehensible enough. But the article also says things like, 'I know of no Muslim who endorses drug taking', in effect denying the heroin *jihad* being waged in towns throughout England, the Muslims knowing that widespread heroin use destroys communities, which is their aim.

It also says, 'A great crime was committed on 11 September [2001]. To associate the faith of Islam with it is unacceptable.'

This was not written by a Muslim but by MacShane!

And his financial corruption was accompanied by political policies that have destroyed Rotherham. The sums involved in his frauds are minuscule by comparison with the sums - and the suffering - he has cost Rotherham through incompetence, malice and corruption. Millions of pounds have been lost or wasted. High levels of violent and fiscal crime have been fostered, and immeasurable harm done to the culture and institutions of the town.

Rotherham is one of the councils that did not protect vulnerable girls in their care from the attentions of Muslim rape gangs. Muslim men raped and abused white girls while the authorities intervened on behalf not of the victims but of the criminals. A father was arrested when he tried to rescue his daughter from the house in which she was being abused. Another abused girl who pleaded for help was offered Urdu and Punjabi lessons to enable her to better integrate with the 'community' in which her abusers were operating. MacShane stood by and said nothing.

Through his policy of fanatically supporting settlers, mainly Muslims, the ancient South Yorkshire town has been turned into a multi-cultural melting pot containing some of the worst elements imaginable, elements that refuse to integrate.

Politically controlled by Muslims, Rotherham now has nine mosques and some of the worst corruption in British history. A Christian chapel and cemetery were acquired by Muslims and the building turned into a furniture warehouse. When sales declined it mysteriously caught fire, not once but twice.

This gives some indication of the level of respect Muslims have for our ancient buildings and our ancestors.

Five other failing Muslim-owned businesses have recently caught fire in Rotherham.

This state of affairs is down to just one person - Denis MacShane.

His lack of judgment does not end at fraud and backing Islam.

A former Europe minister and an ardent Europhile, he continues to write columns for the *Guardian* about Europe and to appear on television programmes as an expert on European affairs. On September 7th 2009 he wrote an article in the London *Evening Standard* in which he proclaimed it was time for Britain to abandon sterling and join the euro, just before the European sovereign-debt crisis started.

Around that time, he also wrote, 'All the old arguments against the euro have fallen away... The euro is not going to collapse ...'

Like the other great traitors, Jack Straw and Ken Livingstone (and I presume George Galloway as well but dwelling on all of them is too distressing), MacShane appears so lacking in judgment, at the same time as being so full of himself, that you wonder at the cause. Are they simply thick or is there something psychologically wrong with them?

People have betrayed their country for all kinds of different reasons - conscience, conviction, love, pride, pique, greed... Our contemporary traitors are beyond understanding. All we know is that our grandchildren will recoil at the very mention of them.

These self-appointed guardians of the conscience of the Western world have sapped Albion from within with their celebration of the unwanted myth of universal brotherhood, never asking themselves if it was wise to throw open our island to such vast hordes. They are traitors just as much as the Bishop of Margus, who in 441 with his own hands opened the gates of his episcopal city to the besieging Huns. This bishop was rewarded well by Attila. But usually in the end such traitors cannot win; eventually they are judged and condemned either way, by their own people if the resistance is successful or by the invaders if it is they who triumph.

Conquerors usually want a pure conquest. Traitors from a defeated foe seem to taint the victory, render it less noble. So excuses have to be found to discredit and disown them; or not bother with any pretence at legality, the course taken by the invading King Canute in the eleventh century, when, after his victory in a decisive battle that had been made possible by the treacherous Earl of Mercia fleeing with his contingent, he righteously slew the earl as a reward for his treason.

'I promised,' said Canute, 'to set thy head higher than other men's, and I have kept my word.' The trunkless head was set on the gates of London. The trunk was thrown into the Thames from a high window in the upper storey of the royal apartments of an ancient fortified palace jutting over the river. (The earldom of Mercia was given over to a man named Leofric, the husband of Lady Godiva, whose later legendary ride through Coventry was in support of complaints about his taxes.)

If only our contemporary traitors had realised that no one, not even the enemies whose cause they joined, was going to thank them for their treachery! That the foe will marginalise their contribution, distort their names, obscure their treacherous lives!

If only they had considered that Dante placed traitors in the central circle of Hell, to join the disembowelled Prophet!

FLYING THE UNION MOHAMMED
Jack's not all right

JACK is a fine old English Christian name. Originally a diminutive of John, during the Middle Ages it was so common it was used as a general term for 'man' or 'boy'. A remnant of this is in the saying, 'Every man Jack.' This omniscience is still reflected in fairy stories, nursery rhymes, aphorisms and proverbs. It permeates the English language. Even street ice-cream vendors in the late nineteenth century were called 'cream ice Jacks', though they were more likely to be named Giacomo.

Oscar Wilde declared the name Jack 'has no music' and used one young man's efforts to change it to Ernest as the plot for his most famous play. But parents obviously disagree. It has remained the most popular name for baby boys in Britain, taking top spot for at least the last thirteen years, when records began.

Experts say that the enduring appeal of the name Jack is because it sounds trustworthy. 'When we do our research, mothers tell us Jack suggests honesty, trustworthiness and hard work. A Jack will be popular and have a strong character, but he will also be good,' said Faye Mingo, who compiles the research on names for Bounty.com, a parenting club.

In the last couple of years however a strong contender for top place has emerged - Mohammed. In its various spellings, it has taken the name of Islam's prophet to second place.

The implications of this for Albion are dire. The Islam ideology being Stalinist, as soon as the *imams* get absolute power in England all challenges to the dominance of Mohammed as the main English name will have to be destroyed. Like Stalin's perceived enemies, the name Jack will be erased from history. Just as Stalin issued decrees to change history as it suited him, so the *imams* will pronounce a *fatwa* banning Jacks. Text books will be burnt and re-written.

We are already re-writing our history and changing our customs to please the ethnics. In 2000 the Commission on the Future of Multi-Ethnic Britain published a report that asked for Britain to be declared a multi-cultural and 'multi-faith' society, by which it seems they meant a multi-racial society with no special acknowledgement being made to the British. The right of Anglican bishops to sit in the legislature is now called into question, while the terms of the monarch's ancient coronation oath, in which the new sovereign pledges to maintain the laws of God and 'the true Profession of the Gospel and the Protestant Reformed Religion Established by Law', are under debate.

Prince Charles has already said that when he becomes king he wants his subsidiary title to be changed from 'Defender of the Faith', originally a 1521 papal bestowal reflecting the sovereign's position as the head of Christianity in England, to 'Defender of Faith'. He said he hoped to be the defender of all faiths. The original Latin phrase, *Fidei Defensor*, is referred to on all current British coins by the abbreviation F D. The Royal Mint's decision in 1849 to omit reference to the phrase from the 'Godless florin' caused such a scandal that it was re-instated. In 1953, while still a dominion of the Commonwealth, Pakistan dropped the title in recognition of the contradiction between its overwhelmingly Muslim population and having a monarch as the defender of the Christian faith.

Like all children everywhere, the future children of Albion will be raised on fairy tales. The *Koran* will naturally be the main one, being almost nothing but fairy tales, but they will also listen spellbound to the gripping tale of Mohammed and the Beanstalk.

They will sing two nursery rhymes that have their origins in Somerset. Little Jack Horner, who put in his thumb and pulled out a plum, is said to be based on a man of that name in the sixteenth century who conspired to have the Abbot of Glastonbury hanged for treason, after which he acceded to his manor, the plum in question. Despite this historical background, he will have to be renamed Mohammed Horner.

Another Somerset legend sets the story of Jack and Jill in the village of Kilmersdon, where to this day there is a Jack and Jill Hill. Why anyone would sink a well at the top of a hill, and how you would draw water from it, are questions in need of answers, but anyway children will soon be singing about Mohammed and Jill going up the hill to fetch a pail of water.

They will also chant the rhyme about how Mohammed Sprat could eat no fat and his wife could eat no lean - so, between them, you see, they licked the platter clean; and every evening before going to bed watch the popular children's television programme Mohammedanory. When they are behaving naughty their parents will tell them to 'Mohammed it in'.

As they enter puberty it will increasingly be a case of 'I'm all right, Mohammed' and 'Up ladder, Mohammed, I'm on board' and in adolescence they will be rebuffed by girls who will tell them to 'Hit the road, Mohammed.' The flash ones among them will be known as Mohammed-the-lads. Many will naturally be interested in football, and want to know all about the famous players of the past, such as Bobby and Mohammed Charlton and the Newcastle United legend Wor Mohammedie Milburn.

They will also learn to drive a car of course, and to do such necessary things as change wheels, how you need to mohammed up the vehicle with a mohammed that you could buy in Halfords. If the puncture happens in freezing weather they will curse Mohammed Frost. Anyone good with his hands in general will be known as a Mohammed-of-all-trades.

They will learn all about wildlife, recognising such common birds as the thieving mohammedaw. Villages will have to be renamed. A Devon village just outside Exeter will become Mohammed-in-the-Green, and a Scottish village south of Glasgow will be Mohammedton.

Though the reigning *imams* will have to be careful when it comes to English history and its many revolts, schoolchildren might read a version of such events as the great insurrection of 1450 and of its leader,

Mohammed Cade. The Victorian serial killer in London's East End might warrant a paragraph, the notorious Mohammed the Ripper.

But if members of the recent Labour government are hoping for a favourable mention in these history books, to be commemorated with honour by the triumphant Muslims because it was they who allowed them uncontrolled entry in to this country, where, urged on by their religious leaders for political reasons, they are multiplying at ten times the rate of the indigenous people, they cannot rely on it. The man who more than anyone else was responsible will be deprived of his identity, erased from memory, falsely known to a country governed by artful theocrats as Mohammed Straw.

WILLIAM THE CONQUERED
2066

NO destiny is harder to describe than one that is unprecedented.

But we'll 'ave a go.

Great is the year and terrible the year of Our Lord 2066. Following a freezing winter comes a scorching summer, abundant with warmth and sun, during which a delegation of top Muslim theocrats led by the Grand Mullah of England, Abdul Bablu, is welcomed into 10 Downing Street for discussions with the new prime minister, Maulana Asmatullah.

The Muslims, with the unwitting assistance of their allies, settlers' descendants in the political wing of the sprawling Black and Minority Ethnic network, have seized power. One item on the agenda is how best to dispose of these allies now that they are superfluous. Attending the meeting to provide suggestions is the England police commissioner, Mahmoud Aziz. Also at number 10 is the London mayor, Zohaib Ahmed. Conditions in the country are discussed, as well as the leanings of certain indigenous politicians. Essentially this aspect of the discussion is about who might usefully be bribed.

In Buckingham Palace meanwhile the doddery old King William is reluctantly preparing to receive another delegation, a dozen Muslim politicians whose convoy of cars is just arriving, the smiling Muslim policemen at the gates shouting, '*Allahu akbar!*' in regional English accents. Those Muslim soldiers of the Household Cavalry who have waived their right to wear a turban while on Palace guard duty remove their bearskins and wag them in the air. Their colleagues wearing a turban make do with thumbs-up signs.

King William sprays on cologne, aware that even after a shower or bath he still smells sourly of old age. He has come to dread his public duties. Dining at functions has become a particular problem, for he often spills soup on himself, staining his lapel. Also, several times during these dinners he has to dry his eyes with his serviette because they are watering. And during coffee he sometimes falls asleep.

He had nodded off just before the Muslims arrived, and had to be woken up by a lackey. His reaction on waking up was panic. He thought no, they should come back another day, he was in no condition to receive visitors, there was nothing to talk about. His panic was caused partly by deafness. He is never certain any more what anyone says. Though he is resigned to the fact that deafness is another of the many irremediable defects of old age, it is still inconvenient and embarrassing at meetings such as the one he is about to endure - indeed, especially at meetings such as this one, for he knows his sole duty today is to listen.

The meeting turns out to be even worse than he expected. The king is aghast at one of the visitors' non-negotiable demands, that his granddaughter marries a Muslim. This will strengthen the legitimacy of what is in effect a conquest. Cursing his deafness, he is not sure he has heard right, and asks them to repeat it, a bit louder. They obligingly do so, almost shouting.

Continuing to speak louder than usual for his benefit, they argue that a similar thing almost happened once. If the crash in the Paris underpass had not occurred, his mother would have married the Muslim boyfriend who also died and they would have had Muslim children, who would have been members of the royal family.

William feels like blurting out that it was precisely to prevent this that the crash was engineered, but feels it would not be diplomatic. And anyway, he is not in a position to refuse. Although it is a sweltering day and they are indoors two of the men are wearing overcoats, and never take their hands out of the pockets, and he had been often enough in war zones all those decades ago to know this is because they are keeping their hand on a gun. In those days, such people were part of his bodyguard. The formal tone of these bearded visitors is tinged with a fundamental hostility.

It is an unpleasant conversation. The king, deaf, a bit senile and still numb from the recent death of his beloved wife Kate, does not fully understand what is happening. He vaguely wonders why all these men in his palace have a bushy beard but a shaved upper lip, and assumes it is simply the current fashion. Their leader, a cleric in Muslim ecclesiastical robes and turban named Ahmed Nadeem, shouts at William, 'A solid government is now at last ruling the land!' He adds that the security of the Crown will be guaranteed, the power of the monarch even strengthened, but that 'a purifying fire will rage through the stinking realm'.

And then, stroking his forest of beard, he loudly announces that the coronation oath will need to be abolished.

Now the king understands.

This loud announcement, more than anything else, signifies to him that a revolution has taken place, that the influence of Muslims in politics is a disease. And that England has now succumbed.

Throughout the eighth and ninth centuries the Archbishops of Canterbury had gradually acquired control over the Church in kingdoms of England other than Kent, and with that control gained influence and power, including conducting the coronation ceremony.

Archbishop Athelm (914-23) composed a coronation service for English monarchs, introducing the actual crown in the ceremony for the first time, and crowning the monarch became one of Canterbury's most valued privileges. It was the discord that arose from the use of the Archbishop of York at a coronation instead of the Archbishop of Canterbury, Thomas Becket, which led to Becket being murdered by four knights in the cathedral in 1170.

In 1953 Archbishop Fisher, robed in white and gold, had said to William's grandmother at her coronation, according to custom: 'Will you to the utmost of your power maintain the Laws of God and the true profession of the Gospel? Will you to the utmost of your power maintain in the United Kingdom the Protestant Reformed Religion established by law? Will you maintain and preserve inviolable the settlement of the Church of England, and the doctrine, worship, discipline, and government thereof, as by law established in England? And will you preserve unto the Bishops and Clergy of England, and to the Churches there committed to their charge, all such rights and privileges, as by law do or shall appertain to them or any of them?'

And Elizabeth had replied, according to custom: 'All this I promise to do. The things which I have here before promised, I will perform, and keep. So help me God.' She solemnly confirmed that one of her titles as the monarch would be 'Defender of the [Christian] Faith'.

In the following decades Prince Charles often said he would like the coronation oath to be changed so that he would be 'Defender of Faith', a champion of all religions; and this was duly done for his coronation.

William now realises that altering the oath, first at his father's coronation and then at his own, was a significant mistake, a concession, like all those concessions over so many decades, regarded as weakness by its supposed beneficiaries, and as a base from which could be demanded more concessions. In the circumstances, the next coronation could not be far off. And now, when only a culture suffused with the doctrines and values of Christianity can save old Albion from the darkness of *sharia*, it will contain no oath at all.

With the discarding of the commitment to Christianity, Charles was discredited, while William himself from the very beginning of his reign was known as William the Conquered.

The monarchy shares many rituals with the Church of England. William remembers at his coronation the sacerdotal robe of gold being placed upon him, in the same ritual that consecrates a Church of England bishop, stiff archaic gold that might have sheathed a Byzantine priest. For how long will these swarthy bearded men with their impassive faces, men supremely self-contained and indifferent, permit such rituals after the removal of the coronation oath? The old world is clearly going. What will replace it? Where will it all end?

After the bearded guests had left the palace, the king, jolted into awareness by the imposition of a foreign ideology, belatedly realises that Islam is the ultimate wickedness and stupidity, an evil and direct threat to civilisation.

'A country is not the land that it holds, but the opinions of the people in it,' he ruefully muses.

'For a century now, too many of those settled in England have owed their allegiance to Islam and their ancestral homelands. Their opinions, which they aggressively proclaim as eternal verities, have destroyed England. Everywhere now instead of harmony there is hideous discord. Instead of peace there is conflict. They are as much aggressors as if they had come wielding weapons. We made the sword we carried blunter and blunter by degrees from feelings of humanity, and now the arm has been lopped from our body with a sharp scimitar.

'In 2010, attempting to allay mounting disquiet, we said, "Muslims only make up five per cent of our population." A decade later we said, "The followers of the Prophet in our country comprise only ten per cent." Ten years after that we said, "The worshippers of Allah among us are only fifteen per cent." Muslims multiplied until they were numerous enough to seize power, as their leaders had always said they would. By an extraordinary combination of circumstances, immigrants from some of the most hellish, backward, corrupt countries in the world have been permitted to take control of England. Why did we allow this to happen? What possessed us? We should have held on to our contempt. It might have steeled us against catastrophe.

'We should never have let these Muslims loose in our own land. We should have done all we could to stop them. We knew that their religion is also their politics. For a hundred years we allowed doom-laden planes to land at our airports, welcoming the invaders, ignoring the threat, enabling our professions and institutions to be swamped by them.'

The old king wipes his constantly weeping eyes. He thinks about all the indigenous writers who, for decades, concerned about their personal safety, wrote about other things, as though anything else mattered, all those trillions of words signifying nothing but cowardice. Journalists, broadcasters, academics and publishers had stayed silent as Islam threatened the basic standards of intellectual life. Fear paralysed their best instincts. The vengeance of foreigners permeated and rotted the whole of society. All that writing! All that struggling to appear clever and witty, purely to entertain for profit or fame, avoiding the grim business of the silent fight to the death.

During those decades, the road to power of Islam was also paved by useful idiots who found compelling the Muslims' petty-minded, moralising interventions in the lives of others, the desire of straggly-bearded men who venerated medieval Bedouins to lord it over everyone else, whose puritanism had an increasingly political slant.

The swarthy settlers stealthily progressed their cultural tyranny from neighbourhood to neighbourhood. When things inevitably did not work out as they promised, they had a get-out clause. The people had not yet embraced Islam with the requisite fervour. As fundamentalism only ever deepens public hypocrisy, not public morality, cynicism will now have become all-pervasive.

It seems inconceivable to William that his kingdom could be taken over by these men wearing joke-shop beards presumably held in place by hooks over the ears. It is as if the Sioux had taken over the American continent or the Picts the Roman Empire.

Long before he became king, he had often seen alarming statistics, but he ignored them. Enjoying himself too much gallivanting round the world with Kate, he never took the trouble to think about them; and now salvation seems to lie only with nationalists, so long reviled, whose activities, through necessity, now include the distribution of arms. Episodes of civil strife have been escalating.

William yearns for bed, for oblivion, and does not know if this is age, grief or the times. 'And,' he muses, 'if the bearded ones hold on despite rebellions and uprisings, they will become the rulers of the English for...' He baulks at the thought. 'Well, I suppose... for ever.'

Only now, too late, will many indigenous people realise what has happened. Ignorant to the end of the extent of their danger and the number of their enemies, only now will they think, 'Really, how stupid! Who could have imagined that there really were so many, that they really did deliberately breed in order to outnumber us! That they really did plan domination, as "the racists" had warned! Did we not have eyes to see?' They now appreciate that for all those decades where there had been political correctness and hypocrisy there should have been polemic so robust that the intellectual inferiority and lack of logic of the Muslims would have been exposed; that there should have been scepticism about the ability of Muslims to integrate long before the belated questioning of their willingness to do so. For all those years, Islam fed on a misplaced respect for the settlers' culture, when implacable rejection of that culture was the only reasonable reaction.

Amazingly, some indigenous leaders are still playing down the gravity of the situation. The pusillanimity that had for a century allowed the enemy to consolidate his forces now hinders preparations to prevent his eventual, and inevitable, grab for absolute power. Calamity of unprecedented magnitude approaches but no steps are taken to meet it. At one moment they are alarmed and feel no measure should be omitted, at another they convince themselves that things are not terrifying. What should be done? Drastic action or no action? Firmness or compromise? The habits of a hundred years of irresolution and lack of realism when facing Islam cannot be broken. Over those fatal decades, our society had hosted the Muslims without questioning their difference to us, without penalising their sullen fanaticism or resisting their enmity. Now, unable to face reality, these leaders shut their eyes, as they had always done. Shutting their eyes is their only action. Those who had ignored past wounds invited the fatal injury. Resistance is left to ordinary folk.

The new rulers try to hide the larval war with distracted decrees, calling the strife mere tumult. But others are calling it an insurrection. The insurgents are mainly indigenous English, compelled to attack their own land as though it were a hostile power.

Internal dissension is the one destructive influence that brings down great countries; and England is split in two. A polarisation has taken place, each side moving further and further apart with nothing to link them, for now there are truly two nations in England. Parliament is full of tension and strife, the struggle starkly between basic democratic principles and an authoritarian theocratic ideology. The two factions do not want to share the same set of customs and the same laws. Unprecedented brawling occurs in the historic debating chamber that is now a battleground of conflicting passions.

Observing different laws is clearly an untenable situation and, after decades of progressive disintegration, cataclysmic conflict looms. News is coming through of the threat of assassinations. Several indigenous politicians are targeted. The *fatwa* has not yet been issued, as Grand Mullah Abdul Bablu is squeamish in the face of the prospect of his vilification by the still mighty USA. He is seeking a way of disposing of his enemies legally, in the full odour of the despised infidel justice...

The takeover of power occurs with some speed, almost artlessly. Acts and laws are passed, edicts issued. A new cabinet post, for religious affairs, is created. The man holding it is Ahmed Nadeem, the cleric who had led the delegation to the palace. Nadeem had recently been recorded on YouTube earnestly taking issue with a genie (who naturally remained unseen off camera).

Nadeem launches a campaign to demolish all churches, with mosques or madrasas erected on their sites where feasible. Some councils object, usually for architectural or history reasons, not religious, but as most councillors in the country are now Muslim it is believed the campaign will be largely successful, especially after the Archbishop of Canterbury, Yoweri Muamba (the second African to hold the post), embracing Grand Mullah Abdul Bablu in front of an assembled crowd at a big meeting, makes him a gift of ten churches, to be turned into mosques. It is the day's most tender and moving moment.

The pious had always been vulnerable to the Muslim priesthood who looked to Mecca. None of the Archbishops of Canterbury for the last eighty years had had a clear basis for their policies on English Islam other than taking the line of least resistance. They were usually to be found nailing their colours to the fence. When the one thing that mattered was to prevent Muslims seizing possession of the country, when resistance was the only reasonable action, all of them, on taking office, kept the policy of appeasing Islam. One recanted, and became known as the Archbishop of re-Canterbury. His successor, seeing that the Muslims had been offended by this defiance, cravenly resumed, and even intensified, the old grovelling. And now their respect for all religion, echoing that of the monarch, had caused the destruction of their own.

233

The town of Canterbury, which attracted pilgrims and tourists from all over the world, will inevitably decline. *The Canterbury Tales* has already have gone out of print for the first time in centuries, its continued publication discouraged by *imams* concerned about the rude bits, despite the salacious scenes and the bawdy stories in the medieval Arabic *Thousand and One Nights* such as 'The Historic Fart', in which a man named Abu Hassan breaks wind at a wedding feast. Returning to his village after years of embarrassed exile, hoping that after all this time it will have been forgotten, the first thing he hears is a mother telling her child, 'You were born on the very night of Abu Hassan's fart'.

In other campaigns, committees of virtuous Muslim citizens are petitioning to change the names of streets, erasing the names of fiendish monarchs and ministers and bloodthirsty soldiers and sailors and replacing them with heroes of Islam; tarpaulin is already in place on Salisbury Plain to cover the pagan Stonehenge; and the sight and sound of 'ham' offends some Muslims so much they have launched a petition to remove it from place-names such as Birmingham and Nottingham.

Ham, naturally, will no longer be available. It is against the law to make, import, sell or eat it, along with bacon, sausages and pork pies. The punishment for breaking this law is a public flogging; but as there is not a single pig left in England such retribution has not been necessary for several years. Tens of thousands of pigs were slaughtered by the state, allegedly to prevent swine flu. Many Muslims were secretly relieved, flu or no flu. The *sharia* court that passed the last sentence ensured the judgment made as big an impact as possible by having it carried out in Melton Mowbray. (Just as the phrase 'on tenterhooks' has continued to be used long after anyone knows what a tenterhook is or was, so Cockneys still use the rhyming slang 'to tell porkies' even though pork pies no longer exist.)

Indigenous people miss their bacon. The famous traditional cooked breakfast fry-up is still advertised as 'full English' by the ethnics who fry and sell it but lacking bacon and pork sausages is really only half-full and is losing its appeal.

In 2010 a young Islamic scholar named Sheikh Rizwan Mohammed decreed, after much earnest debate, that Muslims were allowed to eat *halal* haggis; and a man named Ade Adeluwoye wrote in a blog, 'I believe rice, peas and jerk chicken is an icon of England'.

But the true national dish of the English people now is humble pie.

Knives and forks will have gone out of fashion. Everyone now will eat with their fingers. Following the universal rule that those who adopt a foreign culture observe only its worst manifestations, ignoring moderating nuances and subtleties, and the custom of having meals together seated at a table having long been abandoned, urban indigenous people when eating will now resemble feeding monkeys.

Sumptuary laws will forbid many styles of dress. Municipal swimming baths will all have times set aside exclusively for burkini-clad female Muslims. (Indigenous people no longer use public pools anyway, scared by reports of children at some of them catching an ethnic pox, ophthalmic gonorrhea.)

At night in the public squares Muslims make bonfires of books. *Dark Albion*, an unacknowledged best-seller when first published and now regarded as a classic of dissident literature, is on a long list of proscribed books, its elderly author murdered long ago, shot by a Somalian while waiting for a 108 bus at the top of Westcombe Hill.

The English language will undergo deep changes. It will suffer a heavy infiltration of words from Urdu, which has a lot of Arabic words. 'Fair', which had come to mean not just pale but also beautiful and just, will revert solely to its original meaning.

Restaurant chains such as Pizza Hut that have been taken over by Muslim businessmen will in the month of Ramadan only be open for two hours at dusk.

Non-Muslims officially will have the status of dhimmitude, made subject to a number of humiliating regulations designed to enforce the Koran's command that they 'feel themselves subdued', denied equality of rights and dignity by *sharia* law. In the past in Islamic societies there were periods of tolerance when Christians were able to take part and live normally but the structured discrimination and injustice of the *dhimma* always prevented their full participation and led to periodic persecution and violence.

Following the ancient custom wherever Muslims have seized power, all adult non-Muslim males will have to pay a poll tax, *jizya*, as punishment for not believing in Allah and the sanctity of the Prophet. Payment is sometimes accompanied by a slap in the face to remind the infidel who is in charge.

The English will no longer feel at home in England. Astounded, outraged, they are wounded to the heart by the difference between the land their ancestors had made and the one it has become. Before their eyes the destruction of their customs and the shattering of their world are taking place.

English journalists, minds numbed by decades of political correctness and fear but now faced with the enormous inescapable reality, do not know what to write. Utterly confused, they simultaneously report that the country is close to collapse and that everything is fine, that it is threatened by civil war and that all is normal.

State and religion will again be joined, a system last seen in England in the seventeenth century, after which Christianity was de-politicised and religion became an unthreatening, private matter. The English, suspicious of such enthusiasms as extravagant piety even when they themselves were reasonably religious, will now be in the position of having to show respect to the fervent devotees of an alien religion who, on seizing power, have created a theocracy.

The oppressive influence of this totalitarian religion will be repellent. The English will be so distressed by the indignities of dhimmitude, the burden and humiliation of *jizya*, the new restrictions and at being woken up every morning at 5am by the amplified call to prayer from the nearby mosque, that many will leave the country, straining the resources of the three main countries they flee to - Australia, New Zealand and Canada.

Those who remain will struggle to obey, and in general come to terms with, the new theocracy. As with all totalitarian regimes, there will be now so many crimes against the state it will be difficult to keep pace with them. Most English will be living in the shires. Towns will be dominated by ethnics, many of whom, smug in their security, practise religion as a mere state function. Ambitious men will cynically convert to Islam in the same spirit as many people in the Soviet Union joined the Communist Party, as a career move, patiently overcoming the difficulties placed in their way by bureaucrats who prefer that they remain infidels paying the poll tax.

England will be run by cynics who recognise that slavish obedience is the way to succeed, both politically and financially. The successful men will have benefited, and so will now like the security of the existing arrangement better than the dangerous uncertainties of the previous set-up, even though the upper echelons of the political, legal and financial systems will now be operating largely on the basis of nepotism and bribery. Corruption has crept into every institution. Privileged offices are not awarded on merit but sold. The more successful or higher up men will be the greater their insincerity, their features always carefully arranged in a blend of humility and arrogance, disdain and flattery.

Powerful bureaucrats will exude an air of abstracted benevolence tinged with cunning, a pleasantness masking a secret edge of cruelty. At best there will be a smug paternalism; at worst a dismissive contempt.

They will take perverse pleasure in using more and more Arabic words in their dealings with indigenous people, to confuse and humiliate them, enjoying their discomfiture at their incomprehension, wilfully making communication increasingly difficult. (Muslim shopkeepers however will keep their speech in simple English.)

Feminists and homosexuals will lament their lost rights, decades of struggle negated, ruefully reflecting that everything is relative. Nigerian Muslims who had settled in England illegally in the first place with forged documents will now use their religious connections with rulers and bureaucrats to establish themselves as powerful criminals.

London will be purulent with lies, violence and greed. The mayor, Zohaib Ahmed, following the line of his predecessors of the previous seventy years, continues to assert that its diversity makes it the most vibrant city in the world. Hardly any indigenous Cockneys remain.

And throughout the country, most of the indigenous English who remain in towns will be the lumpen proletariat, blank-eyed swaggering halfwits who behave like drunks even when sober, floppy and heedless, slurring their words and grunting. The new lumpen grunt is not the same as the old working-class dialects. Proud of their extensive tattoos, in all but the coldest weather they will wear nothing but designer loincloths. Their exposed bodies will be something of what the race had been but they will have lost strength and substance, so thin and grey they seem almost transparent, defined only by the tattoos that cover them. The form will still be the same, but faded and diminished. The animating health and vigour will have gone.

Sixteen centuries have passed since Hengist and Horsa and their band of flaxen-haired warriors clambered ashore like excited children by the Thanet cliffs, and, a few decades later, along the same stretch of coast, Augustine arrived with his group of fellow reluctant monks in a more dignified manner. The English race, with its new religion, needed a strong will, proud, disciplined and sustained, to survive at all. England did survive, progressing from tiny settlements to insecure kingdoms to a prosperous country of independent people, achieving success through unique merits. What is happening now is close to racial suicide.

Those who had believed the races would mingle and form a new race will have been proved wrong. So little integration will have taken place the races will have actually grown apart; it will be now easy to believe them of different species.

Compromise will have proved impossible, a cultural no-man's land. Ancestral culture will still be influencing psyche generations after the first settlers came. Indeed, as though recognising they can never fully adapt, many settlers' offspring seem determined to assert the practices of their ancestral homeland to the point of caricature.

The proles will be capricious and undignified, easily provoked into hysteria, any vestige of a sense of pride having been eroded away by the humiliations of dhimmitude. Because English-speakers cannot easily make the 'dh' sound the status will be commonly pronounced 'dimmitude', leading to those of it being known, even among themselves, as 'the dims'.

Some dims will be so out of touch with the world around them they will not be certain what their country is called, confusing it with the name of their town, which is the only world they know. Indeed the name England will now be rarely heard, the dominant Muslims avoiding its use as much as possible as a sort of semi-official policy, arguing, so far only in private among themselves, that as England is no longer the land of the English its name should be changed. Some say it seems a shame to elide centuries of history, while others say it is the will of Allah, and cite the examples of Brittany and Normandy, both of which acquired their new names to reflect the reality of a newly dominant race.

As there are no jobs for the dims anyway the new rulers, to prevent riots, will have retained the Social Security system, so the dims will be under no compulsion to earn a living, and are bored. They will gamble not out of avarice but out of boredom, drink not because they are thirsty but because they are bored, even commit suicide not from despair but frivolously from *ennui*. Frivolity will form the sole consideration of their lives. To justify their subculture of lifelong laziness they will have developed a shallow, convenient philosophy in which work is horrible and absurd; people are born only for pleasure; the essence of human nature is to enjoy oneself, and all the rest is folly. They will regard this trite philosophy as a sort of vision, and not just an excuse for endlessly doing nothing.

In their boredom, their personal relationships will be their main diversion. The relationships will therefore be kaleidoscopic, both intense and shallow, for there is never any mutual interest in them other than the avoidance of the ever-encroaching *ennui*. Family life will have broken down. Couples will seldom stay together for long. The women typically will have several children all by different fathers.

These children will be feral. Scrofulous, rickety or deformed, they will belong to no proper family and the authorities will have abandoned them. Compulsory education will also have broken down, state schools devoting too much time to study of the *Koran* and the teaching of Arabic, and science removed from the curriculum. Health services too will have almost ceased to function, mainly because, despite the exodus of indigenous people, the population will simply be far too great, and diseases once eradicated in England or under control will again spoil many lives and claim many victims. Tuberculosis, re-introduced into the country by settlers from the Indian subcontinent in the first decade of the 21st century, will again ravage towns. HIV, fetched and spread by heterosexual Africans in those same years, will become widespread.

The feral children, left to fend for themselves from an early age, and given little affection, will form gangs, and they will regard their gang as their family.

They will spend much of their time fighting other gangs. Battles will be fought between the gangs of several districts for no reason other than that those of one district have seen a chance to surprise those of another before they are prepared. If no such opportunity presents itself, and no other enemies are around, they will fight among themselves. This will happen rarely however, for there will be usually plenty of other foes to fight - supporters of a rival football club, black gangs, Muslim morality vigilantes...

This feral generation of ignorant, illiterate, diseased bastards called dims, roaming the streets in gangs seeking someone to fight, will in many towns be all that remains of an ancient sturdy race.

Society will be ruled and policed by swarthy sanctimonious men who consult nothing but their old books. If they read of a foolish custom, they consider it a sacred law. From this vile practice of not daring to think for themselves, but of always extracting their ideas from a place and time where no one thinks at all, superstition and myth will, as in that faraway place and distant past, be elevated to the status of a dominant religion. This will curb some of the excesses of capitalism but will also stifle, and often actively suppress, all creativity.

The dims will despise their rulers but keep quiet when a disdainful, haughty official truculently warns them that to persist in a 'bad attitude', meaning to question Islamic beliefs, carries the danger of being regarded as an enemy of the state. Muslims always hated being laughed at and will now be in a position to exact harsh revenge.

Islam will be taking England back to the Dark Ages. A past known under the varnish of museums, seemingly lost irretrievably, is becoming the present. It can be touched and breathed. As in a time-travel machine, during a dizzying flight the years run backwards, the cockpit dashboard showing the years of the third millennium changing to those of the second and stopping at a year numbered in three figures instead of four.

England will have returned to the realm of ignorance.

It will be ruined, its history re-written, its indigenous people remnants of a disinherited race, the likes of me forgotten.

In the ruins, those of the English folk not demoralised by dhimmitude reach out to one another, support each other and organise the resistance. Because of the incredible chronological discrepancy of ideals, the conflict gives the impression of a war between people living in different centuries.